Microsoft® Windows® 98 and Windows® Me

Illustrated Introductory

Disk defragmenter
Mauhnellon — 5531 M&MS 1/3mo

Microsoft® Windows® 98 and Windows® Me

Illustrated Introductory

Steven M. Johnson

Australia • Canada • Mexico • Singapore • Spain • United Kingdom • United States

Microsoft® Windows® 98 and Windows® Me—Illustrated Introductory Edition

Steven M. Johnson

Managing Editor:
Nicole Jones Pinard

Production Editor:
Christine Spillet

Associate Product Manager:
Emeline Elliot

Editorial Assistant
Danielle Roy

Product Manager:
Trisha O'Shea

Developmental Editor:
Trisha O'Shea

Composition House:
GEX, Inc.

QA Manuscript Reviewer:
Alex White, John Freitas

Text Designer:
Joseph Lee, Black Fish Design

Cover Designer:
Doug Goodman,
Doug Goodman Designs

COPYRIGHT © 2001 Course Technology, a division of Thomson Learning. Thomson Learning™ is a trademark used herein under license.

ISBN: 0-619-01870-4

Printed in the United States of America

1 2 3 4 5 6 7 8 9 BM 04 03 02 01 00

For more information, contact Course Technology, 25 Thomson Place, Boston, Massachusetts, 02210.
Or you can visit us on the World Wide Web at www.course.com
ALL RIGHTS RESERVED. No part of this work covered by the copyright hereon may be reproduced or used in any form or by any means—graphic, electronic, or mechanical, including photocopying, recording, taping, Web distribution, or information storage and retrieval systems—without the written permission of the publisher.

For permission to use material from this text or product, contact us by
Tel (800) 730-2214
Fax (800) 730-2215
www.thomsonrights.com

The Illustrated Series Offers the Entire Package for your Classroom Needs

Master Microsoft Office 2000

Master Microsoft Office 2000 with *Microsoft Office 2000—Illustrated Introductory,* students will learn the basics of Microsoft Office 2000 Professional. For deeper coverage, *Microsoft Office 2000—Illustrated Second Course* focuses on the more advanced skills of Office 2000 applications. Illustrated also offers individual applications books on Microsoft Word, Excel, Access, PowerPoint, Publisher, FrontPage, and PhotoDraw. The Illustrated Series offers a growing number of Microsoft approved titles that cover the objectives required to pass the **Office 2000 MOUS** exams. After studying with any of the approved Illustrated titles you will have mastered the Core and Expert skills necessary to pass any Office 2000 MOUS exam.

Check out Computer Concepts and E-Commerce Concepts

Computer Concepts – *Illustrated Brief* or *Introductory, Third Edition,* is the quick and visual way to learn cutting-edge computer concepts. The third edition has been updated to include advances to the Internet and multimedia, changes to the industry, and an introduction to e-commerce and security.

E-Commerce Concepts – *Illustrated Introductory* teaches the basic concepts and language of e-commerce. Designed to teach students to explore and evaluate e-commerce technologies, sites, and issues, *E-Commerce* is the ideal introduction to the quickly developing world of e-commerce. The continually updated Student Online Companion allows students to explore relevant sites and articles, ensuring a complete and current learning experience.

Enhance Any Illustrated Text with these Exciting Products!

Course Technology offers a continuum of solutions to meet your online learning needs. Whether you need an online course enhancement tool, or a customizable Web environment for your distance-learning course, we have the solution for you. Course Technology offers content through 3 Distance Learning Solutions for your classroom experience: MyCourse.com, (hosted by Course Technology) Blackboard and WebCT. 0

MyCourse.com

MyCourse.com is an easily customizable online syllabus and course enhancement tool. This tool adds value to your class by offering brand new content designed to reinforce what you are already teaching. MyCourse.com even allows you to add your own content, hyperlinks, and assignments. For a demonstration please contact your Course Technology sales representative.

WebCT and Blackboard

WebCT and Blackboard are course management tools, which deliver online content for eight –five Course Technology titles. The growing list of titles enables instructors the ability to edit and add to any content made available through WebCT and Blackboard. In addition, you can choose what you want the students to be able to access. The site is hosted on your school campus, allowing complete control over the information. WebCT and Blackboard offer their own internal communication system, offering internal e-mail, Bulletin Boards, and Chat rooms. For more information please contact your Course Technology sales representative.

Create Your Ideal Course Package with CourseKits™

If one book doesn't offer all the coverage you need, create a course package that does. With Course Technology's CourseKits—our mix-and-match approach to selecting texts—you have the freedom to combine products from more than one series.

When you choose any two or more Course Technology products for one course, we'll discount the price and package them together so your students can pick up one convenient bundle at the bookstore.

For more information about any of these offerings or other Course Technology products, contact your sales representative or visit our Web site at: www.course.com.

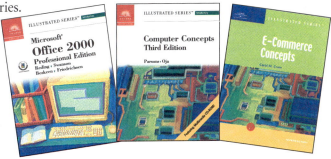

Preface

Welcome to *Microsoft Windows 98 and Windows Me (Millennium Edition)—Illustrated Introductory Edition*. This highly visual text offers users an introduction to *Microsoft Windows 98 and Windows Me*. It also serves as an excellent reference for future use. If you would like additional coverage of Microsoft Windows 98 Second Edition and Windows Me, Course Technology also offers *Microsoft Windows 98 and Windows Me — Illustrated Complete*.

▶ Organization and Coverage

This text contains eight units, which covers both *Microsoft Windows 98 and Windows Me*. Windows 98 Second Edition is an update to Windows 98 and offers the latest Internet, home-networking and hardware technologies. In these units students will learn how to manage files, using both My Computer and Windows Explorer. This text includes steps for Windows 98 users as well as Windows Me users.

▶ About this Approach

What makes the Illustrated approach so effective at teaching software skills? It's quite simple. Each skill is presented on two facing pages, with the step-by-step instructions on the left page, and large screen illustrations on the right. Students can focus on a single skill without having to turn the page. This unique design makes information extremely accessible and easy to absorb, and provides a great reference for after the course is over. This hands-on approach also makes it ideal for both self-paced and instructor-led classes. Each lesson, or "information display," contains the following elements:

Each 2-page spread focuses on a single skill.

Concise text introduces the basic principles discussed in the lesson. Procedures are easier to learn when concepts fit into a framework.

Clear step-by-step directions explain how to complete the specific task. What students will type is in green. When students follow the numbered steps, they quickly learn how each procedure is performed and what the results will be.

Using Scroll Bars

Windows 98 and Me

When you cannot see all of the items available in a window, scroll bars appear on the right and/or bottom edges of the window. Scroll bars allow you to display the additional contents of the window. Figure A-10 shows components of the scroll bars. The vertical scroll bar moves your view up and down through a window; the horizontal scroll bar moves your view from left to right. There are several ways you can use the scroll bars. When you need to scroll only a short distance, you can use the scroll arrows. When you need to scroll more quickly, you can click in the scroll bar above or below the scroll box to move the view up or down one window's height (the line that was at the bottom of the screen moves to the top, and vice versa). Dragging the scroll box moves you even more quickly to a new part of the window. See Table A-7 for a summary of the different ways to use scroll bars. ✏ You can use the scroll bars to view and read the description of each Control Panel program.

Steps

QuickTip
When no scroll bars appear in a window, it means that all the information fits completely in the window.

1. In the Control Panel, click the **down scroll arrow** in the vertical scroll bar, as shown in Figure A-10
   Clicking this arrow moves the view down one line. Clicking the up arrow moves the view up one line at a time.

2. Click the **up scroll arrow** in the vertical scroll bar
   The view moves up one line.

3. Click anywhere in the area below the scroll box in the vertical scroll bar
   The contents of the window scroll down in a larger increment.

4. Click the area above the scroll box in the vertical scroll bar
   The contents of the window scroll back up. To move in even greater increments, you can drag the scroll box to a new position.

QuickTip
If you have a mouse with a wheel button between the left and right buttons, you can roll the wheel button to scroll up and down quickly or click the wheel button and move the mouse in any direction.

5. Drag the **scroll box** in the horizontal scroll bar to the middle of the bar
   The scroll box indicates your relative position within the window, in this case, the halfway point. After reading the Control Panel program descriptions, you restore the Control Panel to its original display.

6. On the Control Panel toolbar, click the **Views button list arrow**, then click **Large Icons**

7. Click **View** on the menu bar, then click **Status Bar**
   The status bar appears at the bottom of the Control Panel.

8. Click **View** on the menu bar, point to **Toolbars**, then click **Text Labels**
   In the next lesson you open a Control Panel program to learn how to work with dialog boxes.

▶ WINDOWS 98 AND ME A-12 GETTING STARTED WITH WINDOWS 98 AND ME

Tips and troubleshooting advice right where you need them—next to the step itself.

The page numbers are designed like a road map.

Every lesson features large-size, full-color representations of what the students' screen should look like after completing the numbered steps.

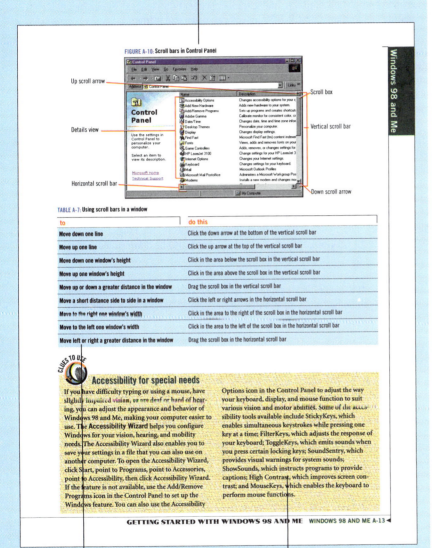

Quickly accessible summaries of key terms, toolbar buttons, or keyboard alternatives connected with the lesson material. Students can easily refer to this information when working on their own projects later.

A Clues to Use box provides concise information that expands upon one component of the major lesson skill or describes an independent task related to the major lesson skill.

Other Features

The two-page lesson format featured in this book provides the new user with a powerful learning experience. Additionally, this book contains the following features:

▶ **Real-World Case**

The case study used throughout the textbook, a fictitious coffee company called Wired Coffee Company, is designed to be "real-world" in nature and introduces the kinds of activities that students will encounter when working with *Microsoft Windows 98 and Windows Me*. With a real-world case, the process of solving problems will be more meaningful to students.

▶ **End-of-Unit Material**

Each unit concludes with a Concepts Review that tests students' understanding of what they learned in the unit. The Concepts Review is followed by a Skills Review, which provides students with additional hands-on practice of the skills. The Skills Review is followed by Independent Challenges, which pose case problems for students to solve. At least one Independent Challenge in each unit asks students to use the World Wide Web to solve the problem as indicated by a Web Work icon. The Visual Workshops that follow the Independent Challenges help students develop critical thinking skills. Students are shown completed Web pages or screens and are asked to recreate them from scratch.

▶ **Customer Feedback**

The Illustrated Series responded to Customer Feedback by adding a **Project Files List** at the back of the book for easy reference, and by changing the **red font in the steps to green** for easier reading, as well as adding new conceptual lessons to units to give students the extra information they need when learning.

VII

Instructor's Resource Kit

The Instructor's Resource Kit is Course Technology's way of putting the resources and information needed to teach and learn effectively into your hands. With an integrated array of teaching and learning tools that offers you and your students a broad range of technology-based instructional options, we believe this kit represents the highest quality and most cutting edge resources available to instructors today. Many of these resources are available at **www.course.com**. The resources available with this book are:

Instructor's Manual   Available as an electronic file, the Instructor's Manual is quality-assurance tested and includes unit overviews, detailed lecture topics for each unit with teaching tips, an Upgrader's Guide, solutions to all lessons and end-of-unit material, and extra Independent Challenges. The Instructor's Manual is available on the Instructor's Resource Kit CD-ROM, or you can download it from **www.course.com**.

Course Test Manager   Designed by Course Technology, this Windows-based testing software helps instructor's design, administer, and print tests and pre-tests. A full-featured program, Course Test Manager also has an online testing component that allows students to take tests at the computer and have their exams automatically graded.

Course Faculty Online Companion   You can browse this textbook's password-protected site to obtain the Instructor's Manual, Solution Files, Project Files, and any updates to the text. Contact your Customer Service Representative for the site address and password.

Project Files   Project Files contain all of the data that students will use to complete the lessons and end-of-unit material. A Readme file includes instructions for using the files. Adopters of this text are granted the right to install the Project Files on any standalone computer or network. The Project Files are available on the Instructor's Resource Kit CD-ROM, the Review Pack, and can also be downloaded from **www.course.com**.

Solution Files   Solution Files contain every file students are asked to create or modify in the lessons and end-of-unit material. A Help file on the Instructor's Resource Kit includes information for using the Solution Files.

Figure Files   Figure files contain all the figures from the book in bitmap format. Use the figure files to create transparency masters or in a PowerPoint presentation.

Brief Contents

	Exciting New Products	V
	Preface	VI

Windows 98 and Me	Getting Started with Windows 98 and Me	WINDOWS 98 AND ME A-1
	Working with Windows Programs	WINDOWS 98 AND ME B-1
	Managing Files Using My Computer	WINDOWS 98 AND ME C-1
	Managing Folders and Files Using Windows Explorer	WINDOWS 98 AND ME D-1
	Customizing Windows Using the Control Panel	WINDOWS 98 AND ME E-1
	Exploring the Internet with Microsoft Internet Explorer	WINDOWS 98 AND ME F-1
	Exchanging Mail and News	WINDOWS 98 AND ME G-1
	Managing Shared Files Using a Network	WINDOWS 98 AND ME H-1

Glossary	1
Index	7
Project Files	16

Contents

Exciting New Products	V
Preface	VI

Windows 98 and Me

Getting Started with Windows 98 and Me — WINDOWS 98 AND ME A-1

Starting Windows and Viewing the Windows Desktop	WINDOWS 98 AND ME A-2
Using the Mouse	WINDOWS 98 AND ME A-4
Getting Started with the Windows Desktop	WINDOWS 98 AND ME A-6
Moving and Resizing Windows	WINDOWS 98 AND ME A-8
Moving and resizing the taskbar	WINDOWS 98 AND ME A-9
Using Menus and Toolbars	WINDOWS 98 AND ME A-10
Using Scroll Bars	WINDOWS 98 AND ME A-12
Accessibility for special needs	WINDOWS 98 AND ME A-13
Using Dialog Boxes	WINDOWS 98 AND ME A-14
Using Windows Help	WINDOWS 98 AND ME A-16
Context-sensitive help	WINDOWS 98 AND ME A-17
Shutting Down Windows	WINDOWS 98 AND ME A-18
Logging off Windows	WINDOWS 98 AND ME A-19
Concepts Review	WINDOWS 98 AND ME A-20
Skills Review	WINDOWS 98 AND ME A-21
Independent Challenges	WINDOWS 98 AND ME A-22
Visual Workshop	WINDOWS 98 AND ME A-24
Using the mouse with the Internet	WINDOWS 98 AND ME A-25
Accessing the Internet from the Active Desktop	WINDOWS 98 AND ME A-25

Working with Windows Programs — WINDOWS 98 AND ME B-1

Starting a Program	WINDOWS 98 AND ME B-2
Opening and Saving a WordPad Document	WINDOWS 98 AND ME B-4
About saving files	WINDOWS 98 AND ME B-5
Editing Text in WordPad	WINDOWS 98 AND ME B-6
Setting paragraph tabs	WINDOWS 98 AND ME B-7
Formatting Text in WordPad	WINDOWS 98 AND ME B-8
Setting paragraph indents	WINDOWS 98 AND ME B-9
Using Paint	WINDOWS 98 AND ME B-10
Copying Data Between Programs	WINDOWS 98 AND ME B-12
Printing a Document	WINDOWS 98 AND ME B-14
Printer properties	WINDOWS 98 AND ME B-15

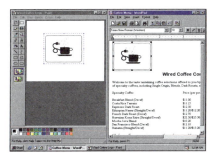

Contents

Playing a Video Clip or Sound ....**WINDOWS 98 AND ME B-16**
   Playing media from the Internet ....**WINDOWS 98 AND ME B-17**
Creating a Movie ....**WINDOWS 98 AND ME B-18**
   Creating a slide show ....**WINDOWS 98 AND ME B-19**
Concepts Review ....**WINDOWS 98 AND ME B-20**
Skills Review ....**WINDOWS 98 AND ME B-21**
Independent Challenges ....**WINDOWS 98 AND ME B-22**
Visual Workshop ....**WINDOWS 98 AND ME B-24**

Managing Files Using My Computer   WINDOWS 98 AND ME C-1

Understanding File Management ....**WINDOWS 98 AND ME C-2**
   What is a file hierarchy? ....**WINDOWS 98 AND ME C-3**
Opening and Viewing My Computer ....**WINDOWS 98 AND ME C-4**
   Formatting a disk ....**WINDOWS 98 AND ME C-5**
Viewing Folders and Files ....**WINDOWS 98 AND ME C-6**
   Viewing image and picture files ....**WINDOWS 98 AND ME C-7**
Creating a Folder ....**WINDOWS 98 AND ME C-8**
   Compressing files ....**WINDOWS 98 AND ME C-9**
Moving Files and Folders ....**WINDOWS 98 AND ME C-10**
   Sending files and folders ....**WINDOWS 98 AND ME C-11**

Deleting and Restoring Files and Folders ....**WINDOWS 98 AND ME C-12**
   Recycle Bin properties ....**WINDOWS 98 AND ME C-13**
Creating a Shortcut to a File ....**WINDOWS 98 AND ME C-14**
   Placing shortcuts on the Start menu ....**WINDOWS 98 AND ME C-15**
Displaying Drive Information ....**WINDOWS 98 AND ME C-16**
   Backing up files ....**WINDOWS 98 AND ME C-16**
Concepts Review ....**WINDOWS 98 AND ME C-18**
Skills Review ....**WINDOWS 98 AND ME C-19**
Independent Challenges ....**WINDOWS 98 AND ME C-21**
Visual Workshop ....**WINDOWS 98 AND ME C-24**

Managing Folders and Files Using Windows Explorer   WINDOWS 98 AND ME D-1

Viewing the Windows Explorer Window ......**WINDOWS 98 AND ME D-2**
   Changing folder options ....**WINDOWS 98 AND ME D-3**
Opening and Viewing Folders in
Windows Explorer ....**WINDOWS 98 AND ME D-4**
Customizing the Windows
Explorer Window ....**WINDOWS 98 AND ME D-6**
   Using the status bar ....**WINDOWS 98 AND ME D-7**
Creating and Renaming Folders in
Windows Explorer ....**WINDOWS 98 AND ME D-8**
Finding a File ....**WINDOWS 98 AND ME D-10**
   Performing an Advanced Search ....**WINDOWS 98 AND ME D-10**

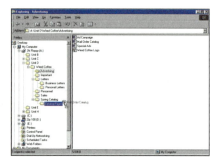

Copying and Moving a File to a Folder	WINDOWS 98 AND ME D-12
Finding files or folders using the History folder	WINDOWS 98 AND ME D-13
Restoring a Deleted File Using Undo	WINDOWS 98 AND ME D-14
Customizing a folder	WINDOWS 98 AND ME D-16
Displaying a thumbnail of a graphic	WINDOWS 98 AND ME D-17
Concepts Review	WINDOWS 98 AND ME D-18
Skills Review	WINDOWS 98 AND ME D-20
Independent Challenges	WINDOWS 98 AND ME D-21
Visual Workshop	WINDOWS 98 AND ME D-24

Customizing Windows Using the Control Panel — WINDOWS 98 AND ME E-1

Customizing the Active Desktop	WINDOWS 98 AND ME E-2
Adding a new Web item to the Active Desktop	WINDOWS 98 AND ME E-3
Changing the Desktop Background and Screen Saver Settings	WINDOWS 98 AND ME E-4
Changing the Desktop Scheme	WINDOWS 98 AND ME E-6
Applying a desktop theme	WINDOWS 98 AND ME E-7
Setting the Date and Time	WINDOWS 98 AND ME E-8
Changing the size of the desktop	WINDOWS 98 AND ME E-9
Working with Fonts	WINDOWS 98 AND ME E-10
Installing a font	WINDOWS 98 AND ME E-11
Managing Power Options	WINDOWS 98 AND ME E-12
Adding a Scheduled Task	WINDOWS 98 AND ME E-14
Adding new hardware and software to Windows	WINDOWS 98 AND ME E-15
Customizing the Taskbar	WINDOWS 98 AND ME E-16
Starting a program as a taskbar button	WINDOWS 98 AND ME E-17
Customizing the Start Menu	WINDOWS 98 AND ME E-18
Rearranging Start menu items	WINDOWS 98 AND ME E-19
Concepts Review	WINDOWS 98 AND ME E-20
Skills Review	WINDOWS 98 AND ME E-21
Independent Challenges	WINDOWS 98 AND ME E-23
Visual Workshop	WINDOWS 98 AND ME E-24

Exploring the Internet with Microsoft Internet Explorer — WINDOWS 98 AND ME F-1

Understanding Web Browsers	WINDOWS 98 AND ME F-2
The history of the Internet and World Wide Web	WINDOWS 98 AND ME F-3
Starting Internet Explorer	WINDOWS 98 AND ME F-4
Connecting to the Internet	WINDOWS 98 AND ME F-5
Exploring the Browser Window	WINDOWS 98 AND ME F-6
Getting help with Internet Explorer	WINDOWS 98 AND ME F-7

Contents

Opening a Web Page and Following Links ....**WINDOWS 98 AND ME F-8**
   Understanding a Web address ....**WINDOWS 98 AND ME F-9**
Adding a Web Page to the Favorites List ......**WINDOWS 98 AND ME F-10**
   Organizing favorites ....**WINDOWS 98 AND ME F-11**
Making a Web Page Available Offline ....**WINDOWS 98 AND ME F-12**
   Saving a Web page ....**WINDOWS 98 AND ME F-13**
Changing Your Home Page and Adding
a Link Button ....**WINDOWS 98 AND ME F-14**
   Viewing and maintaining a History list ....**WINDOWS 98 AND ME F-15**
Searching the Web ....**WINDOWS 98 AND ME F-16**
   Searching for people on the Web ....**WINDOWS 98 AND ME F-17**
Previewing and Printing a Web Page ....**WINDOWS 98 AND ME F-18**
   Setting up the page format ....**WINDOWS 98 AND ME F-19**
Concepts Review ....**WINDOWS 98 AND ME F-20**
Skills Review ....**WINDOWS 98 AND ME F-21**
Independent Challenges ....**WINDOWS 98 AND ME F-23**
Visual Workshop ....**WINDOWS 98 AND ME F-24**

Exchanging Mail and News   **WINDOWS 98 AND ME G-1**

Starting Outlook Express ....**WINDOWS 98 AND ME G-2**
   Starting Outlook Express from your
   Web browser ....**WINDOWS 98 AND ME G-3**
Exploring the Outlook Express Window ....**WINDOWS 98 AND ME G-4**
   Getting help in Outlook Express ....**WINDOWS 98 AND ME G-5**
Adding a Contact to the Address Book ....**WINDOWS 98 AND ME G-6**
Composing and Sending E-mail ....**WINDOWS 98 AND ME G-8**
   Attaching a file to an e-mail message ....**WINDOWS 98 AND ME G-9**
Retrieving, Reading, and Responding
to E-mail ....**WINDOWS 98 AND ME G-10**
   Printing e-mail messages and contacts ......**WINDOWS 98 AND ME G-11**
Managing E-mail Messages ....**WINDOWS 98 AND ME G-12**
   Diverting incoming e-mail to folders ....**WINDOWS 98 AND ME G-13**
Selecting a News Server ....**WINDOWS 98 AND ME G-14**
Viewing and Subscribing to a Newsgroup ..**WINDOWS 98 AND ME G-16**
   Filtering unwanted newsgroup messages ..**WINDOWS 98 AND ME G-17**
Reading and Posting News Messages ....**WINDOWS 98 AND ME G-18**
   Deleting old news messages ....**WINDOWS 98 AND ME G-19**
Concepts Review ....**WINDOWS 98 AND ME G-20**
Skills Review ....**WINDOWS 98 AND ME G-21**
Independent Challenges ....**WINDOWS 98 AND ME G-23**
Visual Workshop ....**WINDOWS 98 AND ME G-25**

Managing Shared Files Using a Network   **WINDOWS 98 AND ME H-1**

Understand network services ....**WINDOWS 98 AND ME H-2**
   File permission properties ....**WINDOWS 98 AND ME H-3**

Copying and Moving a File to a Folder	**WINDOWS 98 AND ME D-12**
Finding files or folders using the History folder	**WINDOWS 98 AND ME D-13**
Restoring a Deleted File Using Undo	**WINDOWS 98 AND ME D-14**
Customizing a folder	**WINDOWS 98 AND ME D-16**
Displaying a thumbnail of a graphic	**WINDOWS 98 AND ME D-17**
Concepts Review	**WINDOWS 98 AND ME D-18**
Skills Review	**WINDOWS 98 AND ME D-20**
Independent Challenges	**WINDOWS 98 AND ME D-21**
Visual Workshop	**WINDOWS 98 AND ME D-24**

Customizing Windows Using the Control Panel   WINDOWS 98 AND ME E-1

Customizing the Active Desktop	**WINDOWS 98 AND ME E-2**
Adding a new Web item to the Active Desktop	**WINDOWS 98 AND ME E-3**
Changing the Desktop Background and Screen Saver Settings	**WINDOWS 98 AND ME E-4**
Changing the Desktop Scheme	**WINDOWS 98 AND ME E-6**
Applying a desktop theme	**WINDOWS 98 AND ME E-7**
Setting the Date and Time	**WINDOWS 98 AND ME E-8**
Changing the size of the desktop	**WINDOWS 98 AND ME E-9**
Working with Fonts	**WINDOWS 98 AND ME E-10**
Installing a font	**WINDOWS 98 AND ME E-11**
Managing Power Options	**WINDOWS 98 AND ME E-12**
Adding a Scheduled Task	**WINDOWS 98 AND ME E-14**
Adding new hardware and software to Windows	**WINDOWS 98 AND ME E-15**
Customizing the Taskbar	**WINDOWS 98 AND ME E-16**
Starting a program as a taskbar button	**WINDOWS 98 AND ME E-17**
Customizing the Start Menu	**WINDOWS 98 AND ME E-18**
Rearranging Start menu items	**WINDOWS 98 AND ME E-19**
Concepts Review	**WINDOWS 98 AND ME E-20**
Skills Review	**WINDOWS 98 AND ME E-21**
Independent Challenges	**WINDOWS 98 AND ME E-23**
Visual Workshop	**WINDOWS 98 AND ME E-24**

Exploring the Internet with Microsoft Internet Explorer   WINDOWS 98 AND ME F-1

Understanding Web Browsers	**WINDOWS 98 AND ME F-2**
The history of the Internet and World Wide Web	**WINDOWS 98 AND ME F-3**
Starting Internet Explorer	**WINDOWS 98 AND ME F-4**
Connecting to the Internet	**WINDOWS 98 AND ME F-5**
Exploring the Browser Window	**WINDOWS 98 AND ME F-6**
Getting help with Internet Explorer	**WINDOWS 98 AND ME F-7**

Contents

Opening a Web Page and Following Links .... **WINDOWS 98 AND ME F-8**
   Understanding a Web address .... **WINDOWS 98 AND ME F-9**
Adding a Web Page to the Favorites List ...... **WINDOWS 98 AND ME F-10**
   Organizing favorites .... **WINDOWS 98 AND ME F-11**
Making a Web Page Available Offline .... **WINDOWS 98 AND ME F-12**
   Saving a Web page .... **WINDOWS 98 AND ME F-13**
Changing Your Home Page and Adding
a Link Button .... **WINDOWS 98 AND ME F-14**
   Viewing and maintaining a History list .... **WINDOWS 98 AND ME F-15**
Searching the Web .... **WINDOWS 98 AND ME F-16**
   Searching for people on the Web .... **WINDOWS 98 AND ME F-17**
Previewing and Printing a Web Page .... **WINDOWS 98 AND ME F-18**
   Setting up the page format .... **WINDOWS 98 AND ME F-19**
Concepts Review .... **WINDOWS 98 AND ME F-20**
Skills Review .... **WINDOWS 98 AND ME F-21**
Independent Challenges .... **WINDOWS 98 AND ME F-23**
Visual Workshop .... **WINDOWS 98 AND ME F-24**

Exchanging Mail and News — **WINDOWS 98 AND ME G-1**

Starting Outlook Express .... **WINDOWS 98 AND ME G-2**
   Starting Outlook Express from your
   Web browser .... **WINDOWS 98 AND ME G-3**
Exploring the Outlook Express Window .... **WINDOWS 98 AND ME G-4**
   Getting help in Outlook Express .... **WINDOWS 98 AND ME G-5**
Adding a Contact to the Address Book .... **WINDOWS 98 AND ME G-6**
Composing and Sending E-mail .... **WINDOWS 98 AND ME G-8**
   Attaching a file to an e-mail message .... **WINDOWS 98 AND ME G-9**
Retrieving, Reading, and Responding
to E-mail .... **WINDOWS 98 AND ME G-10**
   Printing e-mail messages and contacts ...... **WINDOWS 98 AND ME G-11**
Managing E-mail Messages .... **WINDOWS 98 AND ME G-12**
   Diverting incoming e-mail to folders .... **WINDOWS 98 AND ME G-13**
Selecting a News Server .... **WINDOWS 98 AND ME G-14**
Viewing and Subscribing to a Newsgroup .. **WINDOWS 98 AND ME G-16**
   Filtering unwanted newsgroup messages .. **WINDOWS 98 AND ME G-17**
Reading and Posting News Messages .... **WINDOWS 98 AND ME G-18**
   Deleting old news messages .... **WINDOWS 98 AND ME G-19**
Concepts Review .... **WINDOWS 98 AND ME G-20**
Skills Review .... **WINDOWS 98 AND ME G-21**
Independent Challenges .... **WINDOWS 98 AND ME G-23**
Visual Workshop .... **WINDOWS 98 AND ME G-25**

Managing Shared Files Using a Network — **WINDOWS 98 AND ME H-1**

Understand network services .... **WINDOWS 98 AND ME H-2**
   File permission properties .... **WINDOWS 98 AND ME H-3**

Examining Network Computer Properties	**WINDOWS 98 AND ME H-4**
Viewing network properties	**WINDOWS 98 AND ME H-5**
Opening and Viewing a Network	**WINDOWS 98 AND ME H-6**
Setting up a network at home	**WINDOWS 98 AND ME H-7**
Creating a Shared Folder	**WINDOWS 98 AND ME H-8**
Password protection	**WINDOWS 98 AND ME H-9**
Mapping a Network Drive	**WINDOWS 98 AND ME H-10**
Creating a network or dial-up connection	**WINDOWS 98 AND ME H-11**
Copying and Moving Shared Files	**WINDOWS 98 AND ME H-12**
Network traffic	**WINDOWS 98 AND ME H-13**
Opening and Editing a Shared File	**WINDOWS 98 AND ME H-14**
Opening read-only files	**WINDOWS 98 AND ME H-15**
Disconnecting a network Drive	**WINDOWS 98 AND ME H-16**
Network paths	**WINDOWS 98 AND ME H-16**
Concepts Review	**WINDOWS 98 AND ME H-18**
Skills Review	**WINDOWS 98 AND ME H-20**
Independent Challenges	**WINDOWS 98 AND ME H-21**
Visual Workshop	**WINDOWS 98 AND ME H-24**

Glossary	1
Index	7
Project Files	16

Read This Before You Begin

Differences Between Microsoft® Windows® 98 and Windows® Me

This book is written for Microsoft Windows 98 Second Edition and Windows Millennium Edition (Me). Some of the features and dialog boxes between the two Windows versions may look and function differently. When there are differences between the two versions of the software, steps written specifically for Windows 98 end with the notation (98) and steps for Windows Millennium end with the notation (Me).

Project Files

To complete the lessons and end-of-unit material in this book, students need to obtain the necessary project files. Please refer to the instructions on the front inside cover for various methods of getting these files. Once obtained, the user selects where to store the files, such as to the hard disk drive, network server, or Zip disk.

- **Using Copies:** For Units C, D, and H that work with managing folders and files using My Computer and Windows Explorer, make sure students use a *copy* of the Project Files instead of the originals. Using a copy of the Project Files will allow students to work through the lessons again in the future.

- **Restore Settings:** In order to work through the lessons in this book, students need to change operating system and program settings. The lessons make every attempt to restore the operating system and program settings, but please be aware that your initial settings might be different than the ones in this book.

Windows Settings

Each time you start Windows 98 or Windows Me, the operating system remembers previous settings, such as the Control Panel options. When you start Windows 98 or Windows Me, your initial screen might look different than the ones in this book. For the purposes of this book, make sure the following settings in Windows 98 and Windows Me are in place before you start each unit.

- Set the Open each folder in the same window option button in the Folder Options dialog box. (See "Customizing the Active Desktop" in Unit C for instructions.)

- Set the Double-click to open an item (single-click to select) option button in the Folder Options dialog box.

- In addition to the programs installed during the typical Windows installation, the following Windows programs should also be installed: Clipboard Viewer, Character Map, and Backup. If a program is not available, use the Add/Remove Programs icon in the Control Panel to install the program. (See "Adding new hardware and software to Windows" in Unit C for more information.)

To Use Print Screen

Click [Print Screen], open a graphics capable program such as Microsoft Paint, click Edit on the menu bar, and click Paste to paste the screen into Paint.

Windows 98 and Me

Getting
Started with Windows 98 and Me

Objectives

- Start Windows and view the Windows desktop
- Use the mouse
- Get started with the Windows desktop
- Move and resize windows
- Use menus and toolbars
- Use scroll bars
- Use dialog boxes
- Use Windows Help
- Shut down Windows

Microsoft Windows 98 and Millennium Edition (Me), is an **operating system**, a computer program that controls the basic operation of your computer and the programs you run on it. **Programs**, also known as **applications**, are task-oriented software you use to accomplish specific tasks, such as word processing, managing files on your computer, and performing calculations. When you work with Windows 98 and Me, you will notice many **icons**, small pictures on your screen intended to be meaningful symbols of the items they represent. You will also notice **windows** (thus the name of the operating system), rectangular frames on your screen that can contain several icons, the contents of a file, or other usable data. A **file** is an electronic collection of information, such as a resume or a database of addresses. This use of icons and windows is called a **graphical user interface** (**GUI**, pronounced "gooey"), meaning that you interact ("interface") with the computer through the use of graphics: icons and other meaningful words, symbols, and windows. This unit introduces you to basic Windows skills.

Windows 98 and Me

Starting Windows and Viewing the Windows Desktop

When you first start Windows, you see the Windows Active Desktop. The **Active Desktop** is an on-screen version of a regular desk, containing all the information and tools you need to accomplish your tasks. From the desktop, you can access, store, share, and explore information in a seamless manner, whether it resides on your computer, a network, or the Internet. (The **Internet** is a worldwide collection of over 40 million computers linked together to share information.) The desktop is called "active" because (unlike other Windows desktops) it allows you to access the Internet and view Internet content directly from it. Figure A-1 and Figure A-2 show what the desktop looks like when you start Microsoft Windows 98 and Millennium Edition (Me) for the first time. The bar at the bottom of your screen is called the **taskbar**; it allows you to start programs and switch among currently running programs. (At the moment, none are running.) At the left end of the taskbar is the **Start button**, which you use to start programs, find and open files, access Windows Help, and so on. Next to the Start button on the taskbar is the **Quick Launch toolbar**, which contains buttons you use to quickly start Internet related programs and show the desktop. Use Table A-1 to identify the icons and other elements you see on your desktop. Windows 98 and Me automatically starts when you turn on your computer. If Windows is not currently running, follow the steps below to start it now.

1. **Turn on your computer**
   Windows automatically starts and the desktop appears, as shown in Figure A-1 and Figure A-2. If you are working on a network at school or at an office, you might see a network password dialog box. If so, continue to Step 2. If not, continue to the next lesson.

   ##### Trouble?
   If you don't know your password, ask your instructor or technical support person for assistance.

2. **In the User name box, type your username, then type your password in the Password box**
   When you enter a valid password, you receive privileges to use the network.

3. **Click OK**
   Only asterisks appear as you type the password. This helps to prevent other people from learning your password. When you type a valid password, you receive privileges to use the network. When you start Windows, the Welcome to Windows dialog box might appear, depending on your startup settings.

   ##### QuickTip
   To open this dialog box, click the Start button, point to Programs, point to Accessories, point to System Tools (98) or Entertainment (Me), then click Welcome to Windows.

4. **In the Welcome to Windows (98) or Windows Millennium Edition Preview (Me) dialog box, click the Show this screen at startup check box to clear it, then click Exit or the Close button**
   Once the password is accepted, the Windows desktop appears on your screen, as shown in Figure A-1 and Figure A-2.

FIGURE A-1: Windows Active Desktop for Windows 98

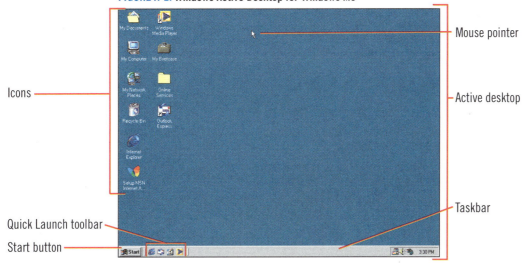

FIGURE A-2: Windows Active Desktop for Windows Me

TABLE A-1: Elements of the Windows Active Desktop

desktop element	allows you to	desktop element	allows you to
My Computer	Work with different disk drives and printers on your computer system	My Briefcase	Keep various copies of documents updated between computers
Network Neighborhood (98) or My Network Places (Me)	Work with different disk drives and printers on a network	Online Services folder	Store programs to access online services such as America Online
Outlook Express	Start Outlook Express, an electronic mail program	Setup MSN Internet Access	Start setup program for The Microsoft Network, an online service
Connect to the Internet	Create a connection to the Internet using a phone or network	Taskbar	Start programs and switch among open programs
Recycle Bin	Delete and restore files	Start button	Start programs, open documents, find a file, and more
Internet Explorer	Start Internet Explorer, a program you use to access the Internet	Quick Launch Toolbar	Show the desktop, start Internet Explorer, start Outlook Express, and start Windows Media Player (Me)
My Documents folder	Store programs, documents, graphics, or other files	Windows Media Player (Me)	Start Windows Media Player, a video and sound program

GETTING STARTED WITH WINDOWS 98 AND ME

Windows 98 and Me

Using the Mouse

A **mouse** is a handheld input device you roll across a flat surface (such as a desk or a mousepad) to position the **mouse pointer**, the small symbol that indicates the pointer's relative position on the desktop. When you move the mouse, the mouse pointer on the screen moves in the same direction. The shape of the mouse pointer changes to indicate different activities. Table A-2 shows some common mouse pointer shapes. Once you move the mouse pointer to a desired position on the screen, you use the **mouse buttons**, shown in Figure A-3, to "tell" your computer what you want it to do. Table A-3 describes the basic mouse techniques you use frequently when working in Windows. Try using the mouse now to become familiar with these navigational skills.

Steps

1. **Place your hand on the mouse, locate the mouse pointer ▷ on the desktop, then move the mouse back and forth across your desk**
   As you move the mouse, the mouse pointer moves correspondingly.

   > **Trouble?**
   > If pointing to the icon highlights it, you are not using default Windows 98 and Me settings. Consult your instructor or technical support person. This book assumes you are using Windows default double-click mouse settings.

2. **Move the mouse to position the mouse pointer over the My Computer icon 🖳 in the upper-left corner of the desktop**
   Positioning the mouse pointer over an icon or over any specific item on the screen is called **pointing**.

3. **Press and release the left mouse button**
   The act of pressing a mouse button once and releasing it is called **clicking**. The icon is now highlighted, or shaded differently than the other icons on the desktop. The act of clicking an item, such as an icon, indicates that you have **selected** it to perform some future operation on it. To perform any type of operation on an icon (such as moving it), you must first select it. Now try a skill called **dragging**, which you use to move icons and other Windows elements.

4. **Point to 🖳, press and hold down the left mouse button, move the mouse down and to the right, then release the mouse button**
   The icon moves with the mouse pointer. This is called dragging. Next you use the mouse to display a shortcut menu.

   > **QuickTip**
   > When a step tells you to "click," it means, by default, to left-click. The direction says "right-click" if you are to click with the right mouse button.

5. **Point to 🖳, then press and release the right mouse button**
   Clicking the right mouse button is known as **right-clicking**. Right-clicking an item on the desktop displays a **pop-up menu**, shown in Figure A-4. This menu displays the commands most commonly used for the item you clicked; the available commands are not therefore the same for every item.

6. **Click anywhere outside the menu to close the pop-up menu**
   Clicking outside the menu in a blank area or pressing [Esc] closes the pop-up menu without performing a command.

   > **QuickTip**
   > You can quickly rearrange icons on the desktop. Right-click an empty area of the desktop, point to Arrange Icons, then click by a Type.

7. **Move 🖳 back to its original position in the upper-left corner of the desktop using the pointing and dragging skills you just learned**

8. **Point to 🖳, then click the left mouse button twice quickly**
   The My Computer window opens, containing several icons. Clicking the mouse button twice is known as **double-clicking**, and it allows you to open the window, program, or file that an icon represents. Leave the desktop as it is, and move on to the next lesson.

WINDOWS 98 AND ME A-4 GETTING STARTED WITH WINDOWS 98 AND ME

FIGURE A-3: Typical mouse

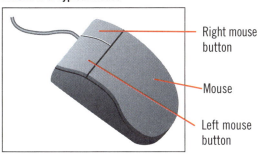

FIGURE A-4: Pop-up menu

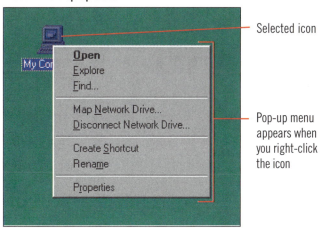

TABLE A-2: Common mouse pointer shapes

shape	used to
▶	Select items, choose commands, start programs, and work with programs
I	Position mouse pointer for editing or inserting text; called the insertion point or cursor
⌛	Indicate Windows is busy processing a command
↔	Position mouse pointer on the border of a window for changing the size of a window
☝	Position mouse pointer for selecting and opening Web-based content

TABLE A-3: Basic mouse techniques

task	what to do
Pointing	Move the mouse to position it over an item on the desktop
Clicking	Press and release the left mouse button
Double-clicking	Press and release the left mouse button twice quickly
Dragging	Point to an item, press and hold the left mouse button, move the mouse to a new location, then release the mouse button
Right-clicking	Point to an item, then press and release the right mouse button

Using the mouse with the Internet

When you use the standard Windows operating system, you click an item to select it and double-click the item to open it. However, when you use the Internet, you point to an item to select it and single-click the item to open it. Because Windows 98 and Me integrates use of the Internet with its other functions, it allows you to choose whether you want to extend the way you click on the Internet to the rest of your computer work. Therefore, Windows 98 and Me gives you two choices for selecting and opening icons using the mouse buttons: single-click (known as the Internet or Web style) or double-click (known as the Classic style). To change from one style to the other in Windows 98, click the Start button on the taskbar, point to Settings, click Folder Options, then click the Web style, Classic style, or Custom option. To perform the same task in Windows Me, click the Start button on the taskbar, point to Settings, click Control Panel, double-click Folder Options, then click the Single-click to open an item (point to select) or Double-click to open an item (single-click to select) option. Windows 98 and Me is set by default to double-click.

Windows 98 and Me

Getting Started with the Windows Desktop

The key to getting started with the Windows desktop is learning how to use the **Start** button on the taskbar. Clicking the Start button on the taskbar displays the Start menu, a list of commands that allows you to start a program, open a document, change a Windows setting, find a file, or display Help information. Table A-4 describes the available commands on this menu that are installed with Windows 98 and Me. As you become more familiar with Windows, you might want to customize the Start menu to include additional items that you use most often and change Windows settings in the Control Panel to customize your Windows desktop. Begin by viewing the Start menu and opening the **Control Panel**, a window containing various programs that allow you to specify how your computer looks and performs.

Steps

1. **Click the Start button on the taskbar**
   The Start menu opens. You use the Settings command on the Start menu to change a Windows system setting.

2. **Point to Settings on the Start menu**
   An arrow next to a menu item indicates a **cascading menu**, or a **submenu**—a list of commands for that menu item. Pointing at the arrow displays a submenu from which you can choose additional commands. The Settings submenu shown in Figure A-5 opens, listing commands to open the Control Panel and Printers; change settings for the taskbar, Start menu, folders, and icons; and update Windows.

3. **Click Control Panel on the submenu**
   The Control Panel shown in Figure A-6 opens, containing icons for various programs that allow you to specify how your computer looks and performs. For Windows Me, a down arrow might appear at the bottom of the list. You can click the down arrow to display hidden menu items. Windows Me uses **Personalized Menus**, which keeps track of which programs you use and hides the programs you have not used recently. Leave the Control Panel open for now, and continue to the next lesson.

> **QuickTip**
> To turn off Personalized Menus, click Taskbar and Start Menu on the Settings list, then click the Use Personalized Menus check box to clear it.

TABLE A-4: Start menu commands

command	description
Windows Update	Connects to a Microsoft Web site and updates your Windows 98 and Me files as necessary
Programs	Opens programs included on the Start menu
Favorites	Connects to favorite Web sites or opens folders or documents that you previously selected; available when the display Favorites feature is turned on in the Taskbar and Start Menu Properties dialog box (Me).
Documents	Opens a list of documents most recently opened and saved
Settings	Allows user preferences for system settings, including Control Panel, printers, taskbar, Start menu, folders (98), icons (98), Active Desktop (98), and Dial Up Networking (Me)
Find (98) or Search (Me)	Locates programs, files, folders, or computers on your computer network, or finds information or people on the Internet
Help	Displays Windows Help information by topic, alphabetical index, or search criteria
Run	Opens a program or file based on a location and filename that you type or select
Log Off	Allows you to log off the system and log on as a different user
Shut Down	Provides options to shut down the computer, restart the computer in Windows mode, set the computer in Stand by mode, restart the computer in MS-DOS mode (98), log off a user and restart the computer (Me), or set the computer in hibernate mode (Me)

FIGURE A-5: Cascading menus

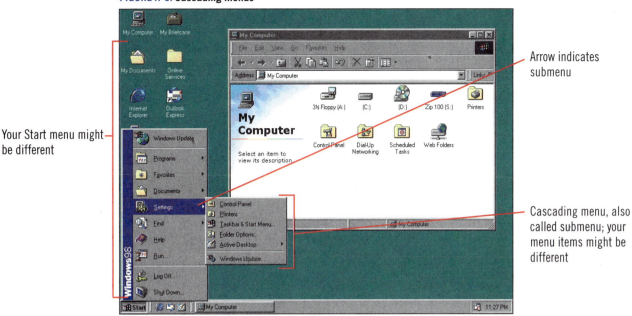

Your Start menu might be different

Arrow indicates submenu

Cascading menu, also called submenu; your menu items might be different

FIGURE A-6: Control Panel

Icons for various programs to change Windows settings

Accessing the Internet from the Active Desktop

One of the important differences between Windows 98 and Me and other versions of Windows is that Windows 98 and Me allows you to access the Internet right from the desktop. This is possible because a program called Internet Explorer is integrated into the Windows 98 and Me operating system. **Internet Explorer** is an example of a **browser**, a computer program designed to access the Internet. Windows 98 and Me adds Web enhancements to the Start menu and the taskbar. The Favorites command on the Start menu makes it easy to access places on the Internet you visit frequently. Commands on the Find (98) or Search (Me) submenu, On the Internet and People, make it easy to find and access places on the Internet you want to visit. To provide additional Internet access, the Quick Launch toolbar, available on the taskbar, helps you launch Internet-related programs and show the desktop. Windows 98 and Me makes it easier than ever to access the Internet.

Windows 98 and Me

Moving and Resizing Windows

One of the powerful things about the Windows operating system is that you can open more than one window or program at once. This means, however, that the desktop can get cluttered with many open windows for the various programs you are using. To organize your desktop, you sometimes must change the size of a window or move it to a different location. Each window, no matter what it contains, is surrounded by a standard border that you can drag to move the window or change its size. Each window also has three standard buttons in the upper-right corner that allow you to change the window's size. Table A-5 shows the different mouse pointer shapes that appear when resizing windows. Try moving and resizing the Control Panel window now.

1. **Click anywhere in the My Computer window, or click the My Computer button on the taskbar**
   The My Computer window moves in front of the Control Panel window. The My Computer window is now **active**; this means that any actions you perform take place in this window. At times, you might want to hide a window so that it isn't visible on the desktop but is still open.

2. **Click the Minimize button in the My Computer window**
   The window no longer appears on the desktop, but you can still see a button named My Computer on the taskbar. When you **minimize** a window, you do not close it but merely reduce it to a button on the taskbar so that you can work more easily in other windows. The button on the taskbar reminds you that the program is still running.

> **QuickTip**
> You can click the Show Desktop button on the Quick Launch toolbar to minimize all open windows and programs and see the desktop.

3. **Point to the title bar on the Control Panel**
   The **title bar** is the area along the top of the window that contains the name of the file and the program used to create it. When a window is active, the title bar color changes from gray to blue. You can move any window to a new location on the desktop by dragging the window's title bar.

4. **With the mouse pointer over any spot on the title bar, click and drag the window to center it on the desktop**
   This action is similar to dragging an icon to a new location. The window is relocated.

> **QuickTip**
> You can double-click the title bar of a window to switch between maximizing and restoring the size of a window.

5. **Click the Maximize button in the Control Panel**
   When you **maximize** a window, it fills the entire screen.

6. **Click the Restore button in the Control Panel**
   The **Restore button** returns a window to its previous size, as shown in Figure A-7. The Restore button only appears when a window is maximized. Now try making the window smaller.

> **QuickTip**
> You can resize windows by dragging any corner, not just the lower left. You can also drag any border to make the window taller, shorter, wider, or narrower.

7. **Position the mouse pointer on the lower-right corner of the Control Panel window until the pointer changes to ↖, as indicated in Figure A-7, then drag the corner up and to the left**
   The window is now resized. In the next lesson you work with the menus and toolbars in the Control Panel, so you can close My Computer now.

8. **Click the My Computer button on the taskbar**
   The My Computer window is now the size it was before you minimized it and is now active. When you finish using a window, you can close it with the Close button.

9. **Click the Close button, located in the upper-right corner of the My Computer window**
   The My Computer window closes. You will learn more about My Computer in later lessons.

FIGURE A-7: Restored Control Panel window

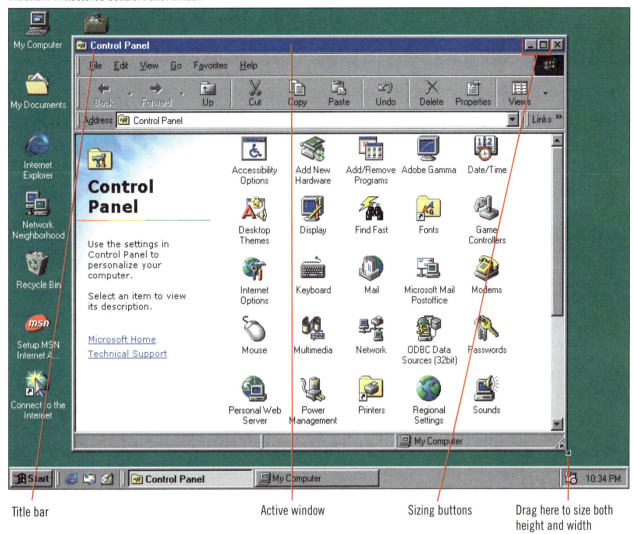

Title bar · Active window · Sizing buttons · Drag here to size both height and width

TABLE A-5: Mouse pointer shapes that appear when resizing windows

mouse pointer shape	use to
↔	Drag the right or left edge of a window to change its width
↕	Drag the top or bottom edge of a window to change its height
↘ or ↙	Drag any corner of a window to change its size proportionally

CLUES TO USE

Moving and resizing the taskbar

In addition to windows, you can also resize and move other elements on the desktop, such as the taskbar, using the methods in this lesson. You can move the taskbar by dragging it to any edge (right, left, top, or bottom) of the desktop. You can also change the size of the taskbar by dragging its edge.

GETTING STARTED WITH WINDOWS 98 AND ME

Windows 98 and Me

Using Menus and Toolbars

A **menu** is a list of commands that you use to accomplish certain tasks. You already used the Start menu to open the Control Panel. A **command** is a directive that provides access to a program's features. Each Windows program also has its own set of menus, which are on the menu bar along the top of the program window. The **menu bar** organizes commands into groups of related operations. Each group is listed under the name of the menu, such as "File" or "Help." To access the commands in a menu, you click the name of the menu. See Table A-6 for examples of items on a typical menu. You can also carry out some of the most frequently used commands on a menu by clicking a button on a toolbar. A **toolbar** contains buttons that are convenient shortcuts for menu commands. ▶ Use a menu and toolbar button to change how the Control Panel window's contents appear.

QuickTip
You can add buttons to or remove them from a toolbar to customize it. To customize the toolbar, click View on the menu bar, point to Toolbars, then click Customize.

1. **Click View on the menu bar**
   The View menu appears, displaying the View commands, as shown in Figure A-8. When you click a menu name, a general description of the commands available on that menu appears in the status bar. On a menu, a **check mark** identifies a currently selected feature (that is, the feature is enabled or "on"). To disable ("turn off") the feature, you click the command again to remove the check mark. A **bullet mark** also indicates that an option is enabled. To disable a command with a bullet mark next to it, however, you must select another command (within the menu section) in its place. In the next step, you select a command.

2. **On the View menu, click Small Icons**
   The icons are now smaller than they were before, taking less room in the window.

3. **Click View on the menu bar**
   The View menu appears, with check marks next to commands. To remove the status bar from the Control Panel, you click Status Bar to turn off the feature.

4. **Click Status Bar**
   The Control Panel appears without the status bar.

5. **Click View on the menu bar, point to Toolbars, then click Text Labels (98)**
   The Control Panel toolbar appears without text labels at the bottom of the buttons. The toolbar at the top of the window includes buttons for the commands that you use most frequently while you work with the Control Panel. When you position the mouse pointer over a button, the name of the button, known as a **ScreenTip**, appears. Use the ScreenTip feature to explore a button on the toolbar. (Windows 98 only)

6. **On the Control Panel toolbar, position the pointer over the Views button to display the ScreenTip**
   Some toolbar buttons appear with an arrow, which indicates the button contains several choices. You click the button arrow to display the choices.

7. **On the Control Panel toolbar, click the Views button list arrow as shown in Figure A-9, then click Details**
   The Details view includes a description of each Control Panel program. In the next lesson you use scroll bars in the Control Panel to view and read the description of each Control Panel program.

▶ WINDOWS 98 AND ME A-10   **GETTING STARTED WITH WINDOWS 98 AND ME**

FIGURE A-8: View menu in the Control Panel

FIGURE A-9: Control Panel toolbars

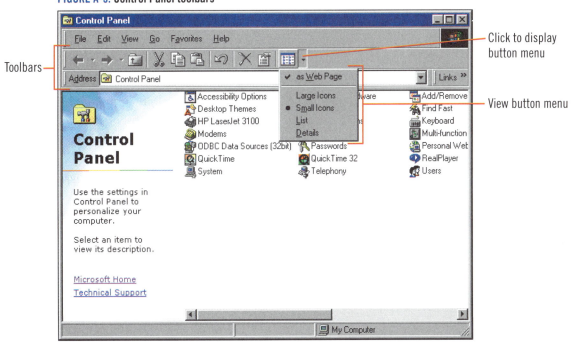

TABLE A-6: Typical items on a menu

item	description	example
Dimmed command	A menu command that is not currently available	Undo Ctrl+Z
Ellipsis	Indicates that a dialog box will open that allows you to select from several options	Save As...
Triangle	Indicates that a cascading menu will open containing an additional list of commands	Zoom ▶
Keyboard shortcut	An alternative to using the mouse for executing a command	Paste Ctrl+V
Underlined letter	Indicates the letter to press while holding down the [Alt] key for a keyboard shortcut	Print Preview

GETTING STARTED WITH WINDOWS 98 AND ME

Windows 98 and Me

Using Scroll Bars

When you cannot see all of the items available in a window, scroll bars appear on the right and/or bottom edges of the window. **Scroll bars** allow you to display the additional contents of the window. Figure A-10 shows components of the scroll bars. The vertical scroll bar moves your view up and down through a window; the horizontal scroll bar moves your view from left to right. There are several ways you can use the scroll bars. When you need to scroll only a short distance, you can use the scroll arrows. When you need to scroll more quickly, you can click in the scroll bar above or below the **scroll box** to move the view up or down one window's height (the line that was at the bottom of the screen moves to the top, and vice versa). Dragging the scroll box moves you even more quickly to a new part of the window. See Table A-7 for a summary of the different ways to use scroll bars. You can use the scroll bars to view and read the description of each Control Panel program.

QuickTip
When no scroll bars appear in a window, it means that all the information fits completely in the window.

1. In the Control Panel, click the **down scroll arrow** in the vertical scroll bar, as shown in Figure A-10
   Clicking this arrow moves the view down one line. Clicking the up arrow moves the view up one line at a time.

2. Click the **up scroll arrow** in the vertical scroll bar
   The view moves up one line.

3. Click anywhere in the area below the scroll box in the vertical scroll bar
   The contents of the window scroll down in a larger increment.

4. Click the area above the scroll box in the vertical scroll bar
   The contents of the window scroll back up. To move in even greater increments, you can drag the scroll box to a new position.

QuickTip
If you have a mouse with a wheel button between the left and right buttons, you can roll the wheel button to scroll up and down quickly or click the wheel button and move the mouse in any direction.

5. Drag the **scroll box** in the horizontal scroll bar to the middle of the bar
   The scroll box indicates your relative position within the window, in this case, the halfway point. After reading the Control Panel program descriptions, you restore the Control Panel to its original display.

6. On the Control Panel toolbar, click the **Views button list arrow**, then click **Large Icons**

7. Click **View** on the menu bar, then click **Status Bar**
   The status bar appears at the bottom of the Control Panel.

8. Click **View** on the menu bar, point to **Toolbars**, then click **Text Labels**
   In the next lesson you open a Control Panel program to learn how to work with dialog boxes.

FIGURE A-10: Scroll bars in Control Panel

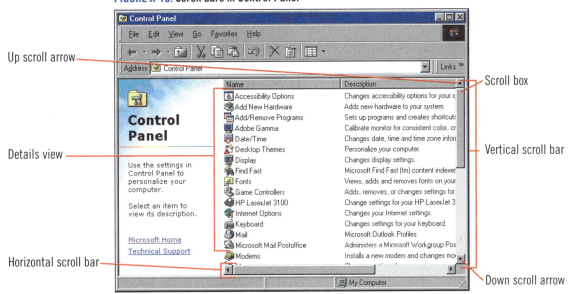

TABLE A-7: Using scroll bars in a window

to	do this
Move down one line	Click the down arrow at the bottom of the vertical scroll bar
Move up one line	Click the up arrow at the top of the vertical scroll bar
Move down one window's height	Click in the area below the scroll box in the vertical scroll bar
Move up one window's height	Click in the area above the scroll box in the vertical scroll bar
Move up or down a greater distance in the window	Drag the scroll box in the vertical scroll bar
Move a short distance side to side in a window	Click the left or right arrows in the horizontal scroll bar
Move to the right one window's width	Click in the area to the right of the scroll box in the horizontal scroll bar
Move to the left one window's width	Click in the area to the left of the scroll box in the horizontal scroll bar
Move left or right a greater distance in the window	Drag the scroll box in the horizontal scroll bar

Accessibility for special needs

If you have difficulty typing or using a mouse, have slightly impaired vision, or are deaf or hard of hearing, you can adjust the appearance and behavior of Windows 98 and Me, making your computer easier to use. The **Accessibility Wizard** helps you configure Windows for your vision, hearing, and mobility needs. The Accessibility Wizard also enables you to save your settings in a file that you can also use on another computer. To open the Accessibility Wizard, click Start, point to Programs, point to Accessories, point to Accessibility, then click Accessibility Wizard. If the feature is not available, use the Add/Remove Programs icon in the Control Panel to set up the Windows feature. You can also use the Accessibility Options icon in the Control Panel to adjust the way your keyboard, display, and mouse function to suit various vision and motor abilities. Some of the accessibility tools available include StickyKeys, which enables simultaneous keystrokes while pressing one key at a time; FilterKeys, which adjusts the response of your keyboard; ToggleKeys, which emits sounds when you press certain locking keys; SoundSentry, which provides visual warnings for system sounds; ShowSounds, which instructs programs to provide captions; High Contrast, which improves screen contrast; and MouseKeys, which enables the keyboard to perform mouse functions.

Windows 98 and Me

Using Dialog Boxes

A **dialog box** is a window that opens when you choose a menu command that is followed by an ellipsis (...). The ellipsis indicates that you must supply more information before the program can carry out the command you selected. Dialog boxes open in other situations as well, such as when you open a program in the Control Panel. In a dialog box, you specify the options you want using a variety of elements. See Figure A-11 and Table A-8 for some of the typical elements of a dialog box. ◆ Practice using a dialog box to control your mouse settings.

Steps

1. **In the Control Panel, double-click the Mouse icon** (You might need to scroll down the Control Panel window to find this icon.)
   The Mouse Properties dialog box opens, shown in Figure A-12. The options in this dialog box allow you to control the configuration of the mouse buttons, select the types of pointers that appear, choose the speed of the mouse movement on the screen, and specify what type of mouse you are using. **Tabs** at the top of the dialog box separate these options into related categories. The tabs in the dialog box vary depending on the mouse installed on the computer.

2. **Click the Buttons tab or the Activities tab**
   This tab has two or more boxes. The first, labeled Button Configuration, has options you can select to make the mouse easier to use for a right-handed or left-handed person. The second, labeled Double-click Speed, has a slider for you to set how fast the mouse pointer responds to a double-click. The slider lets you specify the degree to which the option is in effect—the speed of a double-click. The other boxes vary depending on the Windows version and mouse installed on the computer. Next you experiment with the double-click speed options.

3. **In the Double-click Speed box, drag the slider half way to the right**
   You set the mouse pointer to respond to a fast double-click. You can test the double-click speed in the Test area to make sure it is comfortable for you to use on a regular basis.

4. **Double-click the Test area to the right of the slider until the graphical icon moves**
   As you move the mouse, notice the long pointer trails.

5. **Click the other tabs in the Mouse Properties dialog box, and examine the available options in each category**
   Now, you need to select a command button to carry out the options you selected. The two most common command buttons are OK and Cancel. Clicking OK accepts your changes and closes the dialog box; clicking Cancel leaves the original settings intact and closes the dialog box. The third command button in this dialog box is Apply. Clicking the Apply button verifies the changes you've made and keeps the dialog box open so that you can select additional options. Because you might share this computer with others, it's important to restore the dialog box options to their original settings.

6. **Click Cancel to leave the original settings intact and close the dialog box**

7. **Click the Close button in the upper-right corner of the Control Panel**

FIGURE A-11: Dialog box elements

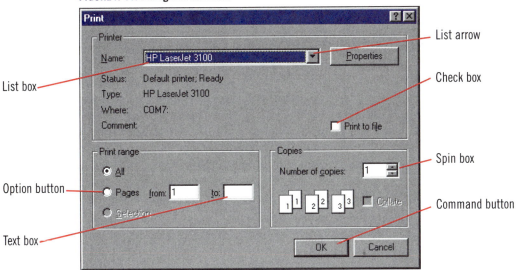

FIGURE A-12: Mouse Properties dialog box

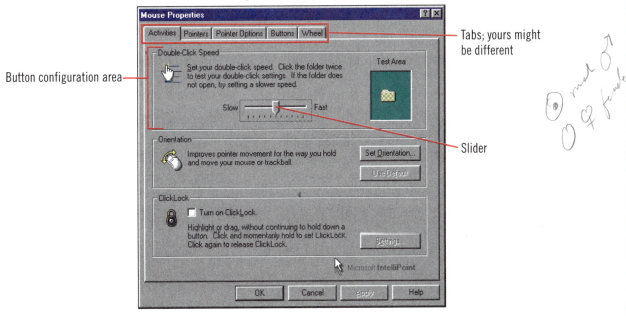

TABLE A-8: Typical items in a dialog box

item	description
Check box	A square box that turns an option on (when the box is checked) and off (when the box is blank)
Command button	A rectangular button with the name of the command on it; it carries out a command in a dialog box
List box	A box containing a list of items; to choose an item, click the list arrow, then click the desired item
Option button	A small circle that selects a single dialog box option (you cannot check more than one option button in a list)
Spin box	A box with two arrows and a text box; allows you to scroll through and choose from numerical increments or type a number
Slider	A shape that you drag to set the degree to which an option is in effect
Tab	A place to organize related options
Text box	A box in which you type text

GETTING STARTED WITH WINDOWS 98 AND ME

Windows 98 and Me

Using Windows Help

When you have a question about how to do something in Windows 98 and Me, you can usually find the answer with a few clicks of your mouse. There are a variety of different ways to access **Windows Help**, which is like a book stored on your computer, complete with an index and a table of contents to make finding information easier. You can click Help on the Start menu to open the main Windows Help dialog box. To get help on a specific program, you can click Help on the program's menu bar. You can also access **context-sensitive help**, help specifically related to what you are doing, using a variety of methods such as pointing to or right-clicking an object. Use Help to learn more about Windows.

Steps

WIN 98

Use the set of steps designed for the Windows version you are using.

1. **Click the Start button on the taskbar, then click Help**
   The Windows Help dialog box opens with the Contents tab in front, shown in Figure A-13. The Contents tab provides a list of Help categories. Each book icon has several "chapters" (subcategories) whose names you can see by clicking the book icon or the name of the Help category next to the book. The Windows Help dialog also includes the Index tab and the Search tab. The Index tab provides you with an alphabetical list of all available Help topics, much like an index at the end of a book. The Search tab helps you locate the topic you need using keywords.

> **QuickTip**
> You can hide the left pane of the Help window to make reading the information easier. Click the Hide button on the Help toolbar to hide the left pane; click the Show button to redisplay it.

2. **Click the Contents tab (if necessary), point to the Exploring Your Computer category, then click to display the subcategories**
   When you point to a Help category, the mouse changes to the hand pointer and the Help category text is selected. The text changes to gray and is underlined. This is similar to the way selecting on the Internet works. You continue to click subcategories to find the Help topic you want.

> **QuickTip**
> To print all or part of the Windows Help information, click the Options button on the Help toolbar, then click Print.

3. **Click the The Windows Desktop subcategory, then click the Getting Started with Windows Desktop Update topic**
   The Help topic appears in the right pane, as shown in Figure A-13. **Panes** divide a window into two or more sections. Read the help information on the Windows desktop. You can move back and forth between Help topics you have already visited by clicking the Back button and the Forward button on the Help toolbar.

4. **Click the Close button in the Windows Help window**
   The Help window closes.

WIN ME

Use the set of steps designed for the Windows version you are using.

1. **Click the Start button on the taskbar, then click Help**
   The Help and Support dialog box opens with a list of Help categories.

2. **Point to the Using Windows Millennium Edition category, then click to display the subcategories**
   When you point to a Help category, the mouse changes to the hand pointer and the Help category text is selected. The text changes to gray and is underlined. This is similar to the way selecting on the Internet works. You continue to click subcategories to find the Help topic you want.

3. **Click the Getting Started with Windows Me category, then click the Learning more about Windows Me Help topic**
   The Help topic appears in the right pane, as shown in Figure A-14. **Panes** divide a window into two or more sections. Read the help information on Windows Me. You can move back and forth between Help topics you have already visited by clicking the Back button and the Forward button on the Help toolbar.

4. **Click the Close button in the Help and Support window**
   The Help window closes.

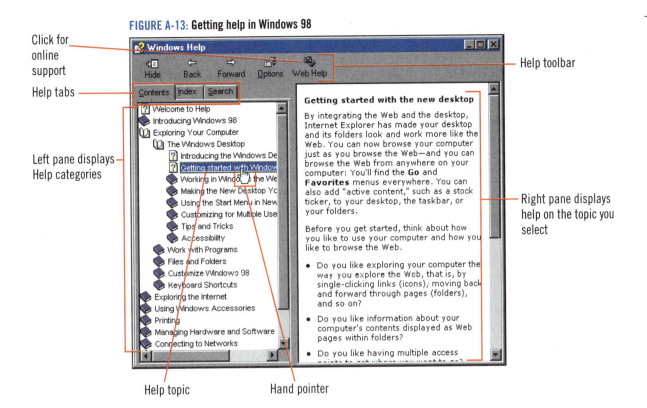

FIGURE A-13: Getting help in Windows 98

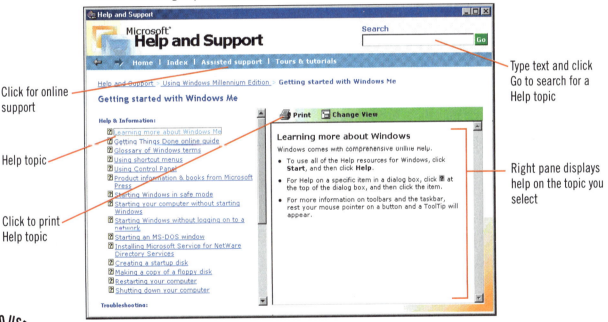

FIGURE A-14: Getting help in Windows Me

Context-sensitive help

To receive help in a dialog box, click the Help button in the upper-right corner of the dialog box; the mouse pointer changes to . Click on the item in the dialog box for which you need additional information. A pop-up window opens, providing a brief explanation of the selected feature. You can also click the right mouse button on an item in a dialog box, then click the What's This? button to display the explanation. In addition, when you click the right mouse button in a Help topic window, you can choose commands to copy and print the contents of the topic. Help windows always appear on top of the currently active window, so you can see Help topics while you work.

Windows 98 and Me

Shutting Down Windows

When you finish working at your computer, you need to make sure to **shut down**, or turn off, your computer properly. This involves several steps: saving and closing all open files, closing all open windows, exiting all running programs, shutting down Windows itself, and, finally, turning off the computer. If you turn off the computer while Windows or other programs are running, you can lose important data. Once you close all files, windows, and programs, you choose the Shut Down command from the Start menu. The Shut Down Windows dialog box opens offering several options, as shown in Figure A-15 (98) or Figure A-16 (Me). See Table A-9 for a description of each option. Depending on your Windows settings, your shut-down options might be different. Close all your open files, windows, and programs, and then exit Windows.

Steps

1. If you have any open windows or programs, click the **Close button** ☒ in the upper-right corner of the window

   Complete the remaining steps to shut down Windows and your computer only if your instructor tells you so.

2. Click the **Start button** on the taskbar, then click **Shut Down**

   The Shut Down Windows dialog box opens as shown in Figure A-15 (98) or Figure A-16 (Me). In this dialog box, you have several options to shut down and restart your computer. You choose the Shut Down option.

3. Click the **Shut Down option button** (98), or click the **What do you want the computer to do? list arrow**, then click **Shut down** (Me), if it isn't already selected

4. If you are working in a lab, click **Cancel** to return to the Windows desktop; if you are working on your own machine or if your instructor tells you to shut down Windows, click **OK** to exit Windows

5. When you see the message "It's now safe to turn off your computer," turn off your computer and monitor

   Some computers power off automatically, so you may not see this message.

TABLE A-9: Shut down options

shut down option	function	when to use it
Stand by	Maintains your session, keeping the computer running on low power	When you want to stop working with Windows for a few moments and conserve power (ideal for a laptop or portable computer)
Shut down	Prepares the computer to be turned off	When you finish working with Windows and you want to shut off your computer
Restart	Restarts the computer and reloads Windows	When you want to restart the computer and begin working with Windows again (your programs may have frozen or stopped working)
Restart in MS-DOS mode (98)	Starts the computer in the MS-DOS mode	When you want to run programs under MS-DOS or use DOS commands to work with files
Hibernate (Me)	Saves your session to disk so that you can safely turn off power; restores your session the next time you start Windows	When you want to stop working with Windows for a while and start working again later; available when the Power Management setting (in the Control Panel) is turned on

FIGURE A-15: Shut Down Windows dialog box for Windows 98

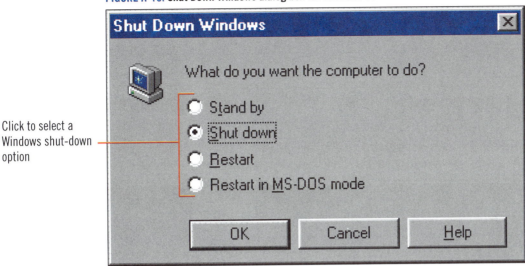

Click to select a Windows shut-down option

FIGURE A-16: Shut Down Windows dialog box for Windows Me

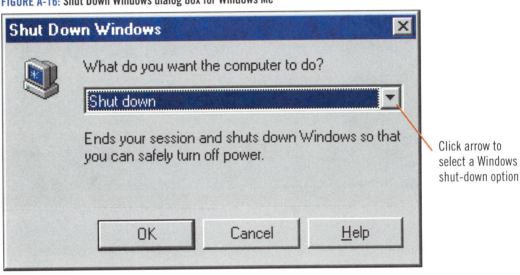

Click arrow to select a Windows shut-down option

Logging off Windows

Many users may use the same computer, so each user has his or her own identity in Windows. This allows many users to use the same computer, keep their files completely private, and customize the operating system for their own preferences. Windows manages these separate identities by giving each user a unique user name and password. To quickly change users of the same computer, you can choose the Log Off command on the Start menu or in the Shut Down Windows dialog box (Me). This command identifies the name of the user who is currently logged on. When you choose this command, Windows 98 and Me shuts down and automatically restarts at the Enter Network Password dialog box. When the new user types a user name and password, Windows starts with that user's configuration settings and network permissions.

Windows 98 and Me

Practice

▶ Concepts Review

Label each element of the screen shown in Figure A-17.

FIGURE A-17

Match each term with the statement that describes its function.

6. Recycle Bin
7. Sizing buttons
8. Start button
9. Taskbar
10. Title bar
11. Mouse

a. Where the name of the program and file appear
b. Where deleted files are placed
c. Displays the Start button and buttons for currently open programs and windows
d. Allows for minimizing, maximizing, and restoring windows
e. The item you click first to start a program
f. Used to point at screen elements and make selections

Practice

Select the best answers from the following lists of choices.

12. The term for moving an item to a new location on the desktop is:
    a. Dragging.
    b. Restoring.
    c. Pointing.
    d. Clicking.
13. The Maximize button is used to:
    a. Scroll slowly through a window.
    b. Reduce a window to a button on the taskbar.
    c. Return a window to its original size.
    d. Expand a window to fill the entire screen.
14. The Minimize button is used to:
    a. Scroll slowly through a window.
    b. Reduce a window to a button on the taskbar.
    c. Return a window to its original size.
    d. Expand a window to fill the entire screen.
15. The Menu bar provides access to a program's functions through:
    a. Commands.
    b. Dialog box elements.
    c. Toolbar buttons.
    d. Scroll buttons.
16. An ellipsis after a menu command indicates:
    a. Another menu will display.
    b. A keyboard shortcut to that command.
    c. The menu command is not currently available.
    d. A dialog box will open.
17. Which is not a method for getting Help?
    a. Click Help on a program's menu bar.
    b. Right-click in a dialog box, then use the Help pointer to point to what you need help with.
    c. Click the Start button on the taskbar, then click Help.
    d. Click the question mark button in a dialog box.

▶ Skills Review

1. **Identify Windows items on the screen.**
    a. Identify and write down as many desktop items as you can, without referring to the lesson.
    b. Compare your results with Figure A-1 and Figure A-2.
2. **Practice using the mouse.**
    a. Move the mouse on your desk, and watch how the mouse pointer moves across the screen.
    b. Point at the My Computer icon on the desktop.
    c. Click the My Computer icon once. Notice the icon's highlighted title.
    d. Press and hold down the mouse button, then drag the My Computer icon to the opposite side of the desktop. Release the mouse button when you finish.
    e. Drag the My Computer icon back to the original location.
    f. Practice clicking and dragging other icons on the desktop.
    g. Double-click the My Computer icon.

Windows 98 and Me Practice

3. **Get started with Windows.**
   a. Click the Start menu.
   b. Point to Settings, then click Control Panel.
4. **Move and resize windows.**
   a. Click the My Computer window.
   b. Click the Minimize button.
   c. Point to the title bar on the Control Panel window, then drag the window to the center of the desktop.
   d. Click the Maximize button.
   e. Click the Restore button.
   f. Position the mouse pointer on any corner of the Control Panel window, and drag to make the window smaller.
   g. Click the My Computer button on the taskbar.
   h. Click the Close button on the My Computer window.
5. **Use menus and toolbars.**
   a. Click View on the menu bar, then click Small Icons.
   b. Click View on the menu bar, then click List.
   c. Click the Views button arrow on the toolbar, then click Details.
6. **Use scroll bars.**
   a. Click below the vertical scroll box.
   b. Click the vertical up scroll arrow.
   c. Drag the horizontal scroll box to the middle of the scroll bar.
   d. Click the View button arrow on the toolbar, then click Large Icons.
7. **Use dialog boxes.**
   a. Double-click the Display icon, then click the Appearance tab.
   b. Click the Scheme list arrow, then select a color scheme.
   c. Click Apply (but don't click OK yet).
   d. Click the Scheme list arrow, then click Windows Standard to restore the former color scheme.
   e. Click OK, then close the Control Panel.
8. **Use Windows Help.**
   a. Click the Start button, then click Help.
   b. Click the Search tab (98), or click in the Search box (Me).
   c. Type **dialog boxes**, then press [Enter].
   d. Double-click To get Help in a dialog box (98), or click Getting Help in a dialog box (Me).
   e. Read the Help topic in the right pane.
   f. Click the Close button.
9. **Shut down Windows.**
   a. Click the Start button, then click Shut Down.
   b. Click the Restart option button (98), or click the What do you want the computer to do? list arrow, then click Restart (Me).
   c. Click OK if you are not working in a lab or if your lab manager approves of shutting down the computer. Otherwise, click Cancel.

▶ Independent Challenges

1. Windows 98 and Me provides extensive online help. At anytime, you can select Help from the Start menu and get the assistance you need. Use the Help options to learn about the topics listed below.

Practice

To complete this independent challenge:

a. Locate and read the help information on the following topics:
Using the Active Desktop, using shortcut menus, adding or removing toolbar buttons, finding a Help topic, and shutting down your computer.
b. If you have a printer connected to your computer, print one or more Help topics.
c. Close the Windows Help window.

2. You are a student in a Windows 98 and Me course. After learning basic Windows 98 and Me Active Desktop skills, you want to learn how to customize the desktop. Use Windows Help to find information on customizing your desktop and then print the related Help topics.

To complete this independent challenge:

a. Start Windows Help.
b. For Windows 98: Display Getting Started Book: Online Version; display Microsoft Windows 98 Getting Started; display Getting Started; display Customizing Your Desktop; and display the topic Choosing a Desktop Style.

For Windows Me: Click Personalizing Your Computer; click Customizing the look of your computer; click Changing the Windows Me desktop; and click Customizing your desktop, taskbar, Start menu & folders to display the topic.
c. Print the topic.
d. Close Windows Help.

3. You can customize many Windows features to suit your needs and preferences. One way you do this is to change the appearance of the taskbar on the desktop.

To complete this independent challenge:

a. Position the mouse pointer over the top border of the taskbar. When the pointer changes shape, drag up to increase the size of the taskbar.
b. Position the mouse pointer over a blank area of the taskbar, and then drag to the top of the screen to move the taskbar.
c. Click the Start button, point to Settings, and click Taskbar & Start menu (98) or Taskbar and Start Menu (Me). On the Taskbar Options tab (98) or General (Me), click the Show Clock check box to deselect the option, click Apply, and then observe the effect on the taskbar.
d. Print the Screen. (Press [Print Screen] to make a paper copy of the screen. Start the Paint program by clicking the Start button, pointing to Programs, pointing to Accessories, then clicking Paint. Click Edit on the menu bar, click Paste to paste the screen into Paint, then click Yes to paste the large image if necessary. Click File on the menu bar, click Print, then click OK in the Print dialog box.)
e. Restore the taskbar to its original setting, size, and location on the screen.

4. You accepted a new job in New York City. After moving into your new home and unpacking your stuff, you decide to set up your computer. Once you set up and turn on the computer, you decide to change the date and time settings to reflect New York's time zone.

To complete this independent challenge:

a. Open the Control Panel window, then double-click the Date/Time icon.
b. Click the Time Zone list arrow.
c. Select Eastern Time (US & Canada) from the list.
d. Change the month and year to September 2001, then click Apply.
e. Print the screen. (See Independent Challenge 3, Step d for screen printing instructions.)
f. Restore the original date and time zone settings, then click OK.
g. Close the Control Panel window.

Windows 98 and Me | **Practice**

▶ Visual Workshop

Re-create the screen shown in Figure A-18, which shows the Windows desktop with My Computer and the Control Panel open. Print the screen. (See Independent Challenge 3, Step d for screen printing instructions.)

FIGURE A-18

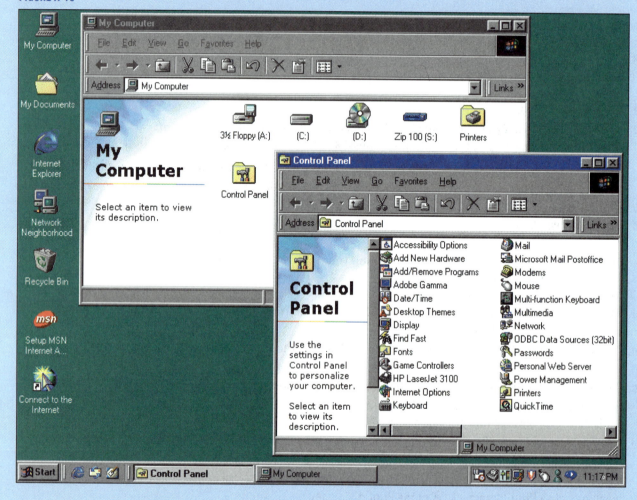

Windows 98 and Me

Working
with Windows Programs

Objectives

- Start a program
- Open and save a WordPad document
- Edit text in WordPad
- Format text in WordPad
- Use Paint
- Copy data between programs
- Print a document
- Play a video clip or sound
- Create a movie

Now that you know how to work with common Windows graphical elements, you're ready to work with programs. Windows comes with several **accessories**: built-in programs that, while not as feature-rich as many programs sold separately, are extremely useful for completing basic tasks. In this unit, you work with some of these accessories. John Casey owns Wired Coffee Company, a growing company that uses Windows 98 and Me. John needs to prepare a new coffee menu, so he plans to use two Windows accessories, WordPad and Paint, to create it. He also wants to use two other multimedia accessories, Media Player and Movie Maker, to play video and sound clips and work with a movie on his computer.

Windows 98 and Me

Starting a Program

A **Windows program** is software designed to run on computers using the Windows operating system. To start a program in Windows, you click the Start button, point to Programs to open the Programs submenu, point to a submenu (if necessary), and then click the program you want to start. In this lesson, you start a Windows Accessory called **WordPad**, a word-processing program that comes with Windows. Throughout the rest of this unit, you work with WordPad and other Windows Accessories to learn essential Windows skills. ➤ John wants to use WordPad to prepare the text of his new coffee menu, so he needs to start this program.

Steps

1. **Click the Start button on the taskbar**
   The Start menu opens.

   > **QuickTip**
   > If a single arrow appears at the top or bottom of the Programs submenu, point to the arrow to scroll up or down the menu to view more elements.

2. **Point to Programs on the Start menu**
   The Programs submenu opens, listing the programs and submenus for programs installed on your computer. WordPad is in the submenu called Accessories.

3. **Point to Accessories on the Programs submenu**
   The Accessories submenu opens, as shown in Figure B-1. Locate WordPad on this submenu. For Windows Me, the Accessories submenu lists a personalized menu of the programs you used most recently. To reduce the number of elements on the Programs submenus and customize your Windows environment, Windows keeps track of which programs you use and hides the programs you have not used recently.

4. **Click the More menu items indicator ⯆ at the bottom of the Accessories submenu (Me), if necessary**
   The full Accessories submenu opens. Locate the WordPad item on this submenu.

   > **Trouble?**
   > If the Toolbar, Format Bar, ruler, or status bar does not appear, click View on the menu bar, then click the element (without a check mark) you want to view.

5. **Click WordPad on the Accessories submenu**
   Your mouse pointer changes momentarily to an hourglass, indicating that you are to wait while Windows starts the WordPad program. The WordPad window then appears on your desktop, as shown in Figure B-2. The WordPad window includes two toolbars, called the Toolbar and **Format Bar**, as well as a ruler, a work area, and a status bar. A blinking line, known as the **insertion point**, appears in the work area of the WordPad window, indicating where new text will appear. The WordPad program button appears in the taskbar, indicating that the WordPad program is now running.

6. **Click the Maximize button in the WordPad window**
   WordPad expands to fill the screen. In the next lesson you open and save a document in WordPad.

FIGURE B-1: Starting WordPad using the Start menu

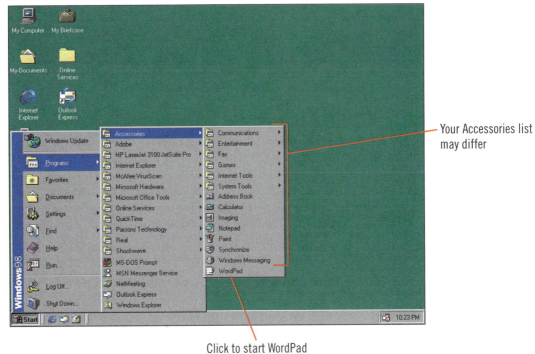

Your Accessories list may differ

Click to start WordPad

FIGURE B-2: Windows desktop with the WordPad window open

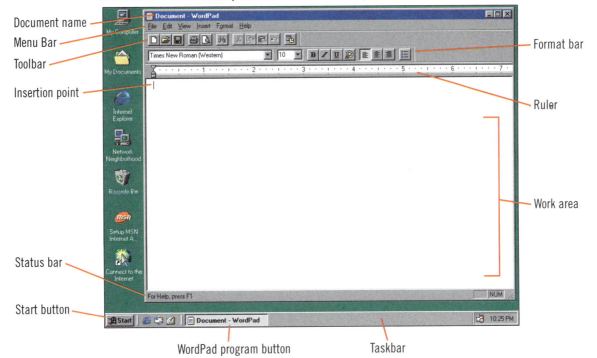

Document name
Menu Bar
Toolbar
Insertion point

Format bar
Ruler

Work area

Status bar
Start button

WordPad program button   Taskbar

Opening and Saving a WordPad Document

A **document** is the piece of work you create using a word-processing program. You can use WordPad to create documents such as letters, memos, and resumes. When you start WordPad, a blank document appears in the work area of the WordPad window, known as the **document window**. You can enter new information to create a new document and save the result in a file, or you can open an existing file and save the document with any changes you made. To prevent any accidental changes to the original document, you can save the document in another file with a new name. This makes a copy of the document, so you can change the new document and leave the original file unaltered. Rather than typing the menu from scratch, John wants to open an existing WordPad document that contains text of the coffee menu and save it with a new name before making any changes to it.

Steps

1. **Click the Open button on the WordPad toolbar**
   The Open dialog box opens, as shown in Figure B-3. In this dialog box, you locate and choose the file you wish to open. The file John created is stored where your Project Files are located.

   Trouble?
   If no filenames appear in the file list, click the Files of Type list arrow, then click Word for Windows.

2. **Click the Look in list arrow, then click the drive and folder where your Project Files are located**
   A list of the files and folders appears in the file list. You can select a file from the file list or type the name of the file you want in the File name text box.

3. **In the file list, click Win B-1, then click Open**
   The file named Win B-1 opens. This is a menu for the coffee company. Save this file with a new name so you don't make any changes to the original file. You use a more descriptive name for the file so you can identify its contents more easily.

   QuickTip
   To provide a consistent place to store all your files, Windows saves all your documents in and opens them and from the My Documents folder on your desktop unless you choose a different location.

4. **Click File on the menu bar, then click Save As**
   The Save As dialog box opens, as shown in Figure B-4. The Save As command allows you to save an existing document under a new name and also in a different folder or drive location.

5. **If Win B-1 is not already selected, click in the File name text box, then select the entire file name by dragging the mouse pointer over it**
   In WordPad, as in most other Windows programs, you must select text before you can modify it. When you **select** text, the selection appears **highlighted** (white text on a black background) to indicate that it is selected. Any action you now take affects the selected text.

6. **Type Coffee Menu to replace the selected text**
   As soon as you start typing, the text you type replaces the selected text.

   QuickTip
   When an existing document is open, you can click the New button on the Toolbar to create a blank new document. The original existing document automatically closes.

7. **Click Save**
   You save the file with a new name, Coffee Menu, in the same folder and drive as the Win B-1 file. The original file, called Win B-1, closes automatically, and the new file name appears in the title bar of the WordPad window.

FIGURE B-3: Open dialog box

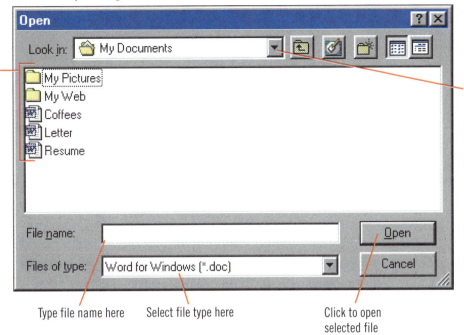

List of files and folders stored in the drive or folder selected in the Look in list box; your list may differ

Click to specify the location of file to be opened

Type file name here   Select file type here   Click to open selected file

FIGURE B-4: Save As dialog box

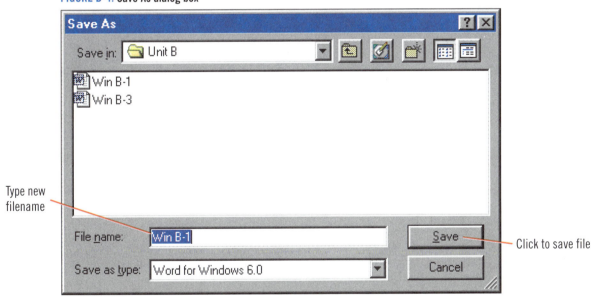

Type new filename

Click to save file

About saving files

Until you save them, the documents you create are stored in the computer's **Random Access Memory (RAM)**. RAM is a temporary storage space whose contents are erased when you turn off the computer. To store a document permanently, you must save it as a file. A file is a collection of information that has a unique name, distinguishing it from other files. You can save files on a **floppy disk** that you insert into the disk drive of your computer (usually drive A: or B:) or a **hard disk**, which is built into the computer (usually drive C:). This book assumes that you will save all of your files on the drive and in the folder where your Project Files are located or on a Project Files Disk, which your instructor provides. Windows lets you save files using names with up to 255 characters, including spaces.

WORKING WITH WINDOWS PROGRAMS

Editing Text in WordPad

Windows 98 and Me

One of the major advantages of using a word-processing program is that you can **edit**, or change, the contents of a document without retyping it. You can also move whole sections of a document from one place to another using the Cut and Paste commands. John wants to add a greeting and change the price of a pound of coffee in the Coffee Menu document. He also wants to change the order of the menu items so that the coffees are listed in alphabetical order.

1. **Press [↓] three times, or click I in the line just above "Specialty Coffees"**
   Figure B-5 shows the insertion point located where you want to insert new text. Repositioning the insertion point in a document (called **navigating**) is an important skill to learn.

   ### Trouble?
   If you make a mistake while typing, press [Backspace] (which deletes the character to the left of the insertion point) repeatedly until you delete your mistake, then retype the text.

2. **Type Welcome to the taste tantalizing coffee selections offered to you by Wired Coffee Company. You will find a variety of specialty coffees, including Single-Origin, Blends, Dark Roasts, and Decaffeinated., then press [Enter]**
   WordPad automatically puts the text that won't fit on one line on the next line, using a feature called **wordwrap**.

3. **In the price of the Breakfast Blend coffee, click to the right of the last digit, 0**
   You need to change this number from "11.90" to "11.00."

4. **Press [Backspace] twice, then type 00**
   Now John wants to rearrange the list so that the coffees are listed in alphabetical order. He needs to move the fourth coffee in the list (Espresso Dark Roast) so it comes before the third (Ethiopian Harrar). To do this, John first must select the name of the fourth coffee; only then he can move the text up the list. You can select text three different ways. You can drag the mouse to highlight the text you want to select. If you need to select just a word, you can double-click it. If you need to select a line or paragraph, you can position the pointer to the left of the first character in the line or paragraph, and then click once to select a line or twice to select an entire paragraph.

   ### QuickTip
   To select the entire paragraph, you can triple-click anywhere in the paragraph.

5. **Position the pointer to the left of the first character in the line "Espresso Dark Roast"**
   The pointer changes from I to ⇗.

6. **Click once**
   With the entire line selected, John can now move the line.

   ### QuickTip
   To view the Clipboard, click the Start button on the taskbar, point to Programs, point to Accessories, point to System Tools, then click Clipboard Viewer.

7. **Click the Cut button ✂ on the Toolbar**
   When selected text is **cut** from a document, Windows removes it from the document and places it on the **Clipboard**, a temporary storage place where it remains available to be pasted elsewhere. When text is **copied**, a copy of it is placed in the Clipboard to be pasted in another location, but the text also remains in its original place in the document.

8. **Press [↑] once to move up one line in the list**
   This is where John wants to paste the line he cut. Selections you paste are inserted at the location of the insertion point.

9. **Click the Paste button 📋 on the Toolbar, then click the Save button 💾 on the Toolbar**
   Figure B-6 shows the information pasted into the list with all the coffees in alphabetical order. You saved the changes you made to the file.

▶ WINDOWS 98 AND ME B-6   **WORKING WITH WINDOWS PROGRAMS**

FIGURE B-5: Positioning the insertion point

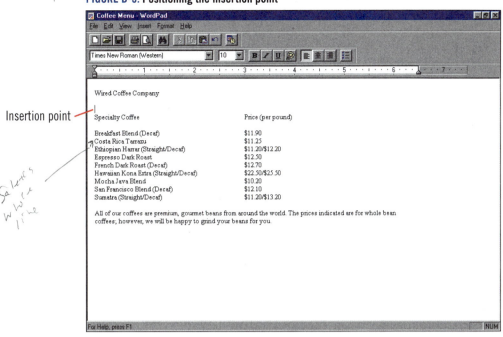

FIGURE B-6: Editing a WordPad file by cutting and pasting

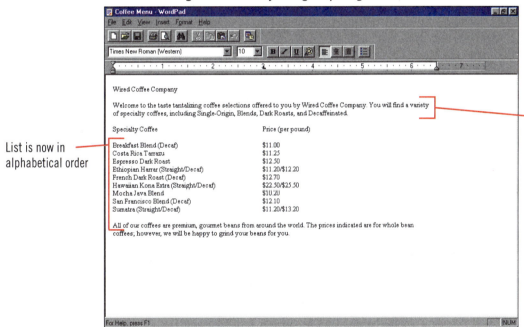

Setting paragraph tabs

In your documents, tabs set how text or numerical data aligns in relation to the edges of the document. A tab stop is a predefined stopping point along the document's typing line. Default tab stops are set every half-inch on the ruler, but you can set multiple tabs per paragraph at any location. Each paragraph in a document contains its own set of tab stops. The default tab stops do not appear on the ruler, but the manual tab stops ⌐ you set do appear. To display the tab stops for a paragraph on the ruler, click the paragraph. To set a tab stop, click the ruler where you want to set it. Once you place a tab stop, you can drag the tab stop to position it where you want. To delete a tab stop, drag it off the ruler. You can also set tabs using the Tabs command on the Format menu.

WORKING WITH WINDOWS PROGRAMS

Formatting Text in WordPad

You can change the **format**, or the appearance, of the text and graphics in a document so that the document is easier to read or more attractive. You can make almost all formatting changes in WordPad using the Format Bar, which appears below the Toolbar in the WordPad window. Table B-1 describes the function of each button on the Format Bar. To format existing text, you select the text you want to format, then select the formatting you want on the Format Bar to format text as you type, position the insertion point where you want to type, select the formatting you want on the Format Bar, then enter text. ✒ John wants to make the Coffee Menu document more attractive by centering the title, bolding it, and increasing its size.

Steps

> **QuickTip**
>
> To insert a special character, such as a trademark, click the Start button on the taskbar, point to Programs, point to Accessories, point to System Tools, then click Character Map. Click a character, click Select, click copy, place the insertion point in your document, and then click the Paste button on the Toolbar.

1. **Select the text Wired Coffee Company**
   Remember that the first step in making any editing change is to select the text you want to change. Then you can carry out the desired command.

2. **Click the Center button on the Format Bar**
   Notice that the title is centered and the button is light gray.

3. **Click the Bold button on the Format Bar**
   The selected material appears in boldface. If you didn't like the way boldface looks, you would click the button again. Buttons act as **toggle** switches—click once to turn on the format feature on, click again to turn it off. Now John wants to italicize the title.

4. **Click the Italic button on the Format Bar**
   Italicizing does not provide the effect that John wants.

5. **Click the Undo button on the Toolbar**
   This command reverses the last change made, such as typing new text, deleting text, and formatting text. Undo cannot reverse all commands (such as scrolling or saving a document), but it is a quick way to reverse most editing and formatting changes.

> **QuickTip**
>
> To change the font type, size, style, and color at the same time, click Format on the menu bar, then click Fonts.

6. **Click the Fonts list arrow on the Format Bar, then click Arial (Western)**
   The **font**, or typeface, of the text changes to Arial.

7. **Click the Font Size list arrow on the Format Bar, then click 14**
   The selected text changes in size to 14 point. One **point** is 1/72 of an inch in height. Whenever you want to know the size of a font on your screen, place the insertion point anywhere in the text and look at the size that appears in the Font Size list box.

8. **Click anywhere in the document (except on the selected text) to deselect the text**
   Figure B-7 shows the centered, bold title with its typeface changed to Arial and its size to 14 point.

9. **Click the Save button on the Toolbar**
   You save the changes made to the Coffee Menu file.

WORKING WITH WINDOWS PROGRAMS

FIGURE B-7: Centered, bold, and enlarged text

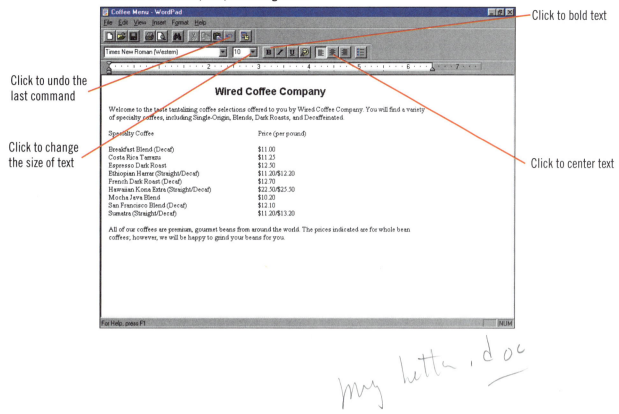

TABLE B-1: Format Bar buttons and list arrows

button or list arrow	function	button	function
Times New Roman (Western)	Select a font		Add or change color
10	Select a font size		Left align
B	Bold		Center align
I	Italic		Right align
U	Underline		Create bulleted list

Setting paragraph indents

The markers on the ruler control the indentation of the current paragraph. The left side of the ruler has three markers. The top triangle, called the **first-line indent marker**, controls where the first line of the paragraph begins. The bottom triangle, called the **hanging indent marker**, controls where the remaining lines of the paragraph begin. The small square under the bottom triangle, called the **left indent marker**, allows you to move the first-line indent marker and the left indent marker simultaneously. When you move the left indent marker, the distance between the hanging indent and the first line indent remains the same. The triangle on the right side of the ruler, called the **right indent marker**, controls where the right edge of the paragraph ends. You can also set paragraph indents using the Paragraph command on the Format menu.

Windows 98 and Me

Using Paint

You use each Windows Accessory to perform a certain task. When it comes to creating and working with images, Paint is a useful Windows Accessory. You can draw images and manipulate them with commands such as rotate, stretch, and invert colors. You can open more than one Windows program at a time, so while WordPad is still running, you can open Paint and work on drawings and images. This is called **multitasking**. John already created a logo for his coffee company. Now he wants to review the logo and revise it as necessary before using it on his promotional materials.

Steps

1. Click the **Start button** on the taskbar, point to **Programs**, point to **Accessories**, click **Paint**, then click the **Maximize button** in the Paint window

   The Paint window opens and is maximized in front of the WordPad window. You can find buttons for frequently used commands in the Paint Toolbox, located along the left edge of the window. Table B-2 describes these tools.

   > **QuickTip**
   > To provide a consistent place to store all your images, Windows Me saves all your image files in and opens them from the My Pictures folder located in the My Documents folder.

2. Click **File** on the menu bar, click **Open**, click the **Look in list arrow**, then click the drive and folder where your Project Files are located

   A list of the files appears.

3. In the file list, click **Win B-2**, then click **Open**

   The file named Win B-2 opens, shown in Figure B-8. If you cannot see the logo on your screen, use the scroll buttons to adjust your view. John decides the logo could use some final modifications. Before he makes any changes, he wants to save this file (with a more meaningful name) so his changes don't affect the original file.

4. Click **File** on the menu bar, click **Save As**, then save the file as **Wired Coffee Logo** on the drive and in the folder where your Project Files are located

   John wants to add a rounded border around the logo. First he selects the proper tool from the Toolbox, and then he can "draw" the border.

   > **QuickTip**
   > You can press and hold down [Shift] while you drag a drawing tool to create a proportional drawing, such as a square or circle.

5. Click the **Rounded Rectangle tool** in the Toolbox, then move the pointer into the Paint work area

   When you move the mouse pointer into the work area, it changes to +, indicating that the Rounded Rectangle tool is active.

   > **Trouble?**
   > If your rounded rectangle doesn't match Figure B-9, click Edit on the menu bar, then click Undo to reverse the last command. If Undo is not available, click the Eraser tool in the Toolbox, drag to erase the rounded rectangle, then repeat Step 6.

6. Beginning above and to the left of the logo, drag + so that a rounded rectangle surrounds the image, then release the mouse button when the pointer is below and to the right of the image, as shown in Figure B-9

   John likes this new look. The logo is complete but John needs to save it.

7. Click **File** on the menu bar, then click **Save**

   Now John can use the logo in his other documents.

WINDOWS 98 AND ME B-10 **WORKING WITH WINDOWS PROGRAMS**

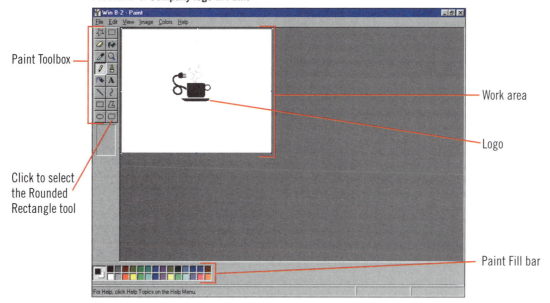

FIGURE B-8: Company logo in Paint

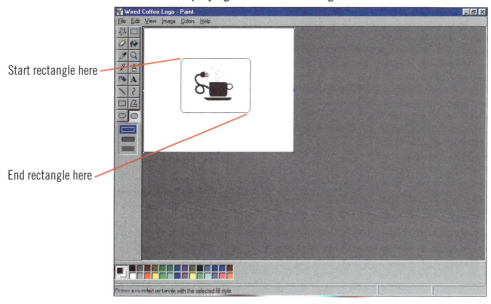

FIGURE B-9: Company logo with rounded rectangle

TABLE B-2: Tools in the Paint Toolbox

tool	description	tool	description
	Selects an irregular shape		Creates dispersed lines and patterns
	Selects a regular shape		Enters text in drawings
	Erases part of a drawing		Draws a straight line
	Fills a shape with a color or texture		Draws a free-form line
	Picks up a color from the picture for drawing		Draws a regular shape
	Magnifies part of an image		Draws an irregular shape
	Draws freehand		Draws an oval or circle
	Designates the size and shape brush to draw with		Draws a rectangle or square with rounded corners

WORKING WITH WINDOWS PROGRAMS

Copying Data Between Programs

One of the most useful features that Windows offers is the ability to use data created in one document in another document, even if the two documents were created in different Windows programs. To work with more than one program or document at a time, you simply need to open them on your desktop. A **program button** on the taskbar represents any window that is open on the desktop. When you want to switch from one open window to another, click the correct program button on the taskbar. If you tile or arrange open windows on the desktop so that they are visible, you can switch among them simply by clicking in the window you want to work in. Just as you worked with the Cut and Paste commands to rearrange text in WordPad, you can use the same commands to move and copy data between two different documents. Table B-3 reviews the Cut, Copy, and Paste commands and their associated keyboard shortcuts. John wants to add the company logo, which he created with Paint, to the Coffee Menu document, which he created with WordPad. First he switches to Paint and copies the logo. Then he switches to WordPad, determines exactly where he wants to place the logo, and pastes the Paint logo into the WordPad document.

Trouble?
If your windows don't appear tiled, click the program button on the taskbar for each program (Paint and WordPad) to ensure that both windows are maximized, then repeat Step 1.

1. **Make sure both WordPad and Paint are open, place the mouse pointer on an empty area of the taskbar, right-click, then click Tile Windows Vertically on the shortcut menu**
   The windows (Paint and WordPad) are next to one another vertically, as shown in Figure B-10, so John can maneuver quickly between them while working.

2. **Click the Paint program button on the taskbar, or click anywhere in the Paint window**
   The Paint program becomes the **active program**. (The title bar changes from gray to blue.)

3. **Click the Select tool in the Toolbox, then drag a rectangle around the coffee logo to select it**
   Dragging with the Select Tool selects an object in Paint for cutting, copying, or performing other modifications.

QuickTip
When windows are tiled, you can drag a selected item from one program window to another to copy the item to the other program window.

4. **Click Edit on the Paint menu bar, then click Copy**
   This copies the logo to the Windows Clipboard. The Copy command is similar to the Cut command you used when working with the coffee list, but when you copy a selection, the original remains intact and a copy is on the Clipboard.

5. **Click the first line of the WordPad document**
   The WordPad program becomes active, and the insertion point is on the WordPad page, where John wants the logo to appear. If you cannot see enough of the page, use the scroll buttons to adjust your view.

6. **Click the Paste button on the WordPad toolbar**
   You paste the logo into the document, as shown in Figure B-11.

7. **Click the Maximize button in the WordPad window, click the Center button on the Format Bar, then click below the logo to deselect it**
   The logo is centered in the document.

8. **Click the Save button on the Toolbar**
   The document is complete and ready for John to print.

9. **Click the Paint program button on the taskbar, then click the Close button in the Paint window**

WINDOWS 98 AND ME B-12 **WORKING WITH WINDOWS PROGRAMS**

FIGURE B-10: Tiled windows

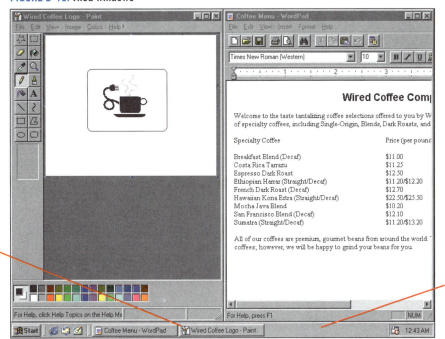

Click to activate the Paint program

Right-click to open pop-up menu and tile windows vertically

FIGURE B-11: Copying a logo between programs

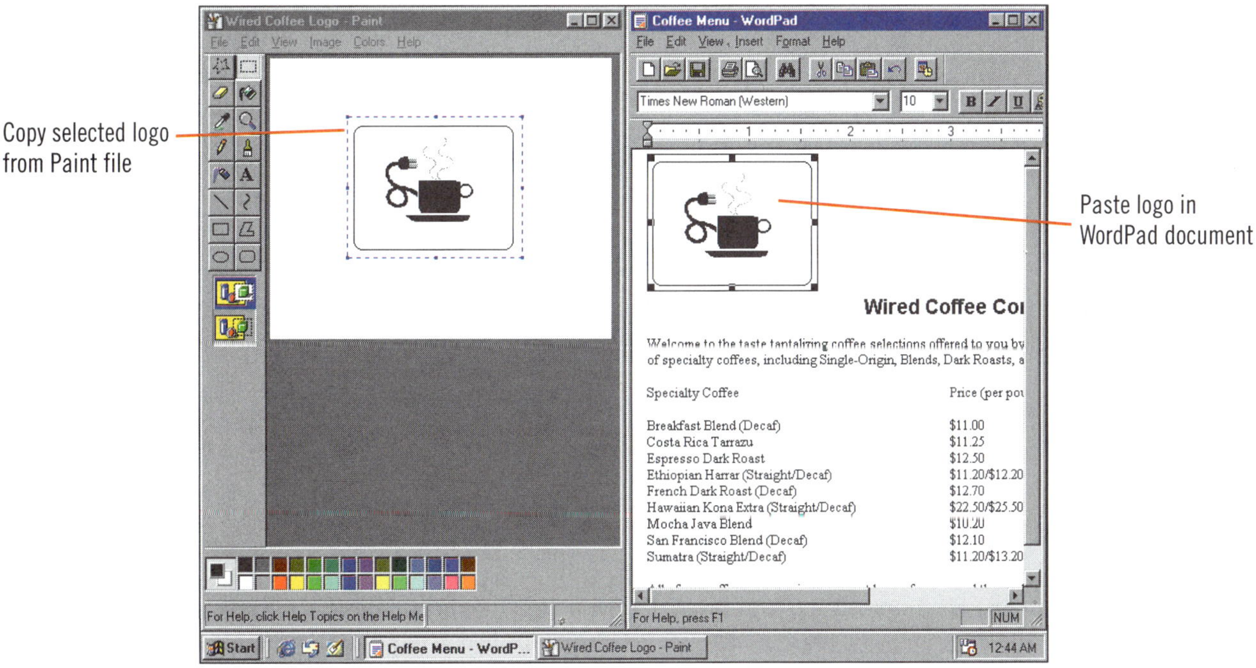

Copy selected logo from Paint file

Paste logo in WordPad document

TABLE B-3: Overview of cutting, copying, and pasting

function	toolbar button	keyboard shortcut	drag-and-drop method
Cut: Removes selected information from a file and places it on the Clipboard	✂	[Ctrl][X]	Press and hold [Shift] as you drag selected text, and it will be moved
Copy: Places a copy of selected information on the Clipboard, leaving the file intact	📋	[Ctrl][C]	Press and hold [Ctrl] as you drag selected text, and it will be copied
Paste: Inserts whatever is currently on the Clipboard in another location (within the same file or in a different file)	📋	[Ctrl][V]	Release the left mouse button

WORKING WITH WINDOWS PROGRAMS

Windows 98 and Me

Printing a Document

Printing a document creates a **printout** or **hard copy**, a paper document that you can share with others or review as a work in progress. Most Windows programs have a print option that you access through the Print dialog box and a Print button on the Toolbar. Although your printing options vary from program to program, the process works similarly in all of them. It is a good idea to use the **Print Preview** feature to look at the layout and formatting of a document before you print it. You might catch a mistake, find that the document fits on more pages than you wanted, or notice formatting that you want to do differently. Making changes before you print saves paper. John decides to preview the coffee menu before printing the document. Satisfied with the result, John prints the Coffee Menu document.

Steps

1. **In the WordPad window, click the Print Preview button on the Toolbar**
   A reduced but proportionate image of the page appears in the Preview window, shown in Figure B-12.

   > **QuickTip**
   > To zoom out from the zoom in position, click the print preview area or click Zoom Out in Print Preview.

2. **Move the mouse pointer (which changes to ⌕ over the logo and click, or click Zoom In in Print Preview**
   The preview image of the page appears larger, easier to see. John notices extra space around the dotted rectangle, the area determined by the **margin** setting, so he is not yet ready to print.

3. **Click Close in Print Preview**
   The Preview window closes and you return to the Coffee Menu document.

4. **Click File on the menu bar, then click Page Setup**
   The Page Setup dialog box opens. In this dialog box, you can change the margin setting to decrease or increase the area outside the dotted rectangle. You can change other printing options here, such as paper size, page orientation, and printer source. Table B-4 describes the Page Setup dialog box options.

5. **Select the number in the Top text box, type 1.25, select the number in the Bottom text box, type 1.25, then click OK**
   You should verify that you like the new margins before printing.

6. **Click**
   The menu margins are smaller.

7. **Click Print in Print Preview**
   The Print dialog box opens, as shown in Figure B-13, showing various options available for printing. Check to make sure the correct printer is specified. If you need to change printers, select a printer. When you are finished, accept all of the settings.

   > **QuickTip**
   > To print a document quickly, click the Print button on the Toolbar. To open the Print dialog box, click File on the menu bar, then click Print.

8. **Click OK**
   The WordPad document prints. While a document prints, a printer icon appears in the status area of the taskbar. You can point to the printer icon to get status information. To close a program and any of its currently open files, select the Exit command from the File menu. You can also click the Close button in the upper-right corner of the program window.

9. **Click the Close button in the WordPad window**
   If you made any changes to the open file and did not save them, you are prompted to save your changes before the program closes.

WORKING WITH WINDOWS PROGRAMS

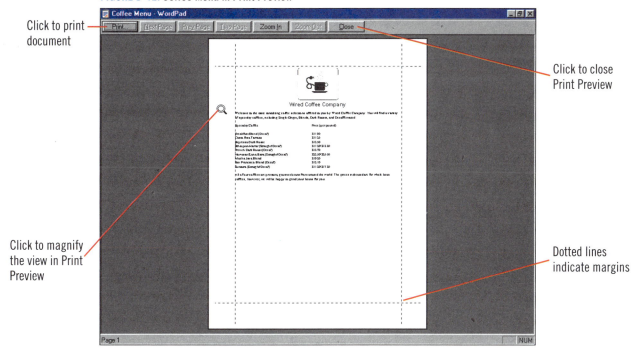

FIGURE B-12: Coffee Menu in Print Preview

- Click to print document
- Click to close Print Preview
- Click to magnify the view in Print Preview
- Dotted lines indicate margins

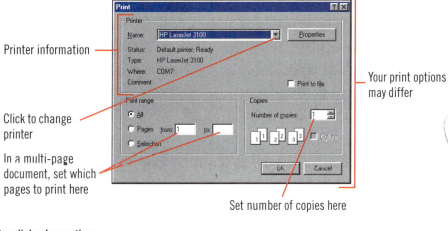

FIGURE B-13: Print dialog Box

- Printer information
- Click to change printer
- In a multi-page document, set which pages to print here
- Your print options may differ
- Set number of copies here

TABLE B-4: Page Setup dialog box options

page setup option	function
Size	Defines the size of the paper on which you want to print
Source	Defines the location of the paper, such as another paper bin or an envelope feeder
Orientation	Allows you to select Portrait (the page being taller than it is wide) or Landscape (the page being wider than it is tall)
Margins	Allows you to define top, bottom, left, and right page margins

Printer properties

You can select Properties from the Print dialog box and adjust several facets of the printing operation. Each printer contains different printer properties. For example, to control the intensity of printed graphics images, you click the Graphics tab, then adjust the Intensity slider. You can also adjust fonts, paper sizes, and other printing dimensions in the Properties dialog box.

Windows 98 and Me

Playing a Video Clip or Sound

Windows comes with a built-in accessory, called **Windows Media Player**, that you can use to play video, sound, and mixed-media files. You can use it to play movies, music, sounds, and other multimedia files from your computer, a CD, a local network, or the Internet. The Windows Media Player delivers high-quality continuous video, live broadcasts, sound, and music playback, known as **streaming media**. You can also copy individual music tracks or entire CDs to your computer and create your own jukebox or playlist of media. With the Windows Media Player, you can modify the media, control the settings, and change the player's appearance (not functionality), known as **skin**. Windows Me comes with Windows Media Player version 7. To make sure you are using the most recent version of Windows Media Player, click Help on the menu bar, then click Check for Player Upgrade or click Windows Update on the Start menu. You must have an open connection to the Internet to perform this check. Windows 98 users should upgrade. When you upgrade, a Windows Media Player icon appears on the desktop and Quick Launch toolbar. John experiments using the Media Player to play a sample video and a sound.

Steps

> **QuickTip**
> To change the skin, click Skin Chooser, select a design, then click Apply Skin.

1. Click the **Start button** on the taskbar, point to **Programs**, point to **Accessories**, point to **Entertainment**, then click **Windows Media Player**
   The Windows Media Player opens, displaying tabs along the left side of the window and player controls that look and function similar to those on a CD player.

2. Click **File** on the menu bar, then click **Open**
   The Open dialog box opens; it contains a list of the files and folders.

3. Click the **Look in list arrow**, click the drive and folder where your Project Files are located, click **Coffee Cup**, then click **Open**
   The Coffee Cup video clip appears in the Windows Media Player, as shown in Figure B-14, and plays.

4. Click **Play** on the menu bar, then click **Repeat**
   You set the video clip to play continuously or "loop."

5. Click the **Play button**, then click the **Stop button** after the video repeats once or twice
   The video clip repeats continuously until you stop it.

> **QuickTip**
> To create a playlist, click the Media Library tab, click the Create Playlist button, type a name, click OK, select a file, click the Add to Playlist button, then click Add to *playlist name*.

6. Click the **Media Player tab**, then click **All Clips**
   All the open videos in the file list appear, as shown in Figure B-15.

7. Click **File** on the menu bar, click **Open**, click the **Look in list arrow**, click the drive and folder where your Project Files are located, click **AM Coffee**, then click **Open**
   The AM Coffee sound clip appears in the Windows Media Player and plays continuously. When you play a sound, a visual effect appears, displaying splashes of color and geometric shapes that change with the beat of the sound.

> **QuickTip**
> To play a music CD, insert the CD in the disc drive and wait for the Windows Media Player to start playing the CD. Double-click a track to play that track.

8. Press and hold **[Tab]**, press **[Enter]** to change the visual effect, then click the **Stop button**
   A new visual effect appears as the sound plays.

9. Click **Play** on the menu bar, click **Repeat** to deselect it, if necessary then click the **Close button** in the Media Player window
   The repeat option turns off, and Windows Media Player closes.

FIGURE B-14: Playing a video clip in Windows Media Player

FIGURE B-15: Viewing files in Windows Media Player

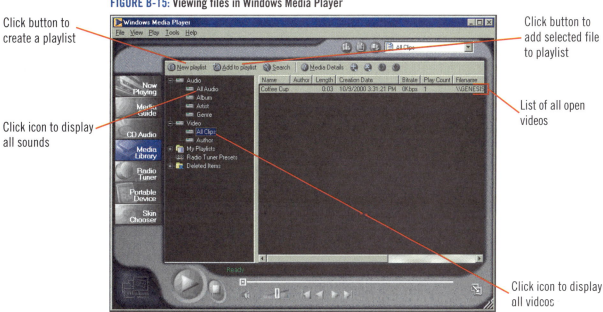

Playing media from the Internet

You can play media available on the Internet, such as videos, live broadcasts, and music tracks. You can stream the media directly from the Web site or by downloading the media file to your computer. When you stream the media, the video or music starts playing while the file is transmitted to you over the Internet. The streaming media is not stored on your computer. To stream media from the Internet, locate the Web site that contains the media you want to play (use the Media Guide tab or Radio Tuner tab), click the link to the media, wait for Windows Media Player to start and the first data to be transmitted and buffered (in a small temporary storage area), then listen to and watch the multimedia. When you download a media file, you wait for the entire file to be transferred to your computer. To download a file, use the Media Guide tab or a Web browser to locate the media you want to download from the Internet, click the Save this file to disk option, click OK, specify the location in which you want to save the file, wait for the file download, then click Close.

WORKING WITH WINDOWS PROGRAMS WINDOWS 98 AND ME B-17

Windows 98 and Me

Creating a movie

Windows Me comes with a built-in multimedia accessory, called **Windows Movie Maker**, which allows you to create your own movies from a variety of sources. You can create a digital movie using a digital video camera or digital Web camera connected directly to your computer. If you don't have a digital device, you can use a video capture card or other device to convert images from an analog video camera, videotape, or television. You organize your clips in a **collection** for use in different movie projects. To create a movie, you assemble the clips from a collection on the storyboard. On the storyboard, you can rearrange and crop parts of the movie. You can also add a fade-in and fade-out transition effect, and add audio tracks, musical soundtracks, background sounds, or narration. When you finish your movie project, Movie Maker can compress the file so it's small enough to attach to and send in an e-mail message. John creates a movie from an existing collection.

Steps

1. Click the **Start button** on the taskbar, point to **Programs**, point to **Accessories**, then click **Windows Movie Maker**, then click exit if necessary to close the tour
   The Movie Maker window opens.

2. Click **File** on the menu bar, click **Import**, click the **Look in list arrow**, click the drive and folder where your Project Files are located, click **Coffee Cup**, then click **Open**
   Movie Maker creates a new collection called Coffee Cup and inserts the Coffee Cup video in the collection.

3. Click **File** on the menu bar, click **Import**, click the **Look in list arrow**, click the drive and folder where your Project Files are located, click **AM Coffee**, then click **Open**
   You add the sound to the Coffee Cup collection.

4. Drag the first video clip onto the first frame of the storyboard
   The first video clip appears in the storyboard, as shown in Figure B-16.

5. Click the **Timeline button** above the storyboard, then drag the **AM Coffee sound** onto the beginning of the audio track below the video clip
   When you drag the sound, an insertion point appears in the audio track to indicate where to place the sound. The sound appears at the beginning of the audio track, as shown in Figure B-17.

6. Click **Play** on the menu bar, then click **Play Entire Storyboard/Timeline**
   As the movie plays, the movie time progresses (in seconds) and a down arrow moves across the Seek Bar to indicate the current location of the movie.

7. Click the **Save Project button** on the Toolbar, click the **Look in list arrow**, click the drive and folder where your Project Files are located, type **Coffee Meltdown**, in the filename text box, then click **Save**
   You save the movie project in a form Windows Movie Maker can recognize. Now, let's save the movie in a form other movie players, such as Windows Media Player, can recognize.

8. Click the **Save Movie button** on the Toolbar, type **Coffee Meltdown** in the Title box and *your name* in the Author text box, then click **OK**
   The Save Movie dialog box asks you to select playback quality settings and enter display information. The default playback quality setting is set to Medium quality (recommended). The playback quality setting affects the file size and the download time, which appear in the dialog box. The Save As dialog box opens.

9. Click the **Save in list arrow**, click the drive and folder where your Project Files are located, click **Save**, click **Yes** to watch the movie, then **close** the Windows Media Player and Windows Movie Maker windows
   The Windows Movie Maker compresses and saves the video, and Windows Media Player plays the video.

QuickTip

To record a video clip, click the Record button, specify the type and quality, click Change Device, click Play, click Record, click Stop, then save the file.

QuickTip

To create a collection, click the New Collection button, name the collection, then click the Record button to create a new video clip, or click File on the menu bar and click Import to import existing video clips.

QuickTip

To create a transition, click the Timeline button, select the clip that you want to fade into, then drag the left border of the clip onto the clip at the left. The farther you drag the clip, the longer the transition.

FIGURE B-16: Movie Maker window

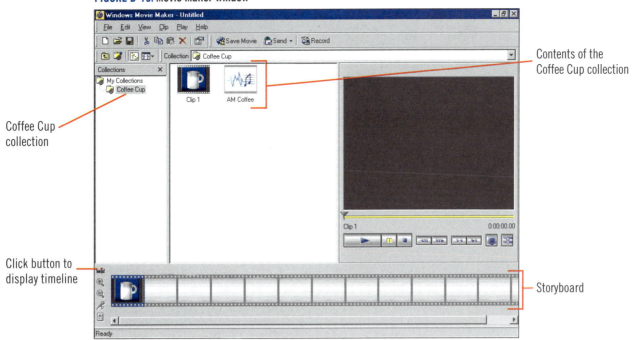

FIGURE B-17: Creating a movie in Windows Movie Maker

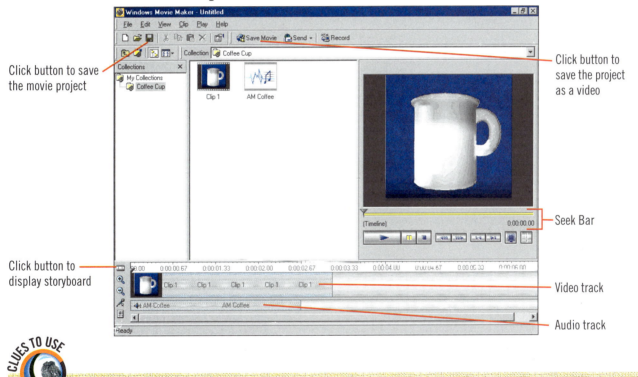

Clues to Use

Creating a slide show

If you have photographs from a digital camera or a scanner, you can create a slide show with Windows Movie Maker. You can also add a soundtrack to the slide show for additional interest. To create a slide show, click File on the menu bar, click Import, select the pictures you want to use, then click Open. Click View on the menu bar, click Options, specify the length of time you want to display each picture, then click OK. Drag the pictures onto the storyboard in the sequence in which you want to display them. Use the Timeline view on the View menu to add transition effects or modify how long to display an individual picture. To create an audio track, click File on the menu bar, click Record Narration to create a track or click Import to a track, then drag the sound clip onto the audio bar where you want to play the clip.

WORKING WITH WINDOWS PROGRAMS

Windows 98 and Me

Practice

▶ Concepts Review

Label each element of the screen shown in Figure B-18.

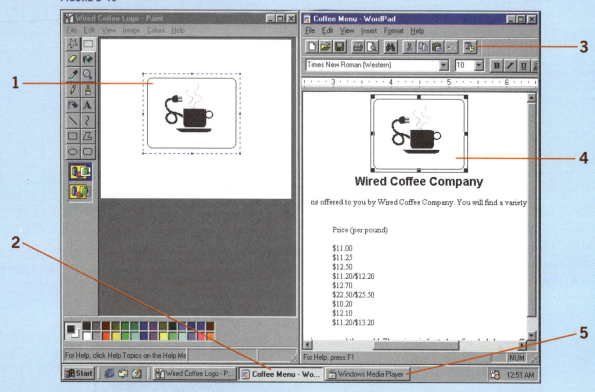

FIGURE B-18

Match each term with the statement that describes its function.

6. Copy
7. Accessories
8. Cut
9. Select
10. Filename

a. Removes selected text or an image from its current location
b. Copies selected text or an image from its current location
c. A set of characters you assign to a collection of information
d. A collection of Windows programs that enable you to perform certain tasks
e. What you must first do to existing text before you can format it

Select the best answers from the following lists of choices.

11. The first step in starting any Windows Accessory is to click:
    a. The Open icon.
    b. The Start button.
    c. The taskbar.
    d. Anywhere on the desktop.

12. What program command makes a copy of a file?
    a. Copy.
    b. Duplicate.
    c. Save.
    d. Save As.

13. When WordPad automatically moves words to the next line, it is called:
    a. Margin.
    b. Tab.
    c. Wordwrap.
    d. Format insert.

Practice

14. **Which of the following is not a way to select text?**
    a. Drag over the text.
    b. Click to the left of the first character in a line of text.
    c. Double-click a word.
    d. Click File on the menu bar, then click Select.
15. **What is the name of the Windows location that stores cut or copied information?**
    a. Start Up menu.
    c. Clipboard.
    b. Hard drive.
    d. Paint.
16. **Which of the following is an option to change the size of the empty border around a document?**
    a. Orientation.
    c. Paper Size.
    b. Margins.
    d. Paper Source.

▶ Skills Review

1. **Open and save a WordPad document.**
    a. Start WordPad.
    b. Open the WordPad file named *Win B-3* from the drive and folder where your Project Files are located.
    c. Save the file as *Choose Coffee* on the drive and in the folder where your Project Files are located.
2. **Edit text in WordPad document.**
    a. Change the spelling of the word "neuances" to "nuances" in the first paragraph.
    b. Insert a space between the characters "r" and "a" in the word, "ora" in the second paragraph.
    c. Delete the word "heavy" in the last line of text, and replace it with "medium".
3. **Format text in WordPad.**
    a. Select all the text in the file named *Choose Coffee*.
    b. Change the text font to Garamond (or another available font), and change its size to 12 point.
    c. Center the title ("Wired Coffee"), and change it to 16-point boldface.
    d. Underline each title ("How to Choose a Coffee" and "How to Taste the Difference"), and change them to 14 point.
    e. Click anywhere in the WordPad window outside of the selected text.
    f. Save the document.
4. **Use Paint.**
    a. Start Paint.
    b. Open the Paint file named *Win B-2* from the drive and folder where your Project Files are located. (This is the same file you used in the lessons.)
    c. Save this file as *Wired Coffee Logo 2* on the drive and in the folder where your Project Files are located.
    d. Draw a circle around the logo.
    e. Use the Undo command or Eraser tool as necessary if the circle doesn't fit around the logo.
    f. Save the file.
5. **Copy data between programs.**
    a. Tile the WordPad and Paint windows vertically. (*Hint*: Maximize both windows first.)
    b. Select the logo in the Paint window.
    c. Copy it to the Clipboard.
    d. In WordPad, insert the cursor at the beginning of the document.
    e. Maximize WordPad.
    f. Paste the logo in the newly inserted blank line.

Windows 98 and Me | Practice

    g. Center the logo.
    h. Save the *Choose Coffee* file.
    i. Close the *Wired Coffee Logo 2 file*, and close Paint.
6. **Print a document.**
    a. Print two copies of the file named *Choose Coffee*.
    b. Close all open documents, then close WordPad.
7. **Play a video clip or sound.**
    a. Start Windows Media Player.
    b. Open the Better Coffee sound from the drive and folder where your Project Files are located.
    c. Play the sound, then close Windows Media Player.
8. **Create a movie.**
    a. Start Windows Movie Maker (Me).
    b. Import the Coffee Cup video and the Better Coffee sound from the drive and folder where your Project Files are located.
    c. Drag the first video clip to frame 1.
    d. Drag the sound clip to the audio track.
    e. Play the movie.
    f. Save the project as *Coffee Time*, give the movie file the same name, and save it with medium quality.
    g. Close Windows Movie Maker.

▶ Independent Challenges

1. You just opened a small, independent bookstore and are working on your inventory. You need to create a list of books that you can use when customers come in and want to know what kind of books you carry. Start WordPad and create a new document that lists the first 10 books in your stock, including the name of your bookstore and its street address, city, state, zip code, and phone number, and for each book, the author's name (last name first), title, and publication date.

    To complete this independent challenge:

    a. Start WordPad.
    b. Enter the heading (the name of the bookstore, address, city, state, zip code, and phone number).
    c. Center the heading information.
    d. Enter the information for at least 10 books, using the Tab key to create columns for the author's name, the title, and the publication date. Be sure that the columns line up with one another.
    e. Proofread your list and correct any errors you may have made.
    f. Italicize the last and first names of each author, and format the title of each book with boldface.
    g. Save the list as *Book Inventory* on the drive and in the folder where your Project Files are located.
    h. Print two copies of the list, and close WordPad.

2. Your parents are celebrating their twenty-fifth wedding anniversary. You want to create an invitation to a party for them. Using WordPad, create an invitation, including the invitation title, your parents' names; date, time, and location of the party (use "35 Crow Canyon Road" for the address); written directions to the party; your name and phone number; and the date to respond by. Using Paint, you then paste a map of the party location onto the invitation. Remember that you can open more than one program at a time and you can easily switch between programs using the taskbar.

    To complete this independent challenge:

    a. Start WordPad and type the information needed for the invitation.
    b. Select the title text and click the Center button on the Toolbar.
    c. Change the title text to 18 point, boldface.

Practice

   d. Change the rest of the text to 14-point Arial.
   e. Save the WordPad document as *Invitation* on the drive and in the folder where your Project Files are located.
   f. Start Paint, then open the *Invitation Map* file from the drive and folder where your Project Files are located.
   g. Copy the map to the Clipboard.
   h. Place the insertion point above the written instructions in the invitation.
   i. Click the Paste button on the Toolbar.
   j. Save the document, preview the document, make any necessary changes, then print the document.
   k. Close WordPad and Paint.

3. As vice president of Things-That-Fly, a kite and juggling store, you need to design a new type of logo, consisting of three simple circles, each colored differently. You plan to use this logo both in the new stationery and in all store advertising. You use Paint to design the logo, and then you paste the logo into a WordPad document and name the document *Stationery*.
   To complete this independent challenge:

   a. Start Paint and create a small circle using the [Shift] key and the Ellipse tool.
   b. Use the Select tool to surround the circle (thereby selecting it), and then select Copy from the Edit menu. Now you can paste the circle, so you don't need to try to redraw the exact same shape.
   c. Select Paste from the Edit menu, and use the mouse to drag the second circle below and a bit to the right of the first.
   d. Select Paste from the Edit menu again, and use the mouse to drag the third circle below and a bit to the left of the first.
   e. For each circle, click the Fill tool in the Toolbox, click the color you want for the circle to be, then click inside the circle you want to fill with that color.
   f. Using the Select tool, select the completed logo, click Edit on the menu bar, then click Copy.
   g. Open WordPad and click the Center button on the Toolbar.
   h. Click the Paste button on the Toolbar, click to the right of the logo to deselect it, press [Enter] twice, then type *Things-That-Fly*.
   i. Using the Format Bar, change the text to 18 point, boldface.
   j. Save the document as *Stationery* on the drive and in the folder where your Project Files are located.
   k. Preview the document, make any necessary changes, then print the document.
   l. Close WordPad and Paint.

4. As creative director at Digital Arts, a computer music company, you need to find sample sounds to include on a demo CD. You use Windows Media Player to open sound files located on your computer and play each one. You also use the Media Library in Windows Media Player to keep track of the sounds you hear and which ones you like best.
   To complete this independent challenge:

   a. Open Windows Media Player.
   b. Open all the sound files in the Media folder (in the Windows folder) on your computer, or play sounds on the Internet using the Media Guide. (*Hint*: You can use the Search Computer For Media command on the Tools menu to help you find the sounds.)
   c. Play each sound file.
   d. Create a playlist as *Media Sounds* in the Media Library.
   e. Add each sound to the playlist.
   f. Play the playlist in the Media Library.
   g. Close Windows Media Player.

Windows 98 and Me | Practice

▶ Visual Workshop

Re-create the screen shown in Figure B-19, which displays the Windows desktop with more than one program window open. You can use the file *Win B-2* for the coffee cup logo. (Save it as *A Cup of Coffee* on the drive and in the folder where your Project Files are located.) Create a new WordPad document, save it as *Good Time Coffee Club* with your Project Files, and enter the text shown in the figure. Print the screen. (Press [Print Screen] to make a copy of the screen, open Paint, click Edit on the menu bar, click Paste to paste the screen into Paint, then click Yes to paste the large image, if necessary. Click File on the menu bar, click Print, then click OK.)

FIGURE B-19

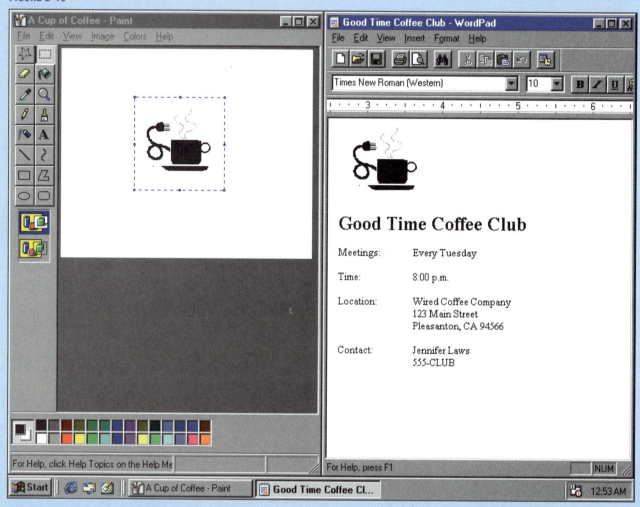

Windows 98 and Me

Managing
Files Using My Computer

Objectives

- ▶ Understand file management
- ▶ Open and view My Computer
- ▶ View folders and files
- ▶ Create a folder
- ▶ Move files and folders
- ▶ Delete and restore files and folders
- ▶ Create a shortcut to a file
- ▶ Display drive information

An important Windows skill for you to learn is **file management**, which involves organizing and keeping track of files and folders. Windows 98 and Me provides you with two file management programs: My Computer and Windows Explorer. You use both of these tools to view the files on your computer and their arrangement. You can also use them to rearrange the files to fit the way that you work by creating new folders and by renaming and deleting files and folders. A **folder** is an electronic collection of files and other folders. This unit concentrates on My Computer, while the next unit focuses on Windows Explorer. In this unit John Casey learns about the files on his computer and how to keep them organized using My Computer.

Understanding File Management

Managing folders and files enables you to locate quickly any file that you created and need to use again. Working with poorly managed files is like looking for a needle in a haystack—it is frustrating and time-consuming to search through several irrelevant, misnamed, and out-of-date files to find the one you want. Figure C-1 shows the files and folders that John uses in the course of running his business.

As you examine the figure, note that file management can help you to do the following:

 Organize folders and files in a file hierarchy, or a logical order, so that information is easy to locate and use

A *file hierarchy* is a logical structure of files and folders, so that files are located in appropriate folders, and folders are located within other folders as necessary, to make everything easy to find. For instance, John stores all of his correspondence files in a folder called Letters. Within that folder are two more folders. One named Business Letters holds all business correspondence. The other, Personal Letters, holds all of John's personal correspondence.

 Save files in the folder in which you want to store them for future use

John has a folder named Sales in which he stores all information about sales for the current year. He also places files related to accounting information in this folder.

 Create a new folder so you can reorganize information

Now that John does more advertising for Wired Coffee Company, he wants to create a new folder to store files related to these marketing efforts.

 Delete files and folders that you no longer need

John deletes files when he's sure he will not use them again, to free disk space and keep his disk organized.

 Create shortcuts

If a file or folder you use often is located several levels down in a file hierarchy (for example, if it is a file within a folder, within a folder), you might take several steps to access it. To save you time in accessing the files and programs you use most frequently, you can create shortcuts to them. A shortcut is a link that you can place in any location to gain instant access to a particular file, folder, or program on your hard disk or on a network. John created a shortcut on the desktop to the Wired Coffee folder. To view or access the contents of his folder, all he needs to do is double-click the shortcut icon on the desktop.

 Find a file when you cannot remember where you stored it

John knows he created a letter to a supplier earlier this week, but now that he is ready to revise the letter, he cannot find it. Using the Search command on the Start menu, he can find that letter quickly and revise it in no time.

 Open a file when you don't know the type of program used to create it (Me)

If John wants to open a file but doesn't know which program to use to open it, he can use the Open With command. To open a file of unknown type, John can right-click the file icon, point to Open With, and then click one of the programs known to open that type of file, or he can click Any Program to open the Open With dialog box, where he can select a program to open the file.

FIGURE C-1: How John uses Windows to organize his files

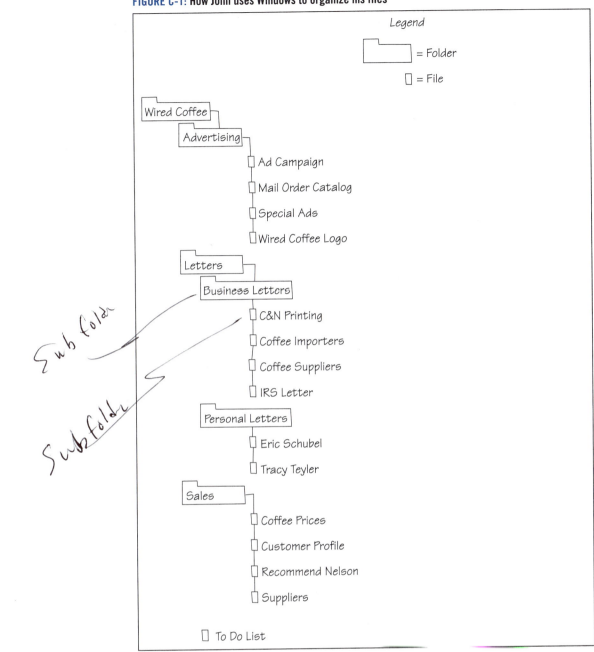

What is a file hierarchy?

Windows allows you to organize folders and files in a file hierarchy, imitating the way you actually store paper documents in real folders. Just as a filing cabinet contains several folders, each containing a set of related documents and several dividers grouping related folders together, a file hierarchy allows you to place files in folders, then place folders in other folders, so that your files are neat and organized. For example, Figure C-1 shows the file hierarchy of the Wired Coffee folder on the drive and folder where your Project Files are located. At the top of the hierarchy is the name of the folder, Wired Coffee. This folder contains several files and folders. The folders are named Advertising, Letters, Business Letters, Personal Letters, and Sales; each contains files and folders related to each of these topics.

Opening and Viewing My Computer

Windows 98 and Me

The key to organizing folders and files effectively within a hierarchy is storing related things together and naming folders informatively. That way, you can get a good idea of what's on your system just by looking at the higher levels of your file hierarchy; you don't have to examine every individual file or memorize a coding system. ✏️ As the previous lesson showed, the file hierarchy on John's disk contains several folders and files organized by topic. Now he uses My Computer to review this organization and see if it needs changes.

Steps

Trouble?
If you are using a Project Disk, make a copy of the disk before you use it and insert it into your disk drive. See your instructor or technical support person for assistance.

1. **Make sure a copy of the disk or drive where your Project Files are located is available, then double-click the My Computer icon** 🖥️
   This icon is usually located in the upper-left corner of the desktop. My Computer opens, displaying the contents of your computer, including all the disk drives and printers, as shown in Figure C-2. Since computers differ, your My Computer window probably looks different. Icons represent drives and folders. Like most other windows, the My Computer window contains a toolbar, a status bar providing information about the contents of the window, a menu bar, and a list of contents.

Trouble?
If the toolbar is not visible, click View on the menu bar, point to Toolbars, then click Standard Buttons.

2. **If necessary, click the Maximize button in the My Computer window**
   This enables you to see the entire toolbar as you work. The toolbar contains a set of buttons that make using My Computer easier. Table C-1 lists what each of these buttons does and how you use them.

3. **Double-click the drive and folder where your Project Files are located**
   You can see the folders contained on the disk drive. When you open a disk drive or folder, the Address bar changes to indicate the new location. The Address bar changed from My Computer to disk drive A (A:\), and the title bar for the My Computer window changed to 3½ Floppy (A:). To see what the folders stored on the disk drive contain, you need to open them. John wants to see what files the Wired Coffee folder contains.

QuickTip
To go from My Computer to Windows Explorer, another file management tool that comes with Windows, right-click any disk or folder icon, then click Explore.

4. **Double-click the Wired Coffee folder**
   You can see the files and folders that the Wired Coffee folder contains. Different types of icon represent files created using different applications. John wants to see what files the Sales folder contains.

5. **Double-click the Sales folder**
   You can now see the files that the Sales folder contains. John created these files using WordPad and saved them in the Sales folder.

Formatting a disk

New floppy disks must be formatted before you can use them. Sometimes the disk is preformatted, but if it is not, you can easily perform this function yourself. To format a floppy disk, select the disk drive in My Computer that contains the disk, click File on the menu bar, then click Format, or right-click the disk drive, then click Format. Specify the disk size and format type, then click Start. If you are formatting a disk that has never been formatted, select the Full format type. If the disk has been formatted once and you simply want to clear its contents, select the Quick format type to reduce the time it takes. Be absolutely certain you want to format a disk before doing so, because formatting removes all data from a disk.

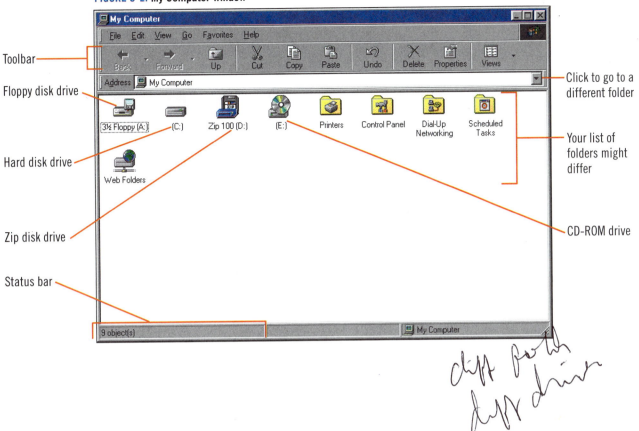

FIGURE C-2: My Computer window

TABLE C-1: My Computer toolbar buttons

Windows 98 button	name	function	Windows Me button	name	function
	Back	Moves back to the previous location you visited		Back	Moves back to the previous location you visited
	Forward	Moves forward to the previous location you visited		Forward	Moves forward to the previous location you visited
	Up	Moves up one level in the file hierarchy		Up	Moves up one level in the file hierarchy
	Cut	Cuts a folder or file		Search	Lets you search for folders or files
	Copy	Copies a folder or file		Folders	Displays a list of folders on your computer
	Paste	Pastes a folder or file		History	Displays a list of recently used folders and files
	Undo	Undoes the most recent My Computer operation		Move To	Moves a folder or file to another folder
	Delete	Deletes a folder or file		Copy To	Copies a folder or file to another folder
	Properties	Shows the properties of a folder or file		Delete	Deletes a folder or file
	Views	Lists the contents of My Computer using different views		Undo	Undoes the most recent My Computer operation
				Views	Displays the contents of My Computer using different views

MANAGING FILES USING MY COMPUTER

Viewing Folders and Files

Once you open one or more folders, you can use buttons on the toolbar to help you move quickly between them in My Computer. If you want to move up one step in the hierarchy, you can click the Up One Level button. Each time you open a folder, Windows 98 and Me keeps track of where you have been. If you want to go back or forward to a folder you already visited, you can click the Back or Forward button. If you want to go to a folder you visited two or more locations ago, you can click the list arrow next to the Back or Forward button to display a menu of places you visited, and then select where you want to go. When you view a folder in the My Computer window, you can use the View button on the toolbar to change the way you view folder and file icons. John moves between folders and changes the way he views folders and files, depending upon the type of information that he needs.

QuickTip
You can also click the Address bar list arrow to move up or down the file hierarchy to another location.

1. **Click the Up button on the toolbar**
   The Wired Coffee folder and its contents appear in the Wired Coffee window. Each time you click the Up One Level button, you move up one step in the hierarchy to the folder that contains the folders and files you currently see on the screen.

2. **Click the again**
   You should now be at the top level of your disk drive file hierarchy and should see several folders. See Figure C-3. Instead of double-clicking the Wired Coffee folder icon again to reopen the folder, you can click the Back button on the toolbar to go back to the previous folder (Wired Coffee) you visited.

3. **Click the Back button on the toolbar**
   The Wired Coffee folder and its contents appear in the My Computer window. At this point, you can open other folders. John opens the Advertising folder to see what's inside.

Trouble?
If Microsoft Word is installed on your computer, the Word icon appears for the files, as shown in Figure C-4. If not, the WordPad icon appears.

4. **Double-click the Advertising folder**
   The Advertising folder and its contents appear in the My Computer window. John wants to go back to the Sales folder. Instead of using the Up One Level button to go back to the Wired Coffee folder and then clicking the Sales folder, you can click the list arrow next to the Back button to display a menu of places you visited, and then select the Sales folder.

5. **Click the Back button list arrow on the toolbar, then click Sales**
   The Back button list arrow, shown in Figure C-4, displays the folders you visited recently. You can click the Forward button on the toolbar to return quickly to the folder that you visited recently. In this case, you can return to the Wired Coffee folder.

QuickTip
You can click File on the menu bar, then click a folder or drive to open a location you visited recently.

6. **Click the Forward button on the toolbar**
   The Wired Coffee folder and its contents appear in the My Computer window. John wants to change the display of icons in the Wired Coffee folder.

7. **Click the Views button list arrow on the toolbar, then click Details**
   In the Details view, the name, size of the object, type of file, and date on which each folder or file was last modified appear, as shown in Figure C-5. This might be the most useful view because it includes a great deal of information about the folder or file, in addition to the icon of the application used to create the file.

8. **Click the Views button list arrow on the toolbar, then click Large Icons**
   The view changes to the Large Icons view. Each time you click the Views button (98), the view changes in the following order: Large Icons, Small Icons, List, Details, and Thumbnails (Me).

FIGURE C-3: Viewing folders and files in Large Icons view

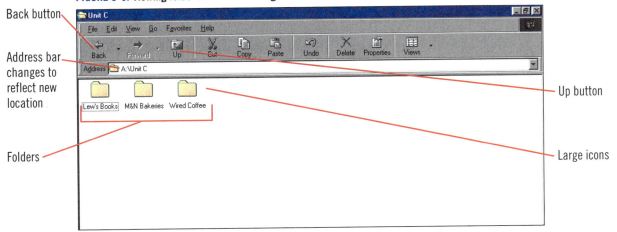

FIGURE C-4: Moving between folders

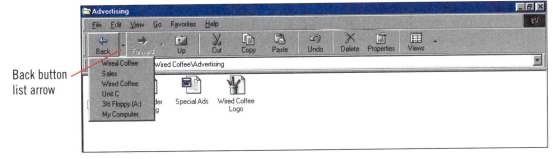

FIGURE C-5: Viewing folders and files in Details view

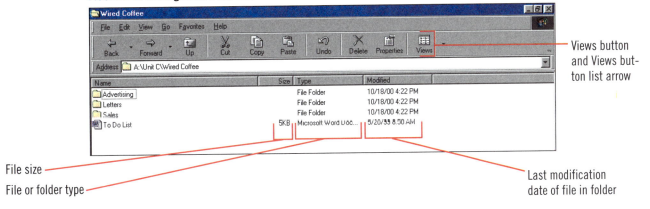

Viewing image and picture files

The My Pictures folder does the same thing for images and pictures as the My Documents folder does for documents—it provides a consistent storage location. The My Pictures folder is the default location for storing images from digital cameras, scanners, and other digital imaging devices. If you store your images and pictures in the My Pictures folder, you can preview a file in the My Computer or Windows Explorer window without opening the file in an editing program. In the My Computer or Windows Explorer window, the right pane contains a file list, which you can view in a number of different formats, including large icons or **thumbnails** (miniature views), and a preview area. Above the preview area is the selected image or picture. For Windows Me, a row of buttons along the top of the preview area allows you to zoom in and zoom out, preview the image or picture in actual size, print the image or picture, and rotate the image or picture. If you want to open the image or picture, you can double-click the file.

MANAGING FILES USING MY COMPUTER

Windows 98 and Me

Creating a Folder

Creating a new folder is a necessary skill for successful file management. Creating a new folder can help you organize and keep track of files and other folders. There are two ways to create a folder in Windows 98 and Me. You can select the New command on the File menu, or you can right-click anywhere in any My Computer window and then select the New command. John needs to create two new folders, one for his To Do List, and the other for information about his employees.

Steps

1. **Click File on the menu bar, point to New, then click Folder**
   A new folder appears in the Wired Coffee window, shown in Figure C-6. All new folders are initially named New Folder. A border appears around the newly created folder, meaning that it is selected and ready to be renamed. Since this folder will hold important files relating to John's work week, he decides to call the folder Important.

2. **Type Important and press [Enter]**
   The folder is now named Important.

3. **Place the mouse pointer anywhere in the Wired Coffee window (except on a file or folder), right-click, then point to New**
   The pop-up menu opens, as shown in Figure C-7.

4. **Click Folder**
   A new folder appears, named New Folder, where you right-clicked the mouse in the My Computer window.

5. **Type Personnel and press [Enter]**
   The My Computer window now has two new folders, shown in Figure C-8. Once you create new folders, you can quickly rearrange them into orderly rows and columns.

6. **Click the View on the menu bar, point to Arrange Icons, then click By Name**
   The folder and file icons in the Wired Coffee folder are sorted by name in alphabetical order and automatically moved in line with the other icons. You can change the way individual files and folders are sorted by using other Arrange Icons options on the View menu. Table C-2 describes these options.

> **QuickTip**
> To rename a folder, right-click the folder you want to rename, click Rename, then type a new name.

TABLE C-2: Options on the View menu for arranging files and folders

option	arranges files and folders
By Name	Alphabetically
By Type	By type, such as all documents created using the WordPad program
By Size	By size, with the largest folder or file listed first
By Date	Chronologically by their last modification date, with the latest modification date listed last
Auto Arrange	Automatically in orderly rows and columns

FIGURE C-6: Creating a new folder

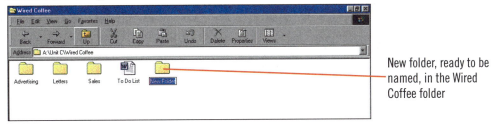

New folder, ready to be named, in the Wired Coffee folder

FIGURE C-7: Right-clicking to display a shortcut menu

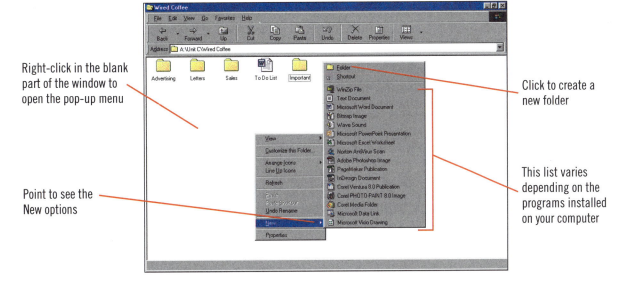

Right-click in the blank part of the window to open the pop-up menu

Point to see the New options

Click to create a new folder

This list varies depending on the programs installed on your computer

FIGURE C-8: Two new folders

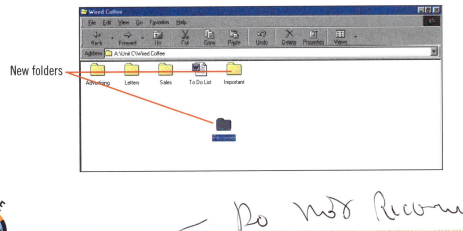

New folders

Compressing files

For Windows Me, you can compress files in special folders that use compressing software to decrease the size of the files they contain. Compressed folders are useful for reducing the files size of standard documents and programs. They are not as useful for storing large graphic files, such as bitmaps. To create and use a compressed folder, right-click a blank area in the folder window of the drive or folder in which you want to create the compressed folder, point to New, click Compressed Folder, type a name for the compressed folder, then press [Enter]. If the Compressed Folder menu item is not available, use the add/remove programs utility windows setup tab in the control panel to install the compression folder feature. A zippered folder icon appears, denoting a compressed folder. Drag the files onto the compressed folder to copy and compress the files.

MANAGING FILES USING MY COMPUTER

Moving Files and Folders

Windows 98 and Me

You can move a file or folder from one location to another using a variety of methods in My Computer (or Windows Explorer). Table C-3 describes methods of moving and copying. If the file or folder and the location where you want to move it are visible in a window or on the desktop, you can simply drag the item from one location to the other. When the location is not visible, you can use the Cut, Copy, and Paste commands on the Edit menu or the buttons on the toolbar. Now that John created a folder (which he named Important) for his weekly tasks, he is ready to move the To Do List file into it. He also needs to move a letter (a recommendation for a new marketing person) currently contained in the Sales folder to the new Personnel folder.

Steps

> **QuickTip**
>
> Dragging a file or folder from one place to another on the same disk moves it; whereas dragging it from one disk to another copies it. If you want to copy the item on the same disk, simply press and hold [Ctrl] while you drag the mouse.

1. **Drag the To Do List file from the Wired Coffee window to the Important folder**
   You remove the icon representing the To Do List file from the Wired Coffee folder and place it in the folder named Important. You move folders in the same manner.

2. **Double-click the Important folder and confirm that you moved the file**
   The folder named Important now contains John's To Do List. John now needs to move the file named Recommend Nelson, a personnel recommendation for one of his employees, from the Sales folder to the Personnel folder.

3. **Click the Back button list arrow on the toolbar, click Sales, then click the Recommend Nelson file to select it**
   Since the Personnel folder is not visible, John uses the Cut and Paste commands to move a file from one folder to another.

> **QuickTip**
>
> If you want to perform a file management operation such as moving or copying more than one file or folder at a time, first select all the files or folders by pressing and holding [Ctrl] and clicking each one. Then perform the operation.

4. **Click Edit on the menu bar, then click Cut**
   You remove the file from its original location and store it on the Windows Clipboard. When you cut or copy a file, the file icon turns gray, as shown in Figure C-9. John moves back to the Wired Coffee folder and then opens the Personnel folder to complete the file move.

5. **Click the Back button on the toolbar, then double-click the Personnel folder**
   John is ready to use the paste command to move the file.

6. **Click Edit on the menu bar, then click Paste**
   You paste the file in the Personnel folder, shown in Figure C-10. After completing the move, John returns to the Wired Coffee folder.

7. **Click to return to the Wired Coffee folder**

Sending files and folders

The Send To command, located on the pop-up menu of any desktop object, lets you "send" (or move) a file or folder to a new location on your computer. For example, you can send a file or folder to a floppy disk to make a quick back-up copy of the file or folder, to a mail recipient as an electronic message, or to the desktop to create a shortcut. You can also use the Send To command to move a file or folder from one folder to another. To send a file or folder, right-click the file or folder you want to send, point to Send To on the pop-up menu, and then click the destination you want. You can determine the options that appear in the Send To command by creating a shortcut to the program or folder you want included and moving it to the SendTo folder, located within the Windows folder.

FIGURE C-9: Preparing to move a file

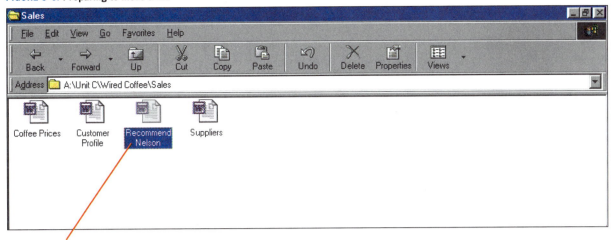

Grayed-out icon indicates file has been cut

FIGURE C-10: Relocated file

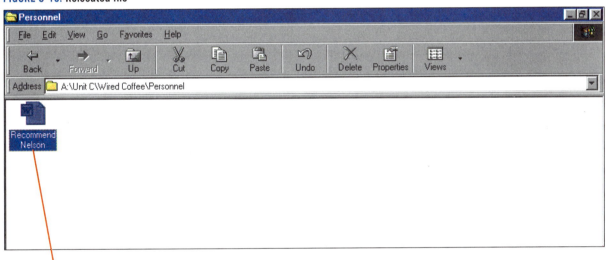

File in its new location

TABLE C-3: Methods for moving and copying files

action	methods
Move	Drag the file or folder to new location on the same disk
	Right-click the file or folder, drag to folder or drive, then click Move Here
	Select the file or folder, click File on the menu bar, click Cut, display a folder or drive
	Click File on the menu bar, then Paste
	Select the file or folder, click the Move To button on the toolbar, click a folder or drive, then click OK (Me)
Copy	Press and hold [Ctrl], then drag the file or folder to new location
	Right-click the file or folder, drag to folder or drive, then click Copy Here
	Select the file or folder, click File on the menu bar, click Copy, display a folder or drive, click File on the menu bar, then Paste
	Select the file or folder, click the Copy To button on the toolbar, click a folder or drive, then click OK (Me)

MANAGING FILES USING MY COMPUTER

Deleting and Restoring Files and Folders

When you organize the contents of a folder, disk, or the desktop, you might find files and folders that you no longer need. You can **delete** these items, or remove them from the disk. If you delete a file or folder from the desktop or from the hard disk, it goes into the Recycle Bin. The **Recycle Bin**, located on your desktop, is a temporary storage area for deleted files. If you delete a file that you still need, you can restore it by moving it from the Recycle Bin to another location. Be aware that if you delete a file from your floppy disk, it is not stored in the Recycle Bin—it is permanently deleted. See Table C-4 for a summary of the deleting and restoring options. To demonstrate how the Recycle Bin works, John first moves a file to the desktop, deletes that file, and then restores it.

Steps

> **Trouble?**
> Click the title bar in the My Computer window, then drag the window to the right to see the Recycle Bin.

1. **Double-click the Advertising folder, click the Restore button in the Advertising window, then move and resize the window as shown in Figure C-11**
   The Advertising folder and its contents appear in the Advertising window. Before you can delete a file from a floppy disk and send it to the Recycle Bin, you need to move the file to the desktop or hard drive. If you want to delete a file directly from a floppy disk with no possibility of restoring it, you can drag the file directly to the Recycle Bin or press [Delete].

> **QuickTip**
> To move files or folders quickly from one disk to another, select the files or folders, press and hold [Shift], then drag the selected items to the new location.

2. **Right-click and hold the Ad Campaign file, drag it to the desktop from the Advertising folder, then click Move Here**
   The file now appears on the desktop, and you can move it to the Recycle Bin, as shown in Figure C-11.

3. **Drag the Ad Campaign file from the desktop to the Recycle Bin (you might have to move the Advertising window), then click Yes, if necessary**
   The Recycle Bin icon should now look like it contains paper.

4. **Double-click the Recycle Bin icon**
   The Recycle Bin window opens. It contains the deleted file. Like most other windows, the Recycle Bin window contains a menu bar, a toolbar, and a status bar. Because John still needs this file he decides to restore it. The contents of the folders overlap, making it difficult for John to see both windows. He must first rearrange the desktop.

5. **Right-click an empty area of the taskbar, then click Tile Windows Vertically**
   This option allows you to see all open windows on the desktop at one time. The Recycle Bin window and the My Computer window appear side-by-side, as shown in Figure C-12.

> **QuickTip**
> Your deleted files remain in the Recycle Bin until you empty it. To empty the Recycle Bin, right-click the Recycle Bin icon, then click Empty Recycle Bin. This permanently removes the contents of the Recycle Bin from your hard disk.

6. **Select the Ad Campaign file in the Recycle Bin window, then drag it back to the Advertising window**
   You restore the file—it is intact and identical to the form it was in before you deleted it.

7. **Click the Close button in the Recycle Bin window**

FIGURE C-11: Selecting a file to drag to the Recycle Bin

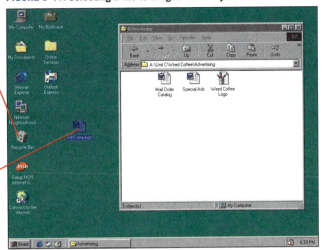

Drag the selection icon here to delete the file

Selected file moved from the Advertising folder to the desktop

FIGURE C-12: Deleted file from the Advertising folder in the Recycle Bin

Contents of your Recycle Bin might differ

TABLE C-4: Deleting and restoring files

ways to delete a file	ways to restore a file from the recycle bin
Select the file, then click the Delete button on the toolbar	Click the Undo button on the Recycle Bin toolbar
Select the file, then press [Delete]	Select the file, click File, then click Restore
Right-click the file, then click Delete	Right-click the file, then click Restore
Drag the file to the Recycle Bin	Drag the file from the Recycle Bin to any location

Recycle Bin properties

You can adjust several Recycle Bin settings by using the Properties option on the Recycle Bin pop-up menu. For example, if you do not want to place files in the Recycle Bin when you delete them, but, rather, want to immediately delete them, right-click the Recycle Bin, click Properties, then click the Do Not Move Files to the Recycle Bin check box to select the option. Also, if you find that the Recycle Bin is full and cannot accept any more files, you can increase the amount of disk space allotted to the Recycle Bin by moving the Maximum Size of Recycle Bin slider to the right. The percentage shown represents how much space the contents of the Recycle Bin takes on the drive.

Creating a Shortcut to a File

It could take you a while to access a file or folder buried several levels down in a file hierarchy. To save time in getting to the items you use frequently, you can create shortcuts. A **shortcut** is a link between two points: a "home" folder which actually stores a file, folder, or program and any other location where you want to access that file or program. The actual file, folder, or program remains stored in its original location; you place the icon representing the shortcut in a convenient location—a folder or the desktop. John always uses his Wired Coffee logo on stationery, flyers, and general advertising materials. Rather than having to take steps to start Paint and then open the file, he simply places a shortcut for this Paint file on the desktop.

1. **In the Advertising folder, right-click Wired Coffee Logo, then click Create Shortcut**
   An icon for a shortcut to the Wired Coffee Logo now appears in the Advertising window. Compare your screen with Figure C-13. All shortcuts are named the same as the files to which they link, but with the words "Shortcut to" in front of the original name. John wants to place the shortcut on his desktop for easy file access.

   Trouble?
   If you cannot see an empty area of your desktop, click the Restore button to resize it.

2. **Right-click and hold the Shortcut to Wired Coffee Logo file, drag it from the Advertising folder to an empty area of the desktop, then click Move Here**
   The shortcut appears on the desktop, as shown in Figure C-14. You can place a shortcut anywhere on the desktop. You should test the shortcut.

   Trouble?
   Depending on your file association settings, the imaging program might open instead of Paint.

3. **Double-click the Shortcut to Wired Coffee Logo icon**
   The Paint program opens with the file named Wired Coffee Logo.

4. **Click the Close button in the Paint window**
   The logo file and the Paint program close. The shortcut to Wired Coffee Logo remains on the desktop until you delete it, so you can use it again and again. If you are working in a lab environment, you should delete this shortcut.

5. **Right-click the Shortcut to Wired Coffee Logo icon**
   When you right-click folders and files (as opposed to the blank area in a window), a pop-up menu opens that offers several file management commands, as described in Table C-5. The commands on your pop-up menu might differ, depending on the Windows features installed on your computer.

6. **Click Delete on the pop-up menu, then click Yes in the Confirm File Delete dialog box**
   You delete the shortcut from the desktop and place it in the Recycle Bin, where it remains until John empties the Recycle Bin or restores the shortcut. When you delete a shortcut, you only remove the shortcut. The original file remains intact in its original location.

7. **Click the Maximize button in the Advertising window**

Placing shortcuts on the Start menu
You can place shortcuts to your favorite files and programs on the Start menu or on a toolbar on the taskbar. To do this, simply drag the folder, file, or program to the Start button or a toolbar on the taskbar, and the item then appears on the first level of the Start menu or on the toolbar.

FIGURE C-13: Creating a shortcut

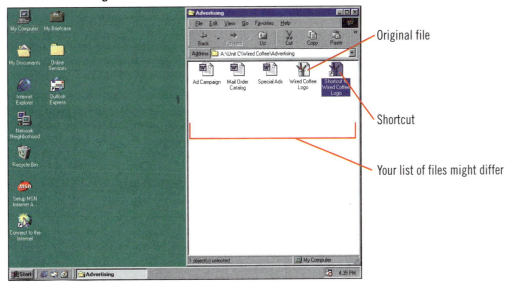

- Original file
- Shortcut
- Your list of files might differ

FIGURE C-14: Dragging a shortcut to a new location

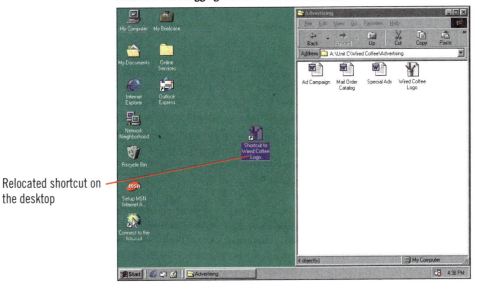

Relocated shortcut on the desktop

TABLE C-5: Shortcut menu options for files and folders

shortcut menu options	description	shortcut menu options	description
Open	Opens the file or folder	Create Shortcut	Creates a shortcut for the file or folder
Open With (Me)	Opens the file with a designated program	Delete	Deletes the file or folder
Explore	Opens a folder or drive in Windows Explorer	Print	Prints the file
Find	Finds files in a folder or drive	Preview (Me)	Previews the selected file
Send To	Sends the file or folder to new location	Rename	Renames the file or folder
Cut	Cuts the file or folder from its original location and places it on the Clipboard	Properties	Displays the properties of the file or folder
Copy	Copies the file or folder to the Clipboard	Sharing	Displays the sharing properties of the folder
Paste	Pastes the file or folder from the Clipboard to a new location		

MANAGING FILES USING MY COMPUTER

Displaying Drive Information

You should know as much about your system as possible. You might have to tell your instructor or technical support person certain information if you encounter a problem with your computer, or you might want to know how much space remains on a disk or want to change a **disk label** (a name you can assign to a hard or floppy disk). When you label a hard disk, the label appears in the My Computer and Windows Explorer windows. Besides checking hard drive or floppy disk information, you can also use Windows tools to check your disks for damage, optimize your disk for better performance, make copies of your disks for safe keeping, and share your disk contents with others. You perform these activities using the Properties command. *John wants to find out how much free space is available on his floppy disk.*

1. **Click the Back button list arrow on the toolbar, then click My Computer**
   John needs to display the 3½ Floppy disk icon in the My Computer window to examine property information.

2. **Right-click the icon in the My Computer window for the drive drive where your Project Files are located**
   The icon representing the 3½ disk drive is highlighted, and the pop-up menu opens.

3. **Click Properties on the pop-up menu**
   The 3½ Floppy (A:) Properties dialog box opens with the General tab in front, as shown in Figure C-15. Click the General tab if it is not the frontmost tab. You can see a graphical representation of the amount of space being used relative to the amount available in the pie chart for the floppy disk.

4. **Click the Label text box if necessary, then type ProjectDisk**
   A disk label can contain up to 11 characters but no spaces.

5. **Click the Tools tab**
   The Tools tab becomes the frontmost tab, as shown in Figure C-16, showing you the utilities that can make Windows work more efficiently: error-checking, backup (98), and defragmentation. You can use the **Defragmentation** feature to speed up the performance of a disk. Defragmenting means rewriting files to the disk in contiguous rather than random blocks. When you click any one of these options, Windows updates you as to when the option was last used on the currently selected disk. Although you use these tools mostly to keep a hard disk healthy, you can use them on a floppy disk as well. Table C-6 describes what each tool does.

> **Trouble?**
> If the Compression tab is not available, use the Add/Remove Programs utility Windows Setup tab in the Control Panel to install the compression folder feature (Me).

6. **Click the Compression tab**
   The Compression tab allows you to compress (reduce the size) of the selected drive to save space.

7. **Click OK**
   The Properties dialog box closes.

8. **Click the Close button in the My Computer window**

Backing up files

The more you work with a computer, the more files you create. To protect yourself from losing critical information, it's important to **back up** (make copies on a separate disk) your files frequently. The Backup option (98) in the disk drive Properties dialog box walks you through a series of dialog boxes to help you back up the files on your hard disk to a floppy or tape drive. You can back up the contents of an entire disk or only certain files.

FIGURE C-15: General tab options in the 3½ Floppy (A:) Properties window

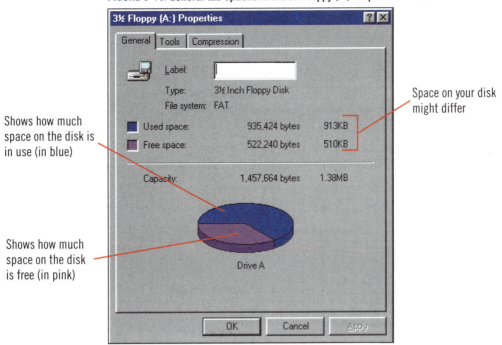

Shows how much space on the disk is in use (in blue)

Shows how much space on the disk is free (in pink)

Space on your disk might differ

FIGURE C-16: Tools tab options in the 3½ Floppy (A:) Properties window

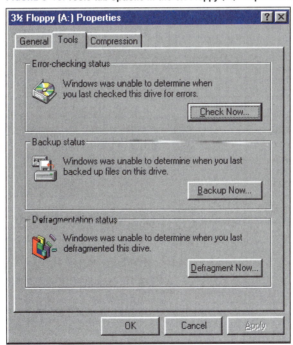

TABLE C-6: Tools in the Properties dialog box

tool	description
Error-checking status	Checks for the last time you checked the disk for damage and, if you want, attempts to correct damaged files
Backup status	Displays the last time you backed up the contents of the disk, and if you want, starts the Windows 98 backup program (Windows Me users can install from Windows Update.)
Defragmentation status	Checks for the last time you optimized the disk, and if you want, starts the Windows Defragmentation procedure

MANAGING FILES USING MY COMPUTER   WINDOWS 98 AND ME C-17

Practice

▶ Concepts Review

Label each element of the screen shown in Figure C-17.

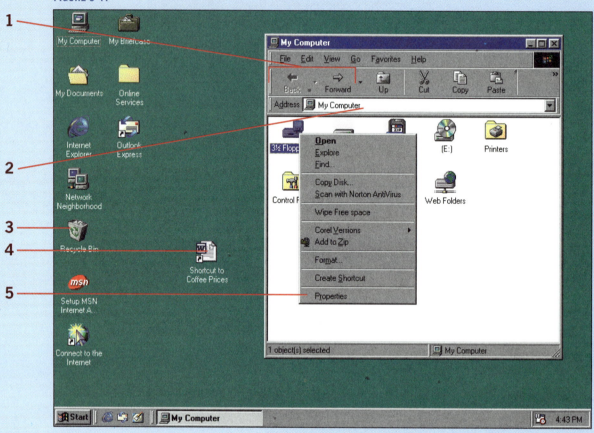

FIGURE C-17

Match each term with the statement that describes its function.

6. My Computer
7. Shortcut
8. File
9. Recycle Bin
10. Folder

a. A link to a file or folder.
b. A file and folder management tool.
c. Location of deleted files.
d. A collection of files and folders.
e. A collection of information.

Practice

Select the best answer from the following list of choices.

11. When you delete a file, place it in:
    a. the Recycle Bin.
    b. the Desktop Container.
    c. My Computer.
    d. Accessories.

12. My Computer is used to:
    a. Delete files.
    b. Add folders.
    c. Manage files and folders.
    d. All of the above.

13. Which of the following is not an option for viewing files and folders?
    a. Filenames
    b. Details
    c. Large icons
    d. Small icons

14. When files and folders are arranged by date, they are arranged by the:
    a. Date they were created.
    b. Date they were last opened.
    c. Current date.
    d. Date they were last modified.

15. When right-clicking a folder, which of the following cannot be done?
    a. Print the contents of the folder
    b. Create a shortcut
    c. Explore the folder
    d. Find a file

▶ Skills Review

1. Open and view My Computer.
    a. Insert your disk where your Project Files are located in the appropriate disk drive, if necessary.
    b. Double-click My Computer.
    c. Click the Maximize button in the My Computer window.
    d. Double-click the 3½ Floppy drive (A: or B:).
    e. Double-click the Wired Coffee folder.
    f. Double-click the Sales folder.

Windows 98 and Me | **Practice**

2. **View files and folders.**
   a. Click the Views button list arrow, then click List.
   b. Click the Up button on the toolbar twice.
   c. Click the Back button on the toolbar.
   d. Open the Personnel folder.
   e. Click the Back button list arrow on the toolbar, then click Sales.
   f. Click the Forward button on the toolbar.
   g. Click View on the menu bar, then click Details.
   h. Click View on the menu bar, then click Large Icons.

3. **Create folders.**
   a. Right-click a blank area of the window, point to New, then click Folder.
   b. Type **Marketing** and press [Enter].
   c. Click View on the menu bar, point to Arrange Icons, then click By Name.

4. **Move files.**
   a. Double-click the Advertising folder.
   b. Click the Mail Order Catalog file.
   c. Click Edit on the menu bar, then click Copy.
   d. Click the Back button on the toolbar.
   e. Double-click the Marketing folder.
   f. Click Edit on the menu bar, then click Paste.
   g. Click the Back button on the toolbar.

5. **Delete and restore files.**
   a. Click the Marketing folder.
   b. Click the Restore button in the window.
   c. Right-click the Marketing folder, drag it to the desktop, then click Move Here.
   d. Drag the Marketing folder from the desktop to the Recycle Bin, then click Yes, if necessary.
   e. Double-click the Recycle Bin.
   f. Right-click an empty area of the taskbar, then click Tile Windows Vertically.
   g. Click File on the Recycle Bin menu bar, click Empty Recycle Bin, then click Yes. (To restore the Marketing folder, you would drag it back to the Wired Coffee folder.)
   h. Click the Close button in the Recycle Bin window.

6. **Create shortcuts.**
   a. Double-click the Advertising folder.
   b. Right-click the Special Ads file, then click Create Shortcut.
   c. Right-click and drag the Shortcut to Special Ads file to the desktop, then click Move Here.
   d. Right-click the Shortcut to Special Ads file, then click Delete.
   e. Click Yes.
   f. Right-click the Recycle Bin icon, then click Empty Recycle Bin.
   g. Click Yes.

Practice

7. Examine disk capacity.
   a. Click the Back button list arrow on the toolbar, then click My Computer.
   b. Right-click the icon representing drive where your Project Files are located in the My Computer window, then click Properties.
   c. Write the capacity of the disk, how much capacity is in use, and how much is available for further use.
   d. Click OK.
   e. Click the Close button in the My Computer window.

▶ Independent Challenges

1. As a manager at Lew's Books and Cappuccino bookstore, you need to organize the folders and files currently on the store's computer. These are on the drive and in the folder where your Project Files are located in the folder named Lew's Books.

To complete this independent challenge:

a. Open My Computer, then open and view the contents of the folder called Lew's Books on the drive and in the folder where your Project Files are located.
b. Using paper and pencil, draw the organization of all folders and files in Lew's Books & Cappuccino.
c. In the Lew's Books folder, create four new folders named *Q1*, *Q2*, *Q3*, and *Q4*.
d. Take the quarterly folders in the 2001 and 2002 folders (2001Q1, 2001Q2, etc.), and place them in the respective Q1, Q2, Q3, and Q4 folders.
e. Create a shortcut for the Collectors' Newsletter file (located in the Letters folder), and place it in the Lew's Books folder.
f. In the folder named Store Locations, create a new folder and name it *New Stores*.
g. Move the New Store Locations file in the Letters folder to the New Stores folder.
h. Using paper and pencil, draw the new organization of all folders and files in the Lew's Books folder.
i. Close My Computer.

Windows 98 and Me | Practice

2. You are vice president of a small carton manufacturing company, Apex Cartons, and you need to organize your Windows folders and files. As with any typical business, you have folders for correspondence (business and personal), contracts, inventory, personnel documents, and payroll information. You may have other folders as well. Your job is to organize these separate folders.

To complete this independent challenge:

a. Open My Computer and create a new folder named *Apex Cartons* on the drive and in the folder where your Project Files are located, within which the rest of the organization of files and folders for this independent challenge will appear.
b. Create a folder named *Manufacturing*.
c. Create a folder named *Material Suppliers*.
d. Create two folders; name one *East Coast* and the other *West Coast*.
e. Move (not copy) the East Coast and West Coast folders into the folder named Material Suppliers.
f. Create a file using WordPad (you don't need to place any text in it), and save it as *Suppliers Bid* in the Manufacturing folder on the drive and in the folder where your Project Files are located.
g. Move the Suppliers Bid file into the Material Suppliers folder.
h. Using paper and pencil, draw the new organization of all folders and files in your Apex Cartons folder.
i. Close My Computer.

3. You and your college roommate decide to start a mail-order PC business called MO PC, and you decide to use Windows to organize the files for the business. Your job is to organize the following folders and files, and to create shortcuts as well.

To complete this independent challenge:

a. Open My Computer and create a new folder named *MO PC* on the drive and in the folder where your Project Files are located, within which the rest of the organization of files and folders for this independent challenge will appear.
b. Create a new folder named *Advertising*.
c. Create a new folder named *Customers*.
d. Use WordPad to create a one-paragraph form letter welcoming new customers, save it as *Customer Letter*, and place it in the Customers folder.
e. Use WordPad to create a list of at least five tasks that need to get done before the business opens, save it as *Business Plan*, and place it in the MO PC folder.
f. Use Paint to create a simple logo, then save it as *MO Logo* in the Advertising folder.
g. Create a shortcut to the MO Logo file.
h. Delete the Business Plan file, and then restore it.
i. Using paper and pencil, draw the new organization of all folders and files in your MO PC folder.
j. Close My Computer.

Practice

4. M & N Bakeries just opened. You are hired to help the owners organize their recipes into different categories and work on the design of their company logo. For this independent challenge, use the files Icing 1, Icing 2, Brownies, Passover & Easter Torte, located in the M&N Bakeries folder on the drive and in the folder where your Project Files are located.

To complete this independent challenge:

a. Open My Computer and open the folder M&N Bakeries on the drive and in the folder where your Project Files are located, within which the rest of the organization of files and folders for this Independent Challenge will appear.
b. Create a folder named *Cakes*.
c. Create a folder named *Flourless Cakes*, and move it into the Cakes folder.
d. Create a folder named *Flour Cakes*, and move it into the Cakes folder.
e. In the M&N Bakeries folder, create a folder named *Cookies & Bars*.
f. Move the Brownies file into the Cookies & Bars folder.
g. Move the Passover & Easter Torte file into the Flourless Cakes folder.
h. Move the Icing 1 recipe file to your desktop, then drag the file to the Recycle Bin.
i. Double-click to open the Recycle Bin, and restore the Icing 1 recipe file to the M&N Bakeries folder on the drive and in the folder where your Project Files are located.
j. Using paper and pencil, draw the new organization of all folders and files in your M&N Bakeries folder.
k. Close My Computer.

Windows 98 and Me | **Practice**

▶ Visual Workshop

Re-create the screen shown in Figure C-18, which displays the My Computer window for the floppy disk drive where your Project Files are located. Use Figure C-1 to help you locate the Coffee Prices file. Print the screen. (Press [Print Screen] to make a copy of the screen, open Paint, click Edit on the menu bar, click Paste to paste the screen into Paint, then click Yes to paste the large image, if necessary. Click File on the menu bar, click Print, then click OK.)

FIGURE C-18

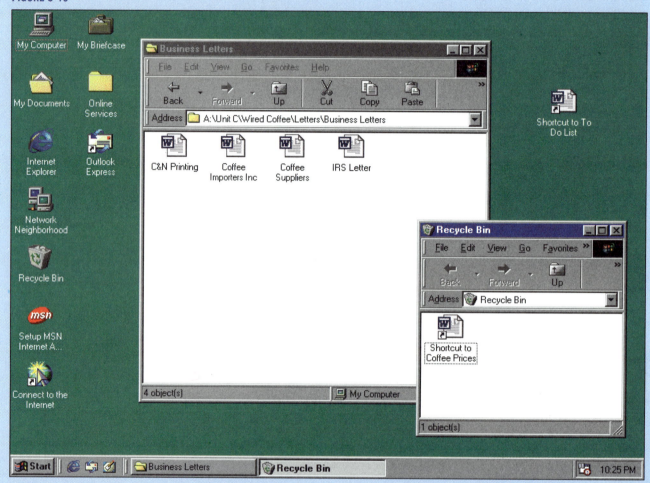

WINDOWS 98 AND ME C-24 **MANAGING FILES USING MY COMPUTER**

Windows 98 and Me

Managing
Folders and Files Using Windows Explorer

Next week 11-12th-01

Objectives

- View the Windows Explorer window
- Open and view folders in Windows Explorer
- Customize the Windows Explorer window
- Create and rename folders in Windows Explorer
- Find a file
- Move and copy a file to a folder
- Restore a deleted file using Undo
- Customize a folder

Windows 98 and Me offers another useful feature for managing files and folders, named Windows Explorer. More powerful than My Computer, Windows Explorer offers more features, and most importantly, allows you to work with more than one computer, folder, or file at once. This is possible because the Windows Explorer window is split into two **panes**, or frames, to accommodate comparison of information from two different locations. You can also use Windows Explorer to copy, move, delete, and rename files and folders, as you can with My Computer. In this unit John Casey uses Windows Explorer to perform some general file management tasks and also to prepare for the upcoming Wired Coffee Spring Catalog.

Viewing the Windows Explorer Window

The most important aspect of the Windows Explorer window is the two panes shown in Figure D-1. The pane on the left side of the screen, known as the **Explorer Bar** (or simply "the left pane"), displays all drives and folders on the computer, and the right pane displays the contents of whatever drive or folder is selected in the Explorer Bar. This arrangement enables you to simultaneously view the overall structure of the contents of your computer (the file hierarchy) and the contents of specific folders within that structure. John wants to gain more experience working in Windows Explorer, so he starts the program and then views the contents of his computer.

Steps

> **Trouble?**
> If you do not see the toolbar, click View on the menu bar, point to Toolbars, then click Standard Buttons to place a check mark next to it and to display the toolbar. Follow the same procedure (clicking Address Bar instead of Standard Buttons) if you don't see the Address Bar.

1. **Click the Start button on the taskbar, point to Programs, point to Accessories (Me), then click Windows Explorer**
   Windows Explorer opens, displaying the contents of your computer's hard drive, as shown in Figure D-1. Note that the contents of your screen vary, depending on the programs and files installed on your computer and also depending on where Windows is installed on your hard disk or network. Windows Explorer has its own toolbar. Below the toolbar is the Address Bar, which you can use to change what is selected in the left pane and therefore what appears in the right pane. Notice that the toolbar and the Address Bar are the same ones used in the My Computer window. Windows 98 and Me provides a consistent look and feel to make accomplishing your tasks easier.

2. **In the Explorer Bar, click the Desktop icon**
   The right pane contains a list of the icons on the desktop. The Address Bar makes it easy to open items on the desktop and the drives, and in the folders and system folders on your computer. As an alternative to using the Address Bar, you can change what appears in the right pane by clicking the drive or folder in the Explorer Bar, which is the left pane. In the same way you can view the contents of your computer using the My Computer window on your desktop, you can also view the contents of your computer using Windows Explorer.

> **QuickTip**
> You can change the size of the left and right panes. Place the mouse pointer on the vertical bar that separates the two panes of the Windows Explorer window. When the mouse changes to ↔, you can drag the line to change the size of each pane.

3. **In the Explorer Bar, click the My Computer icon**
   The right pane contains a list of the drives and system folders on your computer.

4. **Make sure a copy of the disk or drive where your Project Files are located is available— click the Address list arrow on the Address Bar, then click 3½ Floppy (A:) or (B:)**
   The 3½ floppy disk drive opens, as shown in Figure D-2. The right pane of Windows Explorer shows the contents of the drive. You can open a folder or a document in the right pane of Windows Explorer. When you double-click a drive or folder in the right pane, the right pane of Windows Explorer shows the contents of that item. When you double-click a document, the program associated with the document starts and opens the document. You can move back and forth to the last drive or folder you opened using the Back and Forward buttons on the toolbar in the Windows Explorer window just as you did in the My Computer window.

5. **Click the Back button on the toolbar**
   The right pane of Windows Explorer lists the contents of My Computer (the last location you opened in Step 3).

6. **Click the Forward button on the toolbar**
   The contents of the 3½ floppy disk drive reappear in the right pane of Windows Explorer. Leave Windows Explorer open and move to the next lesson.

FIGURE D-1: Displaying the contents of your computer's hard drive

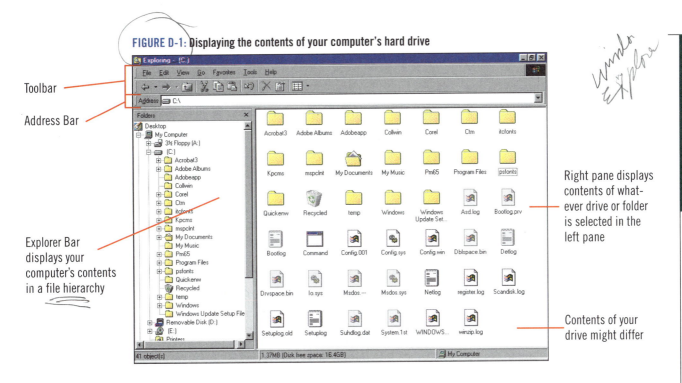

Toolbar

Address Bar

Explorer Bar displays your computer's contents in a file hierarchy

Right pane displays contents of whatever drive or folder is selected in the left pane

Contents of your drive might differ

FIGURE D-2: Contents of the 3½ floppy disk drive for Windows Me

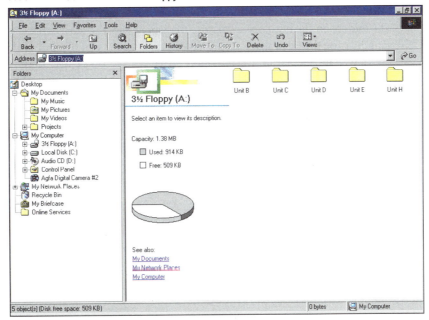

Changing folder options

You can change your view of the current folder in Windows Explorer by changing the folder view settings. You can choose to display the full path of the folder in the Address Bar or title bar, show or hide hidden files and folders in the folder, show the My Documents folder on the desktop, and show pop-up descriptions of folders and desktop items. To change view settings, click Tools on the menu bar, click Folder Options, click the View tab, then click check boxes and option buttons in the Advanced settings window for the settings you want. If you don't like the options you set in the Folder Options dialog box, you can restore the dialog box settings to Windows default settings by clicking Restore Defaults. If you want the new settings to apply to all folders on your computer, click Like Current Folder under Folder views. To restore all folders to original Windows settings, click Reset All Folders.

MANAGING FOLDERS AND FILES USING WINDOWS EXPLORER

Windows 98 and Me

Opening and Viewing Folders in Windows Explorer

The Explorer Bar (the left pane of Windows Explorer) displays your computer's contents in file hierarchy. At the top of the file hierarchy is the desktop, followed by the drives, and then the folders. The dotted gray lines indicate the different levels. You can display or hide the different levels by clicking the plus sign (+) or the minus sign (–) to the left of an icon in the Explorer Bar so that you don't always have to look at the complicated structure of your entire computer or network. Clicking the + to the left of an icon displays (or expands the drive or folder) under the icon the contents of the drive or folder, and clicking the – hides them (or collapses the drive or folder). Clicking the icon itself displays the contents of the item in the right pane. When neither a + nor a – appears next to an icon, the item has no folders in it. (However, it might contain files, whose names you could display in the right pane by clicking the icon.) Using the + and – in the Explorer Bar allows you to display quickly the file hierarchy of the drives and folders on your computer without opening and displaying the contents of each folder. John wants to open the Personnel and Letters folders without opening and displaying the contents of each folder in the file hierarchy.

Steps

1. **Click the – (minus sign) next to the hard drive (C:) icon in the Explorer Bar**
   The folders on the hard drive collapse to display only the hard drive icon. The – changes to a +, indicating the hard drive contains folders. Because you did not click the hard drive icon, the right pane displays the contents of drive A as it did before. John decides to display the folders on the floppy disk drive.

   Trouble?
   If you are using a Project Disk, copy the disk before you use it and insert the copy in your disk drive. For assistance, see your instructor or technical support person.

2. **Click the + (plus sign) next to the 3½ Floppy drive icon in the Explorer Bar**
   The folder on the drive where your Project Files are located expands and appears in the Explorer Bar.

3. **Click the + next to the folder where your Project Files are located in the Explorer Bar, then click the + next to the Wired Coffee folder in the Explorer Bar**
   The folders in the Wired Coffee folder expand and appear in the Explorer Bar, as shown in Figure D-3.

4. **Click the Personnel folder in the Explorer Bar**
   The contents of Personnel folder appear in the right pane, as shown in Figure D-4. When you click a folder in the Explorer Bar, the contents of that folder appear in the right pane of Windows Explorer.

5. **Click the Letters folder in the Explorer Bar, then double-click the Business Letters folder in the right pane of Windows Explorer**
   The Business Letters folder opens, as shown in Figure D-5. The right pane of Windows Explorer shows the contents of the Business Letters folder and the Explorer Bar shows the folders in the expanded Letters folder.

FIGURE D-3: Folders on the 3½ floppy disk drive

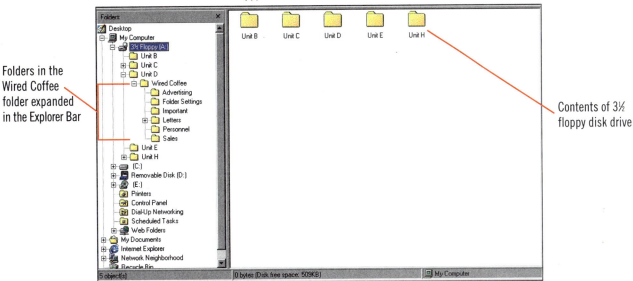

FIGURE D-4: Personnel folder

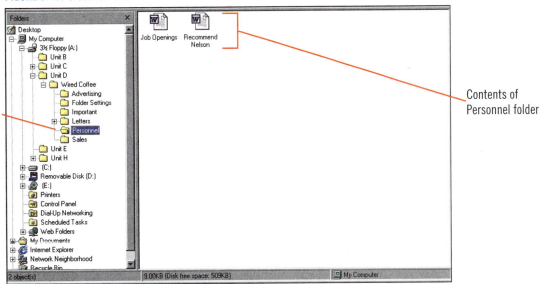

FIGURE D-5: Business Letters folder

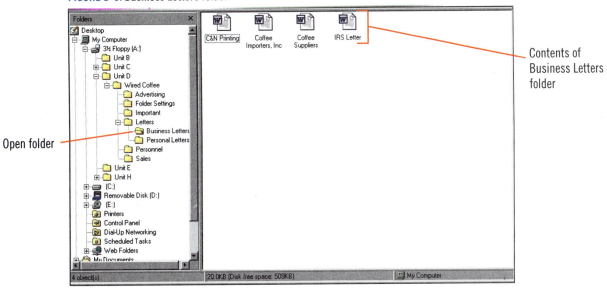

Customizing the Windows Explorer Window

You can display Windows Explorer and your file hierarchy in a variety of different ways, depending on what you want to see and do. For example, if you want to display a lot of files and folders, you can hide the Explorer Bar or the status bar to make more room. If you need to change the way Windows Explorer sorts your files and folders, you can use the column indicator buttons in the right pane of Details view. Clicking one of the column indicator buttons, such as Name, Size, Type, or Modified (date) in Details view, sorts the folders and files by the type of information listed in the column. John wants to find the date he wrote a letter to the coffee suppliers so he decides to sort the files in the Business Letters folder by date.

Steps

1. **Point to Business Letters in the Explorer Bar**
   A ScreenTip appears, displaying the full name of the folder. When you cannot view the entire folder name in the Explorer Bar, you can point to any part of the folder name to display a ScreenTip.

2. **Position the pointer on the vertical bar that separates the two panes of the Windows Explorer window; when the mouse changes to ↔, drag the vertical bar to the right until the full name of each folder appears**

3. **Click the Views button list arrow on the toolbar, then click Details**
   The files and folders with your Project Files (in the 3½ floppy disk drive) appear in Details view, as shown in Figure D-6. John wants to sort his files and folders. First, to see the file and folder information better, he closes the Explorer Bar.

4. **Click the Close button on the Explorer Bar**
   The Explorer Bar closes to provide more room to work with files and folders in the right pane. You can sort by any category listed by clicking the column indicator button located at the top of the folders and files list in the right pane. The files in the Business Letters folder are currently sorted in alphabetical order. John decides to sort the files by date.

5. **Position the pointer between the Name column indicator button and the Size column indicator button; when the pointer changes to ↔, drag to the left or right to display the full name (if necessary), then adjust all the columns to display the full name**
   You know that all file information is completely visible when no ellipses appear after a filename, type, or date. You can sort by any category listed by clicking the column indicator button located at the top of the folders and files list in the right pane. The files in the Business Letters folder are currently sorted in alphabetical order.

QuickTip
Each of the column indicator buttons works as a toggle; clicking once sorts the file in one order, and clicking again reverses the order.

6. **Click the Modified column indicator button**
   You sort the files and folders by their last modification date, from latest to earliest, as shown in Figure D-7.

7. **Click the Name column indicator button**
   You sort the files and folders by name in alphabetical order. John finds the Coffee Suppliers file and sees the date he last modified the file.

8. **Click the View on the menu bar, point to Explorer Bar, then click Folders**
   The Explorer Bar opens and displays folders. In the Explorer Bar, you can also change the display of Internet-related features to search for information, list favorite Web pages, list Web pages you visited in the past, and list channels. You learn more about these Internet-related features in a later lesson.

WINDOWS 98 AND ME D-6   MANAGING FOLDERS AND FILES USING WINDOWS EXPLORER

FIGURE D-6: Windows Explorer in Details view

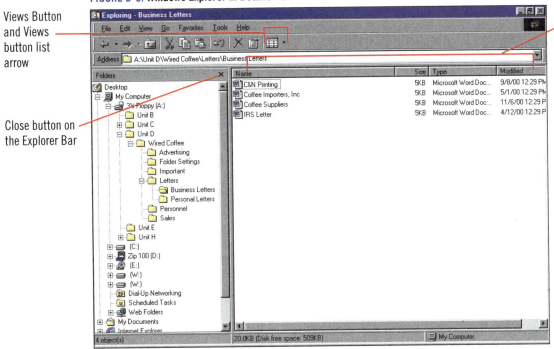

Views Button and Views button list arrow

Close button on the Explorer Bar

Column indicator buttons

FIGURE D-7: Sorting files and folders by date

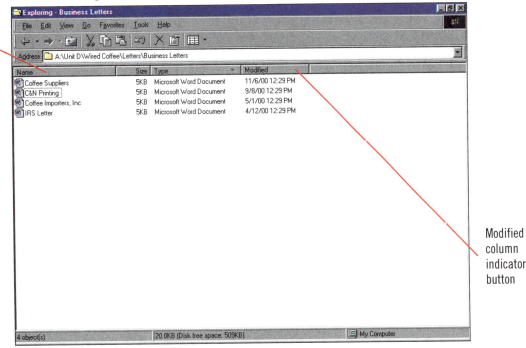

Name column indicator button

Modified column indicator button

Using the status bar

The status bar at the bottom of the Windows Explorer window gives you information about drives, folders, and files on your computer. You can quickly find how many items a drive or folder contains, the total size of its contents, its location on your computer, and (for drives) the amount of free disk space. If you don't want to use the status bar, you can turn it off by clicking View on the menu bar, then clicking Status Bar to remove the check mark.

Creating and Renaming Folders in Windows Explorer

To manage all the files on your computer effectively, you need folders in convenient locations to store related files. You should name each folder meaningfully, so that merely glancing at the folder's name reminds you of its contents. Creating a new folder in Windows Explorer is much like doing so from My Computer. First, select the location where you want the new folder, then create the folder, and finally, name the folder. You can create a folder in Windows Explorer by using the New command on the File menu, or by right-clicking in the right pane, clicking New, then clicking folder. You can rename a folder or file in Windows Explorer using the Rename command. To do this, right-click the file or folder you want to rename, click Rename on the pop-up menu, type the new name, and then press [Enter]. John wants to create a set of new folders to hold the files related to the creation of the Wired Coffee Spring Catalog. He then renames one of the folders.

1. **Click the Wired Coffee folder in the Explorer Bar**
   To create a new folder, you must first select the drive or folder where you want the folder, which in this case is the Wired Coffee folder.

2. **Click File on the menu bar, point to New, then click Folder**
   A new folder, temporarily named New Folder, appears highlighted with a rectangle around the title in the right pane of Windows Explorer, as shown in Figure D-8. To enter a new folder name, you simply type the new name. John names it Spring Catalog.

   Trouble?
   If nothing happens when you type the name, you pressed [Enter] or clicked outside the new folder. Select the folder, click the name "New Folder" so a rectangle surrounds it (with the insertion point inside), then repeat Step 3.

3. **Type Spring Catalog, then press [Enter] or click an empty area in the right pane**
   The Spring Catalog folder appears in both panes, as shown in Figure D-9. John wants to create folders within the Spring Catalog folder.

4. **In the right pane, double-click the Spring Catalog folder**
   Nothing appears in the right pane because the folder is empty; no new files or folders have been created or moved here. Because Spring Catalog is the currently selected folder, it will contain the folders that John creates.

5. **Right-click anywhere in the right pane, point to New on the pop-up menu, then click Folder**
   A new folder, named New Folder, appears in the right pane of Windows Explorer.

6. **Type Catalog Text, then press [Enter]**
   The folder is now named Catalog Text. Notice also the + (or – if the folder is expanded) next to the Spring Catalog folder in the left pane, indicating that this folder contains other folders or files. John decides to change the name of the new folder to Catalog Pages.

   QuickTip
   To rename a file, you can also select the item, click the name so a rectangle surrounds it, type the new name, then press [Enter].

7. **Right-click the Catalog Text folder in the right pane, then click Rename on the pop-up menu, as shown in Figure D-10**
   The folder appears highlighted with a rectangle around the title in the right pane of Windows Explorer.

8. **Type Catalog Pages, then press [Enter]**
   The Catalog Text folder is renamed Catalog Pages.

WINDOWS 98 AND ME D-8   MANAGING FOLDERS AND FILES USING WINDOWS EXPLORER

FIGURE D-8: Newly created folder

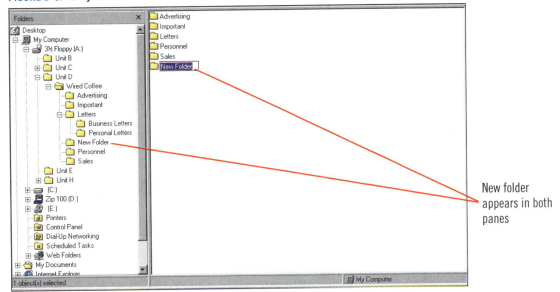

FIGURE D-9: Creating a new folder using right-click method

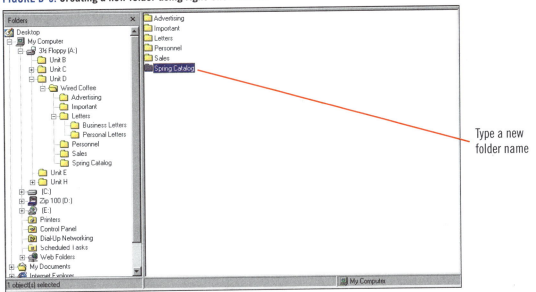

FIGURE D-10: Renaming a folder using right-click method

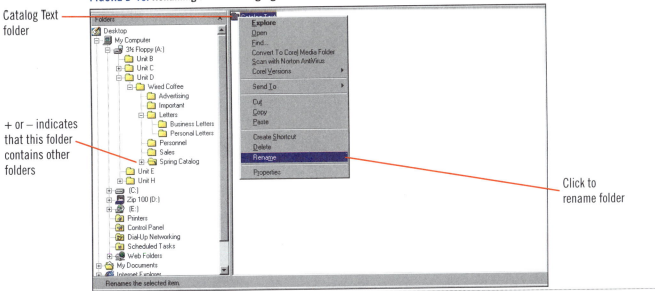

MANAGING FOLDERS AND FILES USING WINDOWS EXPLORER

Windows 98 and Me

Finding a File

Sometimes remembering precisely where you stored a file is difficult. Windows Explorer provides a Find program on the Tools menu to help you find files or folders. The Find program gives you the option to find files or folders by name, location, size, type, and the creation or last modification date. The Find program is also available on the Start menu to help you locate files and folders when you are not using Windows Explorer. To access the Find program on the Start menu, click the Start button on the taskbar, point to Find, and then click Files or Folders. John wants to find a file he created several months ago with a preliminary outline for the Spring Catalog. He cannot remember the exact title of the file or where he stored it, so he needs to do a quick search.

Steps

1. Click **Tools** on the menu bar, point to **Find**, then click **Files or Folders** (98) or click the **Search button** on the toolbar (Me)
   The Find: All Files window opens, shown in Figure D-11. Table D-1 lists the tabs in The Find: All Files window and describes the search options each offers (98). Since John remembers part of the name (but not the location) of the file he needs, he can use the Name & Location tab.

2. Type **Catalog** in the Named text box (98) or in the Search for files or folders named text box (Me)
   You can supply the full name of the folder or file you want to find, or only the part you know for sure. If, for example, John were unsure as to whether or not he saved the file as Spring Catalog or Catalog Outline, he could type Catalog, since he's sure of that part of the name. If John didn't know the name of the file, but did know some text contained in the file, he could enter the text in the Containing text text box. Before you can start the search, you need to indicate where you want the program to search. The Find program initially begins searching in the open folder in Windows Explorer, but you can choose the location you want.

   > **QuickTip**
   > Insert the * (asterisk) wild-card symbol in a filename when you're unsure of the entire name. For example, type S*rs to find not only the file named Suppliers, but also all other files beginning with S and ending with rs (such as Starts and Sportscars).

3. Click the **Look in list arrow**, then click the drive where your Project Files are located

4. Click **Find Now** (98) or **Search Now** (Me)
   The Find program searches all the folders and files on the drive where your Project Files are located and lists those folders and files whose names contain the word "Catalog" in the box at the bottom of the Find: All Files window. The list contains the full names, locations, sizes, types, and the creation or last modification dates of the folders or files.

5. Position the pointer between the In Folder column indicator button and the Size column indicator button; when the pointer changes to ↔, drag to the right to display the location of the file, as shown in Figure D-12
   At this point, John can either double-click the file to start the associated program and open the file, or he can note the file's location and close the Find: Files named Catalog window. He decides to note the file's location and close the window.

6. Click the **Close button** in the Find: Files named Catalog window (98) or click the **Folders button** on the toolbar (Me), then click the **Spring Catalog folder** in the Explorer Bar

TABLE D-1: Tabs in the Find: All Files window for Windows 98

tab	use to
Name & Location	Find the file by name, location, and text the file contains; browse through directories for the file
Date	Search for files created during the previous number of days or months, or between a certain period of time that you specify
Advanced	Search for files by type (such as a WordPad file) or size

▶ WINDOWS 98 AND ME D-10   MANAGING FOLDERS AND FILES USING WINDOWS EXPLORER

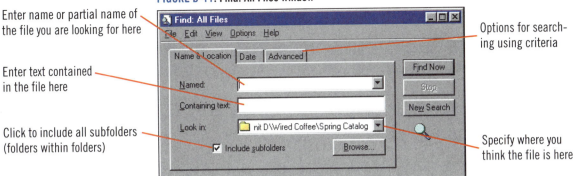

FIGURE D-11: Find: All Files window

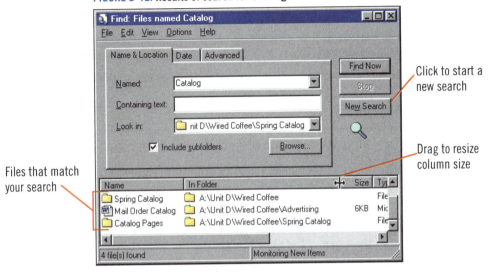

FIGURE D-12: Results of search for Catalog file

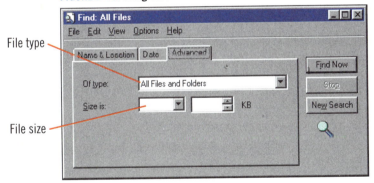

FIGURE D-13: Using advanced search features

Performing an Advanced Search

You can also complete an advanced search that uses criteria, or information, beyond just the name or partial name of the file. If you have no idea what the name or content of the file is, but can recall the type of file (such as a WordPad document), then use the Advanced tab in the Find: All Files window, and select a file type using the Of type list arrow, shown in Figure D-13. When you click Find Now, Windows searches for and display all the files for the type you specify. This can take a long time, although probably less time than recreating the missing files would take. For Windows Me, click the Search button on the toolbar, click Search Options, then click the Date, Type, Size, or Advanced Options check box to perform an advanced search.

MANAGING FOLDERS AND FILES USING WINDOWS EXPLORER

Copying and Moving a File to a Folder

You should always store your files in the appropriate folders. Sometimes this means moving a file from one folder to another (removing it from the first and placing it in the second), and sometimes this means copying a file from one folder to another (leaving it in the first but placing a copy of it in the second). You can move and copy files and folders in several different ways in Windows Explorer. You can use the Cut, Copy, and Paste buttons (98) or the Move To and Copy To buttons (Me) on the Windows Explorer toolbar. Or you can "drag and drop" the file or folder while holding down a mouse button. A third way is to right-click the file or folder and choose the appropriate command from the pop-up menu. John plans to use text from the Mail Order Catalog file (currently located in the Advertising folder) in the Spring Catalog, so he wants to move the Mail Order Catalog file from the Advertising folder to the Catalog Pages folder. He also wants to make a copy of the Wired Coffee Logo file and place it in the Spring Catalog folder.

Steps

1. **Click the + next to the Spring Catalog folder in the Explorer Bar**
   The Spring Catalog folder expands, displaying the folder it contains.

   > **QuickTip**
   > To select files or folders that are not consecutive, press and hold [Ctrl], then click each item.

2. **Click the Advertising folder in the Explorer Bar**
   The right pane of Windows Explorer shows the contents of the folder. When moving or copying files or folders in Windows Explorer, make sure the files or folders you want to move or copy appear in the right pane. To move the Mail Order Catalog file, John drags it from the right pane to the Catalog Pages folder in the Explorer Bar.

3. **Drag the Mail Order Catalog file across the vertical line separating the two panes to the Catalog Pages folder as shown in Figure D-14, then release the mouse button**
   Once you release the mouse button, the Mail Order Catalog file is in the Catalog Pages folder. If you decide that you don't want the file moved, you can move it back easily using the Undo button on the toolbar. Now John copies the Wired Coffee Logo file in the Advertising folder to the Spring Catalog folder.

4. **Point to the Wired Coffee Logo file, press and hold the right mouse button, drag the file across the vertical line separating the two panes to the Spring Catalog folder, then release the mouse button**
   As Figure D-15 shows, the pop-up menu offers a choice of options, including the Copy Here option. You can also right-click a file in the right pane to open a pop-up menu—another way to copy or move the file to a new location.

   > **QuickTip**
   > To copy a file quickly from one folder to another on the same disk, select the file, press and hold [Ctrl], then drag the file to the folder. You can also copy a file from a hard disk to a floppy disk by right-clicking the file, pointing to Send To, then clicking the appropriate disk drive icon.

5. **Click Copy Here**
   The original file named Wired Coffee Logo remains in the Advertising folder, and a copy of the file is in the Spring Catalog folder.

6. **Click the Spring Catalog folder in the Explorer Bar**
   You copy the Wired Coffee Logo file from the Advertising folder (where the original remains) to the Spring Catalog folder.

7. **Click the Catalog Pages folder in the Explorer Bar**
   The folder opens and the Mail Order Catalog file appears in the right pane.

FIGURE D-14: Moving a file from one folder to another

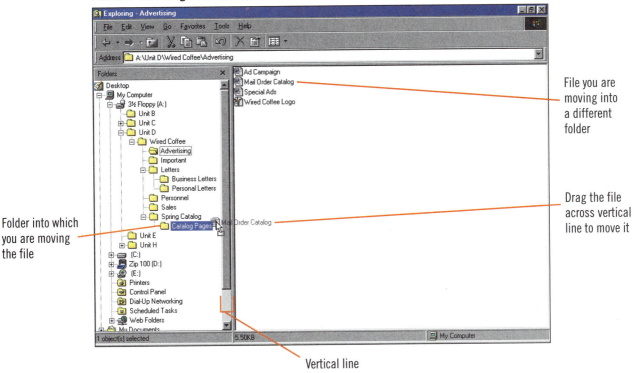

FIGURE D-15: Copying a file from one location to another

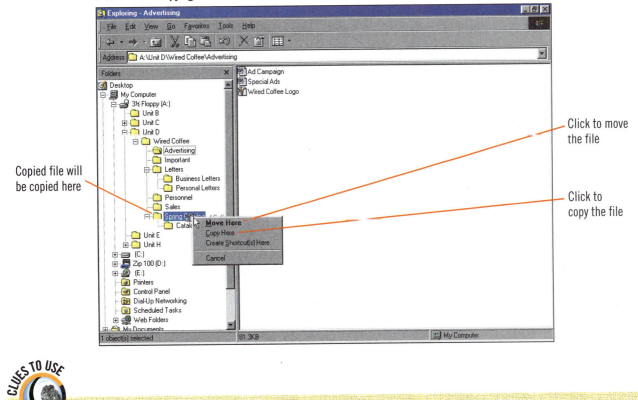

Finding files or folders using the History folder

Windows Me keeps a list of your most recently used files, folders, and network computers in the History folder. To display the History folder, click the History button on the toolbar. You can view the History folder in several ways: by date, by size, by most visited, and by order visited today. In the Explorer Bar, click the View button, then click the view you want.

MANAGING FOLDERS AND FILES USING WINDOWS EXPLORER

Restoring a Deleted File Using Undo

To keep your files and folders manageable, you should delete files and folders you no longer need. The Recycle Bin stores all the items you delete from your hard disk, so that if you accidentally delete an item, you can remove it from the Recycle Bin to restore it, or you can use the Undo command. You cannot restore files and folders that you delete from a floppy disk or that you drag from a floppy disk to the Recycle Bin. Windows does not store items deleted from a floppy disk in the Recycle Bin, but deletes them (after you confirm). See Table D-2 for the various methods of deleting and restoring items. In this lesson, you delete a file and then restore it using the Undo command. Because you cannot restore files deleted from a floppy disk, you start by moving a file from your Project Disk to the desktop.

QuickTip

Some computers are set up not to use the Recycle Bin —deleted files are removed from the hard drive immediately. To check whether your Recycle Bin is in use, right-click the Recycle Bin on the desktop, then click Properties. If the Do not move files to the Recycle Bin check box has a check in it, click the check box to turn off this option.

1. **Click the Spring Catalog folder in the Explorer Bar, then click the + (plus sign) next to the hard drive (C:) icon in the Explorer Bar (98)**
   The contents of the Spring Catalog folder appear in the right pane.

2. **Right-click the Wired Coffee Logo file in the right pane, drag it to the My Documents folder in the Explorer Bar, then click Move Here**
   You move the Wired Coffee file to the My Documents folder.

3. **Click the My Documents folder in the Explorer Bar**
   The My Documents folder is a general folder in which you can store files and folders. When you delete the Wired Coffee Logo file, you store it in the Recycle Bin, and you can restore it using the Undo command.

4. **Scroll to the bottom of the Explorer Bar, drag the Wired Coffee Logo file in the right pane to the Recycle Bin in the Explorer Bar, then click Yes, if necessary**
   You can also right-click the file and then click Delete, or select the file and then press [Delete]. A confirmation dialog box appears. All these methods remove the Wired Coffee Logo from the My Documents folder and store it in the Recycle Bin.

5. **Click the Recycle bin icon in the Explorer Bar**
   The Recycle Bin window opens, as shown in Figure D-16.

QuickTip

To restore an individual file in the Recycle Bin, click the file, then click Restore in the Recycle Bin window (Me).

6. **Click the Undo button on the toolbar**
   You restore the Wired Coffee Logo file to the My Documents folder. The Undo command also lets you reverse multiple actions, so you can use the Undo command again to move the Wired Coffee Logo file back into the Spring Catalog folder on the drive and in the folder where your Project Files are located.

QuickTip

Files and folders that you delete from your hard drive remain in the Recycle Bin until you either restore them or empty the Recycle Bin. To empty the Recycle Bin, right-click it (on the desktop or in Windows Explorer), then click Empty Recycle Bin.

7. **Click again**
   The Wired Coffee Logo file is now back in the Spring Catalog folder.

8. **Scroll to the top of the Explorer Bar if necessary, then click the Spring Catalog folder in the Explorer Bar**
   The contents of the Spring Catalog folder, including the Wired Coffee Logo file, appear in the right pane.

9. **Click View on the menu bar, point to Arrange Icons, then click by Name, if necessary**
   The rearranged items appear sorted by name in the right pane, as shown in Figure D-17.

FIGURE D-16: Recycle Bin Window

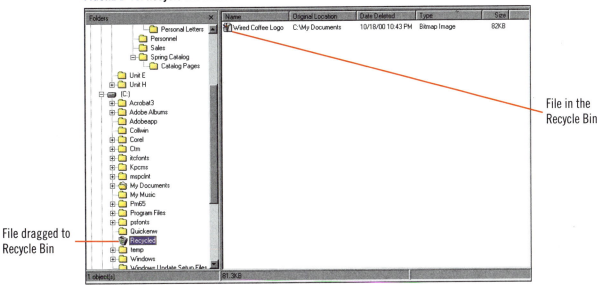

File in the Recycle Bin

File dragged to Recycle Bin

FIGURE D-17: Using Undo to restore a file to its original location

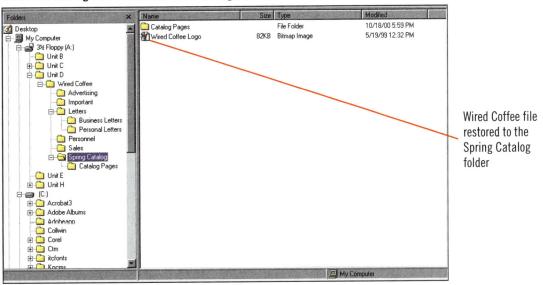

Wired Coffee file restored to the Spring Catalog folder

TABLE D-2: Methods for deleting and restoring files in Windows Explorer

action	methods
Delete	• Right-click the file or folder you want to delete, then click Delete
	• Drag the file or folder to the Recycle Bin
	• Select the file or folder, click File on the menu bar, then click Delete
	• Select the file or folder you want to delete, then press [Delete]
	• Select the file or folder you want to delete, then click the Delete button on the toolbar
Restore	Open the Recycle Bin, and then:
	• Select the file or folder you want to restore, click File on the menu bar, then click Restore
	• Right-click the file or folder you want to restore, then click Restore
	• Drag the file or folder to a new location on the desktop

MANAGING FOLDERS AND FILES USING WINDOWS EXPLORER

Customizing a folder

To make working in Windows Explorer more interesting and appealing, you can customize the way a folder looks when it is open (when its contents appear in the right pane). As you have seen, by default folders appear against a white background. You can change the background color, select a picture to use as a background, or even create your own Web page view of the folder. Windows Explorer comes with a **wizard** (a series of dialog boxes) that walks you through the steps of customizing a folder. John wants to customize the background of the Wired Coffee folder to display the Wired Coffee logo.

1. Click the **Wired Coffee folder** in the Explorer Bar
   The right pane of Windows Explorer contains a list of the contents of the Wired Coffee folder.

2. Click **View** on the menu bar, then click **Customize this Folder**
   The Customize this Folder Wizard opens, as shown in Figure D-18. This wizard helps you change the background appearance of the currently displayed folder. See Table D-3 for a description of the wizard options.

3. Click **Next** (Me), then click the **Choose or edit on HTML template for this folder check box** to clear it if necessary (Me)

4. Click the **Choose a background picture option button** (98) or click the **Modify background picture and filename appearance check box** to select it if necessary (Me), then click **Next**
   Now you need to select a background picture for the Wired Coffee folder. You can select a picture from the list provided, or you can click the Browse button to select a picture stored elsewhere on your computer. John wants to select the Wired Coffee Logo file stored on the drive and in the folder where your Project Files are located, so he clicks the Browse button.

5. Click **Browse**
   The Open dialog box opens, displaying the My Documents folder. John selects the Wired Coffee Logo file on the drive and in the folder where your Project Files are located.

6. Click the **Look in list arrow**, click the drive and folder where your Project Files are located, double-click the **Wired Coffee folder**, double-click the **Advertising folder**, then double-click **Wired Coffee Logo**
   The Wired Coffee Logo file appears in the left pane of the Customize this Folder dialog box and is selected in the list of available background pictures.

7. Click **Next**
   The wizard displays the filename and location of the background picture you selected. You can click the Back button to change the picture selected or click the Finish button to complete the wizard with the selected picture.

8. Click **Finish**
   The right pane of Windows Explorer displays the Wired Coffee logo in the background, as shown in Figure D-19. John finishes working with Windows Explorer, so he closes the program.

9. Click the **Close button** ☒ in Windows Explorer
   Windows Explorer closes.

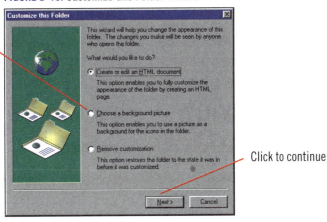

FIGURE D-18: Customize this Folder Wizard

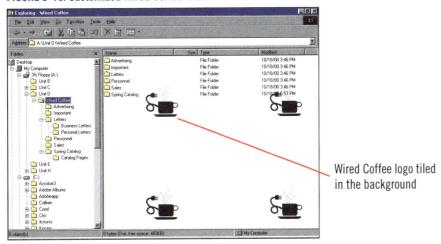

FIGURE D-19: Customized Wired Coffee folder

TABLE D-3: Customize this Folder Wizard options

option	allows you to...
Create or edit an HTML document (98) or Create or edit an HTML template for this folder (Me)	Create or edit an Internet document to view the folder as a Web page (You must know how to use HTML, a computer programming language, to use this option.)
Choose a background picture (98) or Modify background picture and filename appearance (Me)	Change the background color or select a picture as a background for the folder
Remove customization (98)	Remove the previous customization of the folder
Add folder comment (Me)	Add a ScreenTip comment for a folder

Displaying a thumbnail of a graphic

In Windows Explorer for Windows Me you can view a thumbnail version of files in selected folders. A thumbnail is a miniature version of an image often used for quickly browsing through multiple images. Thumbnail versions are available for graphical format only. Click the folder that contains the files you want to view in a thumbnail version. Click View on the menu bar, then click Thumbnails.

Windows 98 and Me Practice

▶ Concepts Review

Label each element of the screen shown in Figure D-20.

FIGURE D-20

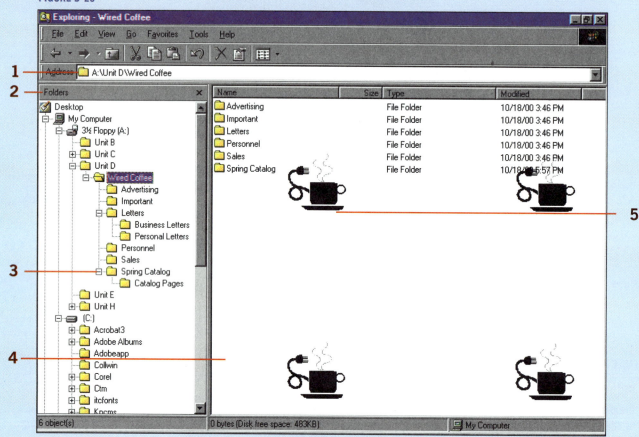

Match each term with the statement that describes its function.

6. Move a file or folder to the Recycle Bin
7. Column indicator
8. Panes
9. + icon
10. Right-click an icon

a. Open pop-up menu
b. Sorts files and folders
c. Icon clicked to expand folder contents
d. Frames that display information from two different locations
e. Delete selected file or folder

WINDOWS 98 AND ME D-18 MANAGING FOLDERS AND FILES USING WINDOWS EXPLORER

Practice

Select the best answers from the following lists of choices.

11. Windows Explorer differs from My Computer in that it allows you to:
    a. Change the view.
    b. Move between folders.
    c. View the overall structure of your computer's contents.
    d. View the contents of a folder or drive.

12. Where is the Explorer Bar located in Windows Explorer?
    a. Folder
    b. Hard drive
    c. Right pane
    d. Left pane

13. In Windows Explorer, which of the following do you click to display the contents of a folder or drive in the Explorer Bar?
    a. [folder icon]
    b. [back arrow icon]
    c. +
    d. –

14. To sort files and folders in Windows Explorer, click:
    a. The Views button list arrow on the toolbar, then click List.
    b. View on the menu bar, then click Arrange.
    c. View on the menu bar, then click Sort.
    d. A column indicator button.

15. Which of the following is NOT a valid search criterion for a file using the Find program?
    a. Date modified
    b. Date opened
    c. Name
    d. Location

16. To copy a folder or file in Windows Explorer:
    a. Press [Ctrl] and drag the folder or file.
    b. Drag the folder or file.
    c. Double-click the folder or file.
    d. Left-click the folder or file, then click Copy.

17. When you move a folder or file, you:
    a. Create and move a copy of the original.
    b. Create and move a shortcut.
    c. Move the original.
    d. Create a copy of the original.

18. Which of the following locations is NOT a valid place from which to delete a file and send it to the Recycle Bin?
    a. Floppy disk
    b. My Documents folder
    c. Hard drive
    d. My Computer

19. Which of the following is NOT a Customize this Folder Wizard option?
    a. Remove customization
    b. Choose a color scheme
    c. Choose a background picture
    d. Create and edit an HTML document

Windows 98 and Me **Practice**

▶ Skills Review

1. **View the Windows Explorer window.**
   a. Insert your disk where your Project Files are located in the appropriate disk drive, if necessary.
   b. Click the Start button on the taskbar, point to Programs, point to Accessories (Me), then click Windows Explorer.
   c. Click the Address list arrow, then click My Computer.
   d. Double-click 3½ Floppy drive (A:) or (B:) to explore the contents of the floppy.
   e. Click the Back button on the toolbar.
   f. Click the Forward button on the toolbar.

2. **Open and view folders in Windows Explorer.**
   a. Click the − next to the hard drive (C:) icon in the Explorer Bar.
   b. Click the + next to the 3½ floppy drive icon in the Explorer Bar.
   c. Click the + next to the Wired Coffee folder in the Explorer Bar.
   d. Click the Personnel folder in the Explorer Bar.
   e. Click the Letters folder in the Explorer Bar.
   f. Double-click the Business Letters folder in the right pane.

3. **Customize the Windows Explorer window.**
   a. Click the Views button list arrow on the toolbar, then click Details.
   b. Click the Close button in the Explorer Bar.
   c. Click the Modified column indicator button.
   d. Click the Name column indicator button.
   e. Click View on the menu bar, point to the Explorer Bar, then click Folders.

4. **Create and rename folders in Windows Explorer.**
   a. Click the Wired Coffee folder in the Explorer Bar.
   b. Right-click a blank area of the right pane of Windows Explorer.
   c. Point to New on the pop-up menu, then click Folder.
   d. Name the folder Money, then press [Enter].
   e. Click File on the menu bar, point to New, then click Folder.
   f. Name this folder Legal, then press [Enter].
   g. Right-click the Money folder, then click Rename.
   h. Rename this folder Financial, then press [Enter].

5. **Find a file.**
   a. Click Tools on the menu bar, point to Find, then click Files or Folders (98), or click the Search button on the toolbar (Me).
   b. Type **IRS** in the Named text box (98) or in the Search for files or folders named text box (Me).
   c. Click the Look in list arrow, then click 3½ Floppy (A:) or (B:).
   d. Click Find Now (98) or Search Now (Me).
   e. Write the location of the IRS Letter file.
   f. Click the Close button in the Find: All Files window (98), or click the Folders button on the toolbar (Me).

▶ WINDOWS 98 AND ME D-20   MANAGING FOLDERS AND FILES USING WINDOWS EXPLORER

Practice

6. **Copy a file from one location to another.**
   a. Locate the IRS Letter file on the drive and in the folder where your Project Files are located.
   b. Drag the IRS Letter file in the right pane to the Financial folder in the Explorer Bar.
   c. Right-click and then drag the Coffee Importers, Inc. file from the Business folder in the right pane to the Legal folder in the Explorer Bar.
   d. Click Copy Here on the pop-up menu.
   e. Click the Legal folder in the Explorer Bar.

7. **Restore deleted files using Undo.**
   a. Click the + next to the hard drive (C:) icon in the Explorer Bar.
   b. Right-drag the Coffee Importers, Inc. file from the Legal folder in the right pane to the My Documents folder in the Explorer Bar, then click Move Here.
   c. Click the My Documents folder in the Explorer Bar.
   d. Scroll to the bottom of the Explorer Bar.
   e. Drag the Coffee Importers, Inc. file from the My Documents folder in the right pane to the Recycle Bin in the Explorer Bar.
   f. Click Yes, if necessary.
   g. Click the Undo button on the toolbar.
   h. Click the Undo button on the toolbar again.
   i. Scroll to the top of the Explorer Bar, then click the Legal folder in the Explorer Bar.

8. **Customize a folder.**
   a. Click the Business Letters folder in the Explorer Bar.
   b. Click View on the menu bar, then click Customize this Folder.
   c. Click Next (Me).
   d. Click the Choose a background picture option button (98), or click the Modify background picture and filename appearance check box to select it (Me).
   e. Click Next, then click Browse.
   f. Select the Wired Coffee Logo file in the Advertising folder on the drive and in the folder where your Project Files are located.
   g. Click Open, then click Next.
   h. Click Finish.
   i. Click the Close button in Windows Explorer.

▶ Independent Challenges

1. You just started Sewing Works, a sewing machine repair business, and you want to use Windows to organize your documents. To meet this challenge, you create on the drive and in the folder where your Project Files are located a set of files relevant to the business and organize them in a set of folders that makes it easy for you to locate what you need when you need it.

To complete this independent challenge:
   a. Create a WordPad file named *Wilson Letter* thanking Mr. Wilson for his business. Save this file and the other files you create on the drive and in the folder where your Project Files are located.

Windows 98 and Me | **Practice**

    b. Create another WordPad file named *Suppliers*. List the following suppliers in the file:

        Apex Sewing Machine Parts
        PO Box 3645
        Tempe, AZ 12345
        Jones Sewing Repair
        18th and 3rd Avenues
        Brooklyn, NY 09091

    c. Create a third WordPad file, and name it *Bills*. List the following information in the file:

Apex	16453	$34.56
Jones	47354	$88.45
Ott	44412	$98.56

    d. On the drive and in the folder where your Project Files are located, create a folder named *Sewing Works*.
    e. In the Sewing Works folder, create three new folders: *Letters*, *Contacts*, and *Accounts*.
    f. Expand the Sewing Works folder in the Explorer Bar.
    g. Move the file named Wilson Letter into the Letters folder, the file named Suppliers into the Contacts folder, and the file named Bills into the Accounts folder.
    h. Open the Letters folder.
    i. Print the screen. (Press [Print Screen] to make a copy of the screen, open Paint, click Edit on the menu bar, click Paste to paste the screen into Paint, then click Yes to paste the large image, if necessary. Click File on the menu bar, click Print, then click OK.)
    j. Close Windows Explorer.

2. As manager of the summer program at a day camp, you need to keep your folders and files organized so you can find information easily and quickly. Your files fall into two main categories: campers and activities. You need to create a folder for each category and place them in a separate folder named Day Camp.

   To complete this independent challenge:

    a. On the drive and in the folder where your Project Files are located, create three folders: *Day Camp*, *Campers*, and *Activities*.
    b. Create a WordPad file named *Camper Data*. Save the file on the drive and in the folder where your Project Files are located. In this file, create information on five campers, including their names, ages, bunks, and favorite sports. Here's a sample of two:

Name	Age	Bunk #	Sports
Bill Moore	11	3	Swimming, Horseshoes
Michael Morley	12	4	Basketball

    c. Move the file named Camper Data into the folder named Campers.
    d. Create a WordPad file named *Activities Overview*. Save the file on the drive and in the folder where your Project Files are located. In this folder, create information on five camp activities, including the activity names, equipment or supplies the children need to supply, number of children, and names of the activity leaders. Here's a sample of two:

Activity	Children provide	Number allowed	Leader
Swimming	Swimsuit, water wings if needed	18	John Lee
Soccer	Shoes, shin guards	24	Madeline Harman

    e. Move the file named Activities Overview into the folder named Activities.
    f. Move the Activities folder and the Campers folder into the Day Camp folder.
    g. Expand the Day Camp folder in the Explorer Bar.
    h. Open the Campers folder.
    i. Copy the Camper Data file to the Activities folder.
    j. Open the Activities folder.

Practice

Windows 98 and Me

   k. Print the screen. (See Independent Challenge 1, Step i for screen printing instructions.)
   l. Close Windows Explorer.

3. The summer fine arts program that you manage has different categories of participation for young adults, including two-week and four-week programs. To keep track of who participates in each program, you must organize two lists into folders. To meet this challenge, you must create new folders, create a list of participants, and then move the lists into folders.

To complete this independent challenge:
   a. On the drive and in the folder where your Project Files are located, create a folder named *Summer Program*.
   b. Within the Summer Program folder, create a folder named *Arts*.
   c. Within the Arts folder, create two other folders named *2 Weeks* and *4 Weeks*.
   d. Create a WordPad file named *2 Weeks Art* on the drive and in the folder where your Project Files are located Include the following information:

Leni Welitoff	2 weeks	painting
Tom Stacey	2 weeks	ceramics and jewelry

   e. Create a WordPad file named *4 Weeks Art* on the drive and in the folder where your Project Files are located. Include the following information:

Kim Dayton	4 weeks	painting and landscape design
Sara Jackson	4 weeks	set construction

   f. Move the files you created into their respective folders, 2 Weeks and 4 Weeks.
   g. Rename the Arts folder *Fine Arts*.
   h. Collapse and expand the Summer Program folder.
   i. Expand the Fine Arts folder.
   j. Open the 4 Weeks folder in the Fine Arts folder.
   k. Print the Screen (See Independent Challenge 1, Step i for screen printing instructions.)
   l. Find the files on the drive and in the folder where your Project Files are located that contain "painting" in the text (not the title).
   m. Print the screen. (See Independent Challenge 1, Step i for screen printing instructions.)
   n. Close Windows Explorer.

4. As head of the graphics department in a small design firm, one of your jobs is to organize the clip art images used by the company. The two categories in which you want to place images are Lines and Shapes. You can place clip art images in more than one category as well. To meet this challenge, you must create several folders and Paint images, then move and copy them to different folders.

To complete this independent challenge:
   a. On the drive and in the folder where your Project Files are located, create three different small Paint images and save them using the names: *Ellipses*, *Lines*, and *Curves*.
   b. On the drive and in the folder where your Project Files are located, create two folders named *Lines* and *Shapes*.
   c. Move the Curves and Lines files into the Lines folder.
   d. Move the Ellipses file into the Shapes folder.
   e. Copy the Curves file into the Shapes folder.
   f. Rename the Ellipses file *Ovals*.
   g. Customize the Lines folder with the Curves file.
   h. Open the Lines folder.
   i. Print the screen. (See Independent Challenge 1, Step i for screen printing instructions.)
   j. Close Windows Explorer.

MANAGING FOLDERS AND FILES USING WINDOWS EXPLORER

Windows 98 and Me | **Practice**

▶ Visual Workshop

Re-create the screen shown in Figure D-21, which displays Windows Explorer. Print the screen. (See Independent Challenge 1, Step i for screen printing instructions.)

FIGURE D-21

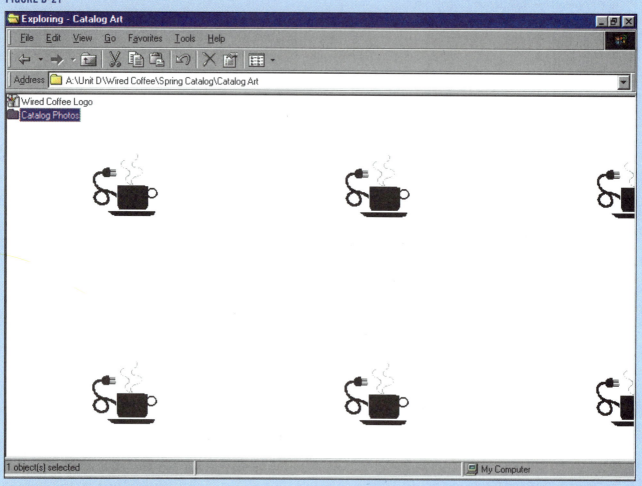

Windows 98 and Me

Customizing
Windows Using the Control Panel

Objectives

- ► Customize the Active Desktop
- ► Change the desktop background and screen saver settings
- ► Change the desktop scheme
- ► Set the date and time
- ► Work with fonts
- ► Manage power options
- ► Add a scheduled task
- ► Customize the taskbar
- ► Customize the Start menu

🛑 *If you are concerned about changing the aspects of Windows 98 and Me at your location and do not wish to customize, simply read through this unit without completing the steps, or click the Cancel button in any dialog box where you could make a change.*

In this unit you'll learn how to customize Windows 98 and Me to suit your personal needs and preferences. You can adjust most Windows features through the **Control Panel**, a central location for changing Windows settings. The Control Panel contains several icons, each of which opens a dialog box for changing the **properties**, or characteristics, of a specific element of your computer, such as the desktop, the taskbar, or the Start menu.

 John Casey needs to change some of the settings on his computer to make his computing environment more attractive and efficient.

Windows 98 and Me

Customizing the Active Desktop

Because more and more people are using the Internet, Windows includes the **Active Desktop**, a feature that allows you to view Web content, or Active Desktop items, on your desktop as you would documents on the Internet, known as **Web pages**. **Active Desktop items** are elements you can place on the desktop to access or display information from the Internet. For example, you can add an Active Desktop item to display stock prices or weather information continuously. Using the Control Panel Display Properties dialog box, you can customize the desktop to display the Active Desktop items you want to use. In addition, you can also change the way you click on desktop icons. For example, in Windows you double-click to open an item. You can change this setting to single-clicking, so your desktop looks and acts like a Web page. John wants to learn how to customize the Active Desktop.

Steps

> **QuickTip**
> To open the Display Properties dialog box from the Control Panel, double-click the Display icon.

1. **Right-click in an empty area on the desktop, point to Active Desktop, then click Customize my Desktop**
   The Display Properties dialog box opens, displaying the Web tab, as shown in Figure E-1. The Web tab provides a list of Active Desktop items and previews of those items.

> **QuickTip**
> You can quickly disable all Active Desktop items from the desktop by right-clicking the desktop, pointing to Active Desktop, then clicking View as Web Page (98) or Show Web Content (Me) to remove the check mark.

2. **Click the View my Active Desktop as a web page check box to select it (98) or the Show Web content on my Active Desktop check box to select it (Me), if necessary**
   To enable or disable (turn on or off) Web content on the Active Desktop, you select or deselect the check box.

3. **Click an Active Desktop item check box to select it, then click Apply**
   The Active Desktop item, such as the Microsoft Investor Ticker or the Internet Explorer Channel Bar, appears in the preview display as a box and on the desktop. To enable or disable (turn on or off) items on the Active Desktop, you select or deselect the Active Desktop item check boxes.

4. **Click the same Active Desktop item check box to deselect it, then click OK**
   You remove the Active Desktop item from the preview display and the desktop. Besides enabling and disabling Active Desktop items, you can also change the way you select and open folders and icons on the desktop and in My Computer and Windows Explorer.

5. **Click the Start button on the taskbar, point to Settings, then click Folder Options (98) or Control Panel and double-click Folder Options icon (Me)**
   The Folder Options dialog box opens, displaying the General tab. The option buttons in the dialog box determine how you click on desktop icons, browse folders, and view Web content. Your desktop can look classic like Windows 95 (you click to select an item) or have the style of a Web page, or the Internet (you point to select an item).

6. **Click Settings (98), then click the Single-click to open an item (point to select) option button**
   The Custom Settings dialog box (98) or the Folder Options dialog box (Me) appears, as shown in Figure E-2.

7. **Click OK (98), click Apply, then point to an icon on the desktop**
   You select the desktop icon using the single-click, or Web style.

> **QuickTip**
> To view a window as a Web page with a panel along the left—the default for Windows Me—click the Views button on the toolbar, then click as Web Page (98).

8. **Click Settings (98), then click the Double-click to open an item (click to select) option button**
   This restores the original folder options.

9. **Click OK (98), click Close (98) or OK (Me), then click the Close button in the Control Panel (Me)**
   The Folder Options dialog box closes.

FIGURE E-1: Display Properties dialog box

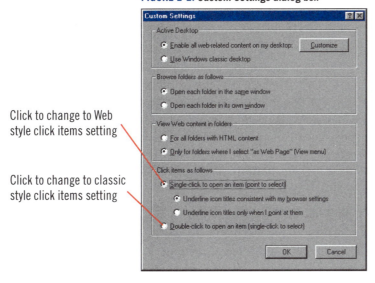

Click check box to hide all Active Desktop items

Click to add or remove Active Desktop items

Click check box to display the Active Desktop items

Click to change how you click on desktop items (98)

FIGURE E-2: Custom Settings dialog box

Click to change to Web style click items setting

Click to change to classic style click items setting

Adding a new Web item to the Active Desktop

You can add new desktop items, live Web content, or pictures to your Active Desktop. Right-click in an empty area on the desktop, point to Active Desktop, then click Customize My Desktop. Click the View my Active Desktop as a Web page check box (98) or the Show Web content on my Active Desktop check box (Me) to select it, then click New. To add a new desktop item, click Yes (98) if necessary or Visit Gallery (Me) to access and display Microsoft's Active Desktop Gallery on the Internet, as shown in E-3, select the item which you want to add, then click Add to Active Desktop. To access and display a Web page, you must to be connected to the Internet.

FIGURE E-3: Microsoft's Active Desktop Gallery

Windows 98 and Me

Changing the Desktop Background and Screen Saver Settings

You can also change how your Windows desktop looks using the Display Properties dialog box. You can adjust the desktop's **background**, the basic surface on which icons and windows appear. You can use a **screen saver**, a moving display that protects your monitor from burn-in, which can occur when there is no movement on your screen for a long time. You can also assign a password to your screen saver to prevent others from using your computer. ⬧ John wants to choose a background for his desktop and set one of the standard screen savers to start when his computer remains idle for more than five minutes.

Steps

1. **Click the Start button on the taskbar, point to Settings, then click Control Panel**
   The Control Panel opens, as shown in Figure E-4. Each icon represents an aspect of Windows that you can change to fit your own working habits and personal needs.

   > **QuickTip**
   > You can also open the Display Properties dialog box by right-clicking in an empty area of the desktop, then clicking Properties.

2. **Double-click the Display icon 🖳 in the Control Panel**
   The Display Properties dialog box opens with the Background tab active, as shown in Figure E-5.

3. **In the Wallpaper section, click the up or down scroll arrow, then click Coffee Bean (or a wallpaper of your choice if this one is not available on your system)**
   The preview window shows how the wallpaper will look on your screen. **Wallpaper** is a picture that serves as your desktop's background. Acceptable formats for wallpaper files are Bitmap (the format of a Paint file) or JPEG (the format of an Internet document). You can use Paint to create new wallpaper designs or change existing ones. Besides the wallpaper, you can also choose a desktop **pattern**, a design that you can modify by clicking the None Wallpaper icon and then clicking the Pattern button.

4. **Click the Display list arrow (98) or Picture Display list arrow (Me), click Tile, then click Apply**
   You can determine how a wallpaper or pattern appears on the screen using the Picture Display list arrow. **Tile** displays the wallpaper picture or pattern consecutively across the screen; **Center** displays the picture or pattern in the center of the screen; and **Stretch** enlarges the picture or pattern and displays it in the center of the screen. The new wallpaper appears on the desktop with the Tile display.

5. **Click (None) in the Wallpaper section, then click Apply to restore the desktop**

6. **Click the Screen Saver tab**
   The default setting is for no screen saver, meaning that no constantly changing image replaces your screen, no matter how long your computer remains idle. Someone who used this machine before you might have already set a screen saver.

   > **QuickTip**
   > To assign a password to your screen saver, click the Password protected check box to select it, then click Apply.

7. **Click the Screen Saver list arrow, then click 3D Flying Objects**
   The 3D Flying Objects screen saver appears in the preview window, as shown in Figure E-6.

8. **In the Wait box, click the up arrow (or down arrow) until it reads 5 minutes**
   This is the amount of time between when your computer detects no mouse or keyboard activity and begins the screen saver.

9. **Click Preview, move the mouse or press any key to stop the preview, then click Apply**
   The entire desktop contains a preview of the screen saver pattern.

FIGURE E-4: Control Panel window

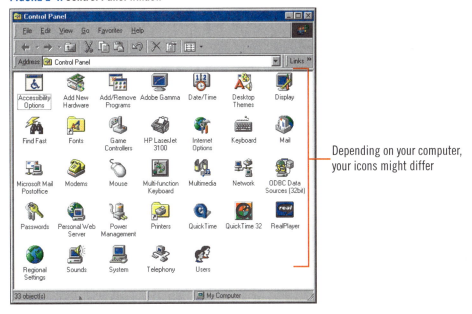

Depending on your computer, your icons might differ

FIGURE E-5: Display Properties dialog box with Background tab

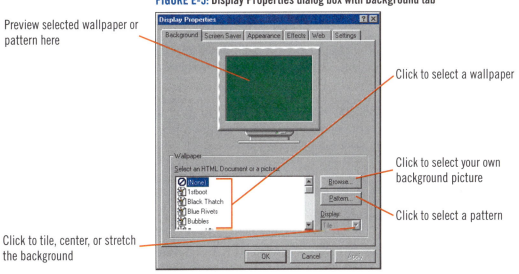

Preview selected wallpaper or pattern here

Click to select a wallpaper

Click to select your own background picture

Click to select a pattern

Click to tile, center, or stretch the background

FIGURE E-6: Display Properties dialog box with Screen Saver tab

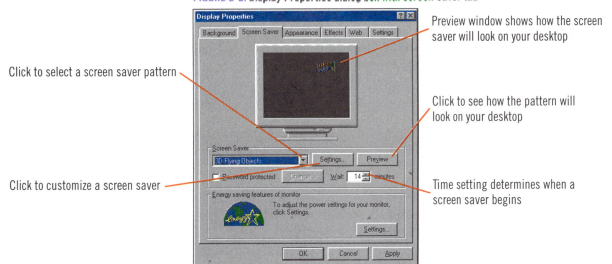

Click to select a screen saver pattern

Preview window shows how the screen saver will look on your desktop

Click to see how the pattern will look on your desktop

Click to customize a screen saver

Time setting determines when a screen saver begins

CUSTOMIZING WINDOWS USING THE CONTROL PANEL

Changing the Desktop Scheme

You can change the appearance of colors, fonts, and sizes used for major window elements such as title bars, icons, menus, borders, and the desktop itself. You can change each item individually, or use a **scheme**, a predefined combination of settings that assures visual coordination of all items. Windows includes many predefined schemes, and you can also create your own. When you create a custom scheme or modify an existing scheme, you save your changes with a unique name. Ray Adams, a visually impaired employee of Wired Coffee, needs a display configuration with window elements larger than standard size and a background color that provides greater contrast with window elements. John decides to create a scheme for Ray, who can switch to the scheme whenever he uses the computer.

Steps

1. Click the **Appearance tab** in the Display Properties dialog box
   The Appearance tab, as shown in Figure E-7, allows you to change the appearance of individual desktop elements, such as the menu bar, message box, and selected text, or to select one of several predefined schemes that Windows provides, and modify it as necessary.

2. Click the **Scheme list arrow**, then click **Windows Standard (extra large)**
   The size of everything in the Preview box increases from standard size to extra large.

3. Click the **Item list arrow**, then click **Desktop**
   Now you can change the desktop color. Notice that the Item size option and Font option are grayed, indicating that these options do not apply to the desktop.

4. Click the **Color list arrow**, then click **light gray color box** in the top row
   You can select from a matrix of different colors. Before you save the scheme, you can apply the scheme to the desktop to see how it looks.

5. Click **Apply**
   The desktop changes but the dialog box remains open. Use the Apply button when you want to test your changes, and the OK button when you want to keep your changes and close the dialog box.

6. Click **Save As**, type **Ray**, then click **OK**
   You save the scheme with the name Ray. Now, anytime Ray wants to use the computer, he can easily select this scheme.

7. Click **Delete** to remove the selected scheme, click the **Scheme list arrow**, click **Windows Standard**, then click **Apply**

8. Click the **Screen Saver tab**, click the **Screen Saver list arrow**, then click **(None)**
   The screen saver turns off.

9. Click **OK**

FIGURE E-7: Display Properties dialog box with Appearance tab

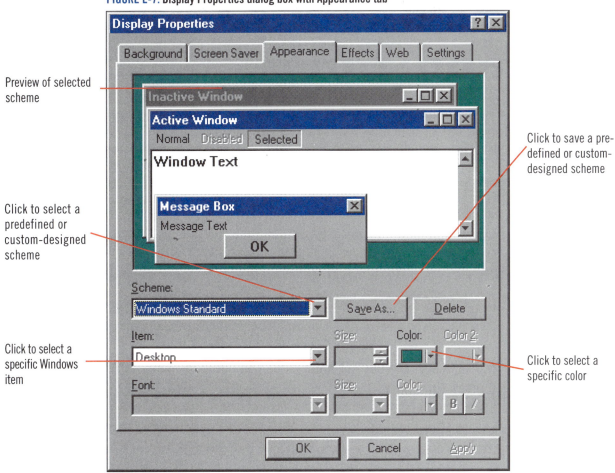

Applying a desktop theme

You can change the entire appearance of the desktop with desktop themes. A desktop theme changes the desktop background, screen saver, mouse pointers, sounds, icons, and fonts based on a set theme, such as baseball, science, sports, travel, or underwater. You can use one of the predefined desktop themes or create your own, as shown in Figure E-8. To apply a desktop theme, click the Start button on the taskbar, point to Settings, click Control Panel to open the Control Panel, double-click the Desktop Themes icon, click the Theme list arrow, select a theme, preview the Screen Saver or Pointers, Sounds, etc., if necessary, select any related options you want, then click OK. If the desktop themes icon is not available, use the Add/Remove Programs utility Windows Setup tab in the Control Panel to install the feature.

FIGURE E-8: Desktop Themes dialog box

Setting the Date and Time

The date and time you set in the Control Panel appear in the lower-right corner of the taskbar. Programs use the date and time to establish when files and folders are created and modified. To change the date and time, you modify the date and time settings in the Date/Time Properties dialog box. In addition to changing the date and time, you can also change their appearance. This is handy if you work on documents from a different country or region of the world. To change the date and time display, you modify the date or settings on the Date/Time tab in the Regional Settings Properties dialog box. John is working on an international document and wants to change his date and time settings.

QuickTip
To open the Date/Time Properties dialog box quickly, double-click the time on the taskbar.

1. **Double-click the Date/Time icon in the Control Panel**
   The Date/Time Properties dialog box opens with the Date & Time tab in front, as shown in Figure E-9. To change the date, you choose the month and year you want in the Date section, and then click the day you want in the calendar. To change the time, you choose the hours, minutes, or seconds you want in the text box in the Time section, and then type a new number or click the up or down arrow to select the new time.

2. **Double-click the current hour in the text box in the Time section, then click the up arrow three times**
   The new time appears in the running clock.

QuickTip
To change the time-zone setting, click the Date & Time tab in the Date/Time Properties dialog box, click the list arrow, and then select the time zone you want.

3. **Click Apply**
   The new time appears in the right corner of the taskbar.

4. **Double-click the current hour, click the down arrow three times, then click OK**

5. **Double-click the Regional Settings icon in the Control Panel**
   The Regional Settings dialog box opens, displaying tabs for Regional Settings, Number, Currency, Time, and Date. Using these tabs, you change the format and symbols used for numbers, currency, time, and date in your files and programs.

6. **Click the Date tab**
   The Date tab appears, displaying the date formats currently being used. You can click the short date or long date list arrows to change the two date formats, as shown in Figure E-10.

7. **Click the Time tab**
   The Time tab appears, displaying the time formats currently being used.

8. **Click OK**

FIGURE E-9: Date/Time Properties dialog box

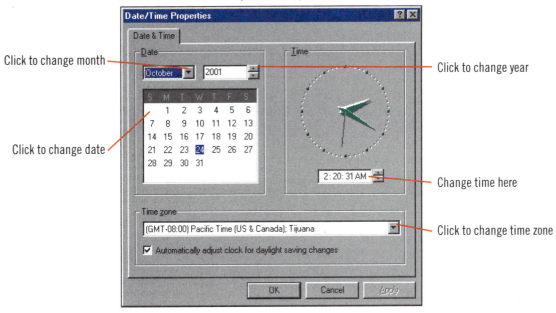

FIGURE E-10: Regional Settings Properties dialog box

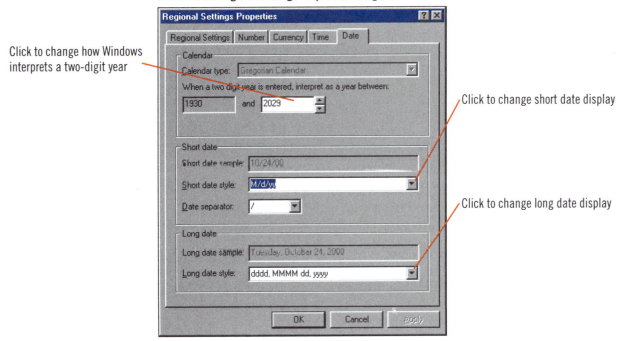

Changing the size of the desktop

You can change the size of the desktop that appears on your monitor. In the Display Properties dialog box, click the Settings tab, then drag the Screen Area slider to the right. The settings available depend upon the hardware that Windows detects during installation. In some cases, settings higher than 640 × 480 or 800 × 600 (such as 1024 × 768) might be available. Note that a higher setting means higher resolution and that more information can fit on the screen.

CUSTOMIZING WINDOWS USING THE CONTROL PANEL WINDOWS 98 AND ME E-9

Windows 98 and Me

Working with Fonts

Everything you type appears in a **font**, a particular design of letters, numbers, and other characters. You might have heard common font names such as Times New Roman, Arial, Courier, or Symbol. Windows comes with a variety of fonts for displaying text and printing documents created with programs that are part of Windows, such as WordPad and Paint. Using the Fonts window, you can view these fonts, compare them to each other, see a sample of how a font appears when printed, and even install new fonts. John wants to examine different fonts to prepare for a flyer he wants to create.

Steps

1. **Double-click the Fonts icon in the Control Panel, then click the Maximize button in the Fonts window if necessary**
   The Fonts window opens. The window lists the fonts available on your system and indicates whether each is a TrueType (98), or an Open Type (Me), or screen font. A **TrueType** or **Open Type font** is based on a mathematical equation that creates letters with smooth curves and sharp corners. A **screen font** consists of **bitmapped characters**, small dots organized to form a letter. Table E-1 lists the various options on the Fonts toolbar and describes what they do.

2. **Click View on the menu bar, then click Hide Variations (Bold, Italic, etc.)**
   The main font styles appear in the Font window, as shown in Figure E-11.

3. **Double-click the Arial font icon**
   As shown in Figure E-12, the window displays information about this font and shows samples of it in different sizes.

4. **Click Print in the Arial (TrueType or Open Type) window, then click OK**
   A copy of the font information prints.

5. **Click Done**
   The Arial (Open Type) window closes.

6. **Click the Similarity button on the Fonts toolbar**
   The Similarity tool helps you find fonts similar to the selected font. All the fonts are listed by how similar they are to Arial, the font listed in the List fonts by similarity to box. You can choose a different font to check which fonts are similar to it by clicking the List fonts by similarity to list arrow, and then selecting the font you want to check.

7. **Click the Large Icons button on the Fonts toolbar, then click the Close button on the Fonts window**
   You return to the Control Panel.

Installing a font

Windows might not come with all the fonts you need or want, but you can purchase additional fonts and install them easily. To install a new font, click Install New Font on the File menu in the Fonts window, indicate the location of the font you want to install (on the hard drive or a floppy disk drive), and then click OK. This installs the new font so it's available in the Fonts window of the Control Panel and in all your Windows programs.

CUSTOMIZING WINDOWS USING THE CONTROL PANEL

FIGURE E-11: Fonts window

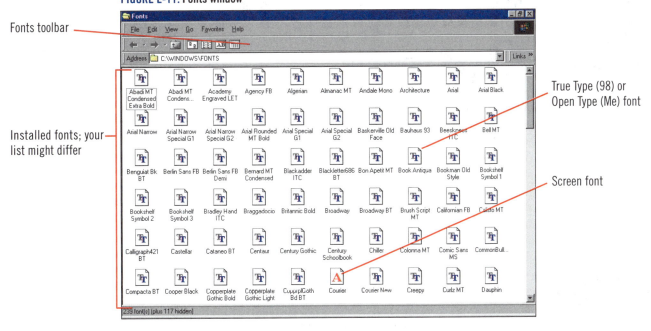

- Fonts toolbar
- Installed fonts; your list might differ
- True Type (98) or Open Type (Me) font
- Screen font

FIGURE E-12: Selected font and how it appears in different sizes

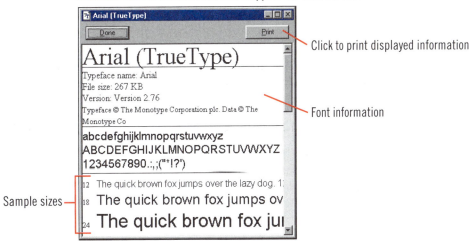

- Click to print displayed information
- Font information
- Sample sizes

TABLE E-1: Fonts toolbar buttons

button	description
←	Moves you back to a previously opened folder
→	Moves you forward to a previously opened folder
↑	Moves up to the next level in the hierarchy of folders
	Lists fonts by large icon
	Lists fonts alphabetically
AB	Lists fonts by similarity to the selected font
	Lists details of fonts, including filename, font name, size, and date last modified

CUSTOMIZING WINDOWS USING THE CONTROL PANEL

Windows 98 and Me

Managing Power Options

You can change power options properties on your computer to reduce the power consumption of your entire system or a specific device. For example, if you often leave your computer for a short time while working, you can set your computer to go into standby, a state in which your monitor and hard disks turn off, after standing idle for a set time. When you bring the computer out of standby, your desktop appears exactly as you left it. Because standby does not save your desktop settings on disk, a power failure that occurs while your computer is on standby can cause you to lose unsaved information. If you are often away from your computer for an extended time or overnight but like to leave the computer on, you can set it to go into hibernation, a state in which your computer first saves everything in memory on your hard disk and then shuts down. When you restart the computer, your desktop appears exactly as you left it. Table E-2 lists common tabs in the Power Options Properties dialog box and describes the power options each offers. During the day, John takes short breaks from his computer to attend meetings, so he wants to change power options for his computer to save power.

Steps

QuickTip

To create your own power scheme, click the Power Schemes tab in the Power Options Properties dialog box, select the Turn off monitor and Turn off hard disks power options you want, click Save As, type a name, then click OK.

1. Double-click the **Power Options icon** in the Control Panel window

   The Power Options Properties dialog box opens with the Power Schemes tab in front, as shown in Figure E-13. A **power scheme** is a predefined collection of power usage settings. You can choose one of the power schemes included with Windows or modify one to suit your needs. The Power Options you see vary depending on your computer's hardware configuration. The Power Options feature automatically detects what is available on your computer and shows you only the options that you can control.

2. Click the **Power schemes list arrow**, then click **Portable/Laptop**

   Settings for the Portable/Laptop power scheme appear in the bottom section of the Power Schemes tab.

3. Click the **Turn off monitor list arrow**, then click **After 1 min**

4. Click **Apply**, then wait one minute without moving the mouse or pressing a key

   After a minute, the screen goes on standby. (The screen is blank.) On standby, your entire computer switches to a low power state where devices, such as the monitor and hard disks, turn off and your computer uses less power.

QuickTip

To show a power option icon in the taskbar, click the Advanced tab, click the Always show icon on the taskbar check box to select it, then click Apply or OK.

5. Move the mouse to restore the desktop

   The computer comes out of standby, and your desktop appears exactly as you left it.

6. Click the **Power schemes list arrow**, click **Always On**, then click **Apply**

   The Turn off monitor and Turn off hard disks options change to reflect power settings for this scheme. The power settings change to Never, the preset option.

7. Click the **Advanced tab**

   The Advanced tab appears, displaying settings to always display the Power Options icon on the taskbar and prompt for a password, as shown in Figure E-14.

8. Click **OK**

WINDOWS 98 AND ME E-12 CUSTOMIZING WINDOWS USING THE CONTROL PANEL

FIGURE E-13: Power Management Properties dialog box

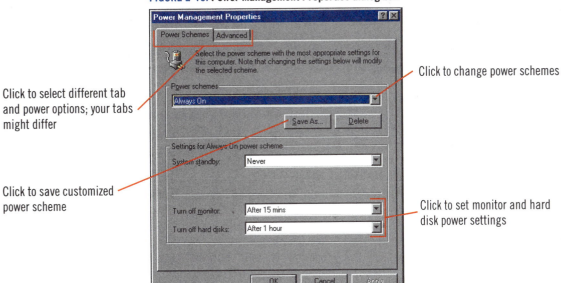

Click to select different tab and power options; your tabs might differ

Click to save customized power scheme

Click to change power schemes

Click to set monitor and hard disk power settings

FIGURE E-14: Advanced power management options

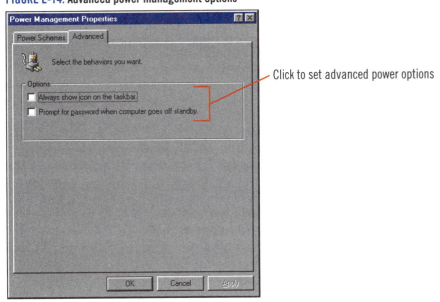

Click to set advanced power options

TABLE E-2: Common Power Options Properties tabs

tab	allows you to
Power Schemes	Change power settings for your monitor and hard disks
Advanced	Change user power options
Hibernate	Turn on and off hibernation; when the Hibernation option is turned on, you can select it when you shut down your computer
UPS	Select and configure an Uninterruptible Power Supply (UPS) device (available depending on the specific UPS hardware installed on your computer)
Alarms	Change settings for low battery notification alarms (available on most laptop computers)
Power Meter	Display power usage details for each battery in your computer (available on most laptop computers)
APM	Turn on or turn off Advanced Power Management (APM) support to reduce overall power consumption (available on most laptop computers)

Windows 98 and Me

Adding a Scheduled Task

Task Scheduler is a tool that enables you to schedule tasks (such as Disk Cleanup, a program that removes unnecessary files) to run regularly, at a time convenient for you. Task Scheduler starts each time you start Windows. When Task Scheduler is running on your computer, its icon appears next to the clock on the taskbar. You can double-click the Task Scheduler icon on the taskbar to open Task Scheduler. With Task Scheduler, you can schedule a task to run daily, weekly, monthly, or at certain times (such as when the computer starts or idles), change the schedule for or turn off an existing task, or customize how a task runs at its scheduled time. Before you schedule a task, be sure that the system date and time on your computer are accurate: Task Scheduler relies on this information to run scheduled tasks. John schedules a task to scan his hard disk for corrupted files.

Steps

QuickTip
To modify a scheduled task, right-click the task you want to modify, and then click Properties.

1. **Click the Start button** on the taskbar, point to **Programs**, point to **Accessories**, point to **System Tools**, then click **Scheduled Task** (98) or double-click the **Scheduled Tasks icon** in the Control Panel window (Me)
   The Scheduled Tasks window opens, as shown in Figure E-15.

2. **Double-click the Add Scheduled Task icon** then click **Next** in the Scheduled Task Wizard dialog box
   The Scheduled Task Wizard displays a list of programs you can schedule to run. If the program or document you want to use is not in the list, you can click Browse to locate the program on your computer disk drive or network.

3. **In the list of programs, click ScanDisk, click Next, click the Weekly option button, then click Next**
   The next Scheduled Task Wizard dialog box opens, as shown in Figure E-16, asking you to select the time and day you want the task to start.

4. **In the Start time box, change the time to one minute ahead of the current time, click the current day of the week check box to select it, then click Next**
   The next Scheduled Task Wizard dialog box opens, might ask you to enter the name and password of the current user. The task will run as if that user started it.

5. **In the Enter the password box, type your password, press [Tab], type your password again, then click Next if necessary**

QuickTip
To stop a scheduled task that is running, right-click the task that you want to stop, then click End Task.

6. **Click Finish**
   The scheduled task appears in the Scheduled Task window, as shown in Figure E-17.

7. **Wait for the scan disk operation to begin, then click Close in the ScanDisk window**

QuickTip
To be notified when a scheduled task does not run, click Advanced on the menu bar, then click Notify Me of Missed Tasks to select the option.

8. **Right-click the ScanDisk icon, click Delete, then click Yes**
   You delete the scheduled task.

9. **Click the Close button on the Scheduled Tasks window, then click the Close button on the Control Panel (Me)**

WINDOWS 98 AND ME E-14   CUSTOMIZING WINDOWS USING THE CONTROL PANEL

FIGURE E-15: Scheduled Tasks window

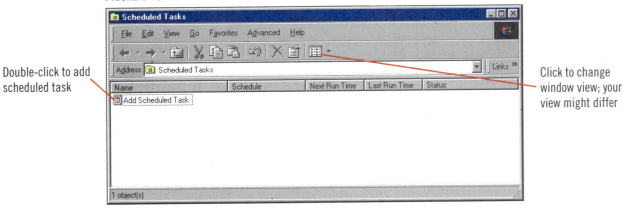

Double-click to add scheduled task

Click to change window view; your view might differ

FIGURE E-16: Scheduled Task Wizard

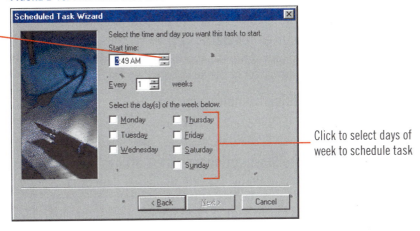

Click to set start time of task

Click to select days of week to schedule task

FIGURE E-17: Task added to Scheduled Tasks window

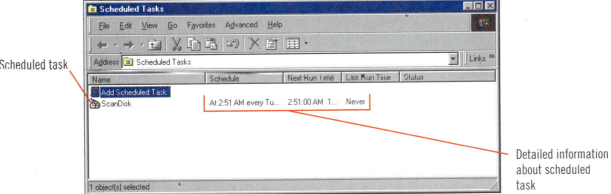

Scheduled task

Detailed information about scheduled task

Adding new hardware and software to Windows

You can add new hardware, such as a printer, and add or remove programs by using tools on the Control Panel. The Add New Hardware and Add/Remove Programs dialog boxes walk you through the necessary steps. To start the add new hardware procedure, double-click the Add New Hardware icon in the Control Panel, then click Next, and follow the prompts. To add or remove a program, double-click the Add/Remove Program icon, click Install, and then follow the prompts. In both cases, Windows should recognize that new hardware needs to be added or that an installation file needs to be executed. To install a Windows accessory or feature, such as Character Map, Compression Folder, or Desktop Themes, double click the Add/Remove Programs icon, click the Windows Setup tab, double-click a category if necessary, click the check box next to the accessory or feature you want to install, then click OK (it might be asking you to insert your windows installation CD).

CUSTOMIZING WINDOWS USING THE CONTROL PANEL

Windows 98 and Me

Customizing the Taskbar

Most often you use the taskbar for switching from one program to another. The taskbar is initially located at the bottom of the Windows desktop. As with other Windows elements, you can customize the taskbar; for example, you can change its size and location, or add or remove toolbars to help you perform the tasks you need to do. Sometimes you need more room on the screen to display a window, and hiding the taskbar helps. You can use the **Auto hide** feature to help you hide the taskbar automatically when you don't need it. John removes and adds a toolbar to the taskbar, and then he learns how the Auto hide feature works.

Steps

QuickTip

You can show the toolbar title or toolbar button names for a toolbar on the taskbar. Right-click an empty area of the toolbar, then click Show Title or Show Text.

1. **Place the mouse pointer in an empty section of the taskbar, right-click the taskbar, then point to Toolbars**
   The Toolbars submenu appears, as shown in Figure E-18. You can add or remove a variety of existing toolbars to the taskbar or create a new one.

2. **Click Quick Launch to deselect it**
   You remove the Quick Launch toolbar from the taskbar. Now you have more room on the taskbar for program buttons.

3. **Click the Start button, point to Settings, then click Taskbar & Start Menu**
   The Taskbar Properties (98) or Taskbar and Start Menu Properties (Me) dialog box opens, displaying the Taskbar Options tab, as shown in Figure E-19. You can change the appearance of items (such as the clock and small icons on the Start menu) on the taskbar or the appearance of the taskbar on the screen.

4. **Click the Auto hide check box to select it**
   You hide the taskbar in the Preview box.

5. **Click OK**
   You hide the taskbar at the bottom of the screen.

6. **Move the mouse pointer to the bottom of the screen**
   While the mouse pointer is at the bottom of the screen, the taskbar appears. When you move the mouse pointer up, you hide the taskbar.

Trouble?

If the Quick Launch toolbar reappears on the right side of the taskbar, position the mouse pointer over the small bar (which changes to ↔) to the left of the Internet Explorer icon, then drag to the left until you reach the Start button.

7. **Right-click in an empty section of the taskbar, point to Toolbars, then click Quick Launch to select it**
   You add the Quick Launch toolbar to the taskbar.

8. **Click the Start button, point to Settings, then click Taskbar & Start Menu**
   The Taskbar Properties (98) or Taskbar Start Menu Properties (Me) dialog box opens.

9. **Click the Auto hide check box to deselect it, then click OK**

CUSTOMIZING WINDOWS USING THE CONTROL PANEL

FIGURE E-18: Removing a toolbar from the taskbar

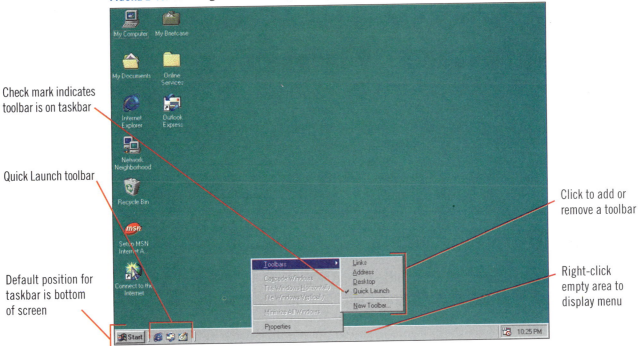

FIGURE E-19: Taskbar Properties dialog box with Taskbar Options tab

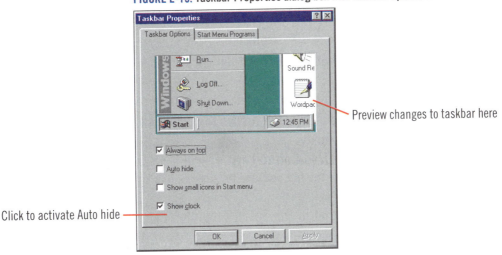

Starting a program as a taskbar button

You can change how Windows displays a program each time you start it using its Start menu shortcut. The program can open in a standard window, in a maximized window, or minimized as a button on the taskbar. Starting a program as a taskbar button is useful for a program you don't need to maximize but want to access quickly. To set a program to start in minimized form, click the Start button on the taskbar, point to Settings, click Taskbar & Start Menu, click the Start Menu Programs tab (98) or Advanced tab (Me). In the Start Menu folder, locate the shortcut to the program you want to start, and then click it. Click File on the menu bar, click Properties, then click the Shortcut tab. Click the Run list arrow, click Minimized, click OK, click File, click Close, then click OK again.

Customizing the Start Menu

Windows 98 and Me

You can add shortcuts to programs, files, or folders to the Start menu, so that instead of navigating several levels of the Start menu to start a program or access a file, you can simply click the Start button and then click the item you want on the Start menu. Of course, adding too many items to the Start menu defeats the purpose. To customize the Start menu for Windows Me further, you can display additional menu items on the Start menu, including Favorites, Log Off, and Administrative Tools, or extend a submenu from the Control Panel, Printers, or Dialup and Network Connections menu items on the Settings submenu. When you extend a menu item, a submenu appears with additional menu items. For example, when you extend the Control Panel, a submenu appears with a menu item for each icon in the Control Panel to provide easy access to each one. Because John works with the Wired Coffee logo so often, he decides to add the file to the Start menu.

Steps

> **QuickTip**
> To remove all recently used documents from the Documents submenu, click the Advanced tab in the Taskbar and Start Menu Properties dialog box, then click Clear.

1. Click the **Start button**, point to **Settings**, click **Taskbar & Start Menu**, then click the **Start Menu Programs tab** (98) or **Advanced tab** (Me)
   The Taskbar Properties (98) or Taskbar and Start Menu Properties (Me) dialog box appears, as shown in Figure E-20. You can use the Start Menu Programs tab to add items to and delete them from the Start menu. To add the Wired Coffee Logo file to the Start menu, you need to specify the file's location.

2. Make sure the disk or drive where your Project Files are located is available, click **Add**, then click **Browse**
   The Browse dialog box opens, where you can navigate to and select a file, folder, or program you want to add to the Start menu.

3. Click the **Look in list arrow**, then click the drive and folder where your Project Files are located
   You need to display all types of files in order to view the Wired Coffee Logo file.

4. Click the **Files of type list arrow**, then click **All Files**
   All Project Files appear.

5. Double-click **Wired Coffee Logo**, then click **Next**
   Once you locate the file, you need to specify its place on the Start menu. John wants the file on the main Start menu.

6. Click **Start Menu** in the Select Program Folder dialog box, click **Next**, click **Finish**, then click **OK**
   Now open the Start menu, and verify that you added the file.

> **QuickTip**
> You can also add an item to the Start menu by creating a shortcut to it (on the desktop or in Windows Explorer, for example) and dragging the icon to the Start button.

7. Click the **Start button**
   The Wired Coffee Logo file now appears at the top of the Start menu, as shown in Figure E-21. To open the Wired Coffee Logo file, all you need to do is click its icon on the Start menu. Now remove this item from the Start menu to return your desktop to its original settings.

8. Press **[Esc]** to close the Start menu, right-click in an empty area on the **taskbar**, click **Properties**, then click the **Start Menu Programs tab** (98) or **Advanced tab** (Me)

9. Click **Remove**, locate and click **Wired Coffee Logo** in the list, click **Remove**, click Yes to confirm the deletion if necessary, click **Close**, then click **OK**
   When the Taskbar Properties dialog box closes, the Wired Coffee shortcut is no longer on the Start menu.

WINDOWS 98 AND ME E-18 CUSTOMIZING WINDOWS USING THE CONTROL PANEL

FIGURE E-20: Taskbar Properties dialog box with Advanced tab (Me)

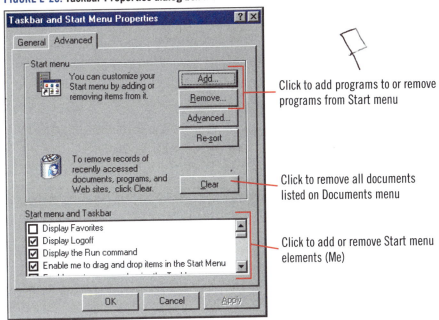

FIGURE E-21: File added to Start menu

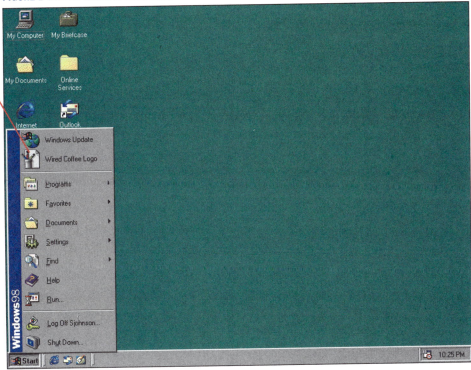

Clues to Use

Rearranging Start menu items

If you don't like the location of an item on the Start menu, you can move the item to a different location by dragging it. A blank line appears as you move the mouse pointer indicating the new location of the item. For example, to move the Windows Explorer menu item from the Programs submenu to the Start menu, open the Start menu, then drag the Windows Explorer item to the Start menu.

CUSTOMIZING WINDOWS USING THE CONTROL PANEL

Windows 98 and Me Practice

▶ Concepts Review

Label each element of the screen shown in Figure E-22.

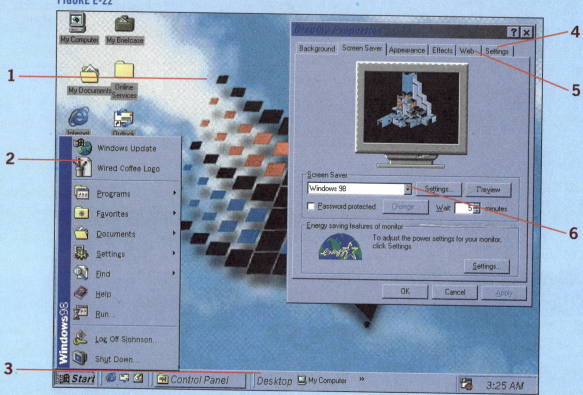

FIGURE E-22

Match each term with the statement that describes its function.

7. Patterns
8. Screen saver
9. Color schemes
10. Control Panel
11. Start menu

a. Preset designs for the desktop
b. Used to start programs and open documents
c. Used to change properties of various elements of a computer
d. Preset combinations of desktop colors
e. Used to prevent damage to the monitor

Select the best answers from the following lists of choices.

12. To customize the Active Desktop, you need to open the:
   a. Desktop Settings dialog box.
   b. Custom Desktop dialog box.
   c. Folder Options dialog box.
   d. Display Properties dialog box.
13. To change the pattern on the desktop from the Display Properties dialog box in the Control Panel, click the:
   a. Appearance tab.
   b. Settings tab.
   c. Background tab.
   d. Screen Saver tab.

Practice

14. An Internet document or Paint file used as a background is called a:
    a. Display.
    b. Shortcut.
    c. Pattern.
    d. Wallpaper.
15. To change the scheme on the desktop from the Display Properties dialog box in the Control Panel, click the:
    a. Effects tab.
    b. Background tab.
    c. Screen Saver tab.
    d. Appearance tab.

▶ Skills Review

1. **Customize the Active Desktop.**
    a. Right-click in an empty area on the desktop.
    b. Point to Active Desktop, then click Customize my Desktop.
    c. Click the Web tab, if necessary.
    d. Click an Active Desktop item check box to select it, then click Apply.
    e. Click an Active Desktop item check box to deselect it, then click OK.
    f. Open the Folder Options dialog box, then click Settings.
    g. Change to single-click mode, then click Apply.
    h. Point to an icon on the desktop, then change back to double-click mode.
    i. Close the Folder Options dialog box and the Control Panel.

2. **Change the desktop background and screen saver settings.**
    a. Click the Start button, point to Settings, then click Control Panel.
    b. Double-click the Display icon.
    c. Click the Background tab, if necessary, then click Blue Rivets in the Wallpaper section.
    d. Click the Screen Saver tab, click the Screen Saver list arrow, click 3D Pipes, then click Preview.
    e. Move the mouse to end the Screen Saver preview.

3. **Change the desktop scheme.**
    a. Click the Appearance tab.
    b. Click the Item list arrow, then click Desktop.
    c. Choose any color you want for the desktop, then click Apply.
    d. Click Save As, type **Fred**, then click OK.
    e. Click Delete.
    f. Click the Scheme list arrow, then click Windows Standard, then click Apply.
    g. Click the Screen Saver tab, click the Screen Saver list arrow, then click (None).
    h. Click the Background tab, click (None) in the Wallpaper section, then click OK.

4. **Set the date and time.**
    a. Double-click the Date/Time icon.
    b. Double-click the number of minutes.
    c. Click the up arrow three times, then click Apply.
    d. Double-click the number of minutes.
    e. Click the down arrow three times, then click OK.

5. **Work with fonts.**
    a. Double-click the Fonts icon.
    b. Double-click a Times New Roman icon.
    c. Click Print, click OK, click Done, then click the Close button.

Windows 98 and Me | Practice

6. **Manage power options.**
   a. Double-click the Power Options icon in the Control Panel.
   b. Click the Turn off monitor list arrow, then click After 1 min.
   c. Click Apply, then wait one minute without moving the mouse or pressing a key.
   d. Move the mouse to restore the desktop.
   e. Click the Turn off monitor list arrow, click Never, then click OK.

7. **Add a scheduled task.**
   a. Open the Scheduled Tasks window.
   b. Double-click the Add Scheduled Task icon, then click Next.
   c. Click Character Map, or another available program click Next, click the One time only option button, then click Next.
   d. Change the time to one minute ahead, select the current day, then click Next.
   e. Type your password, press [Tab], type your password again, then click Next, if necessary.
   f. Click Finish, wait for the task to take place, then click the Close button on the program window.
   g. Right-click the Character Map icon, click Delete, then click Yes.
   h. Close the Scheduled Tasks window.

8. **Customize the taskbar.**
   a. Right-click the taskbar, point to Toolbars, then click Quick Launch to remove that toolbar from the taskbar.
   b. Click the Start button, point to Settings, then click Taskbar & Start Menu.
   c. Click the Auto hide check box to select it, then click OK.
   d. Move the mouse pointer to the bottom of the screen.
   e. Right-click the taskbar, point to Toolbars, then click Quick Launch to add the toolbar back to the taskbar.
   f. Click the Start button, point to Settings, then click Taskbar & Start Menu.
   g. Click the Auto hide check box to deselect it, then click Apply.

9. **Customize the Start Menu.**
   a. Open the Taskbar & Start Menu, then click the Start Menu Programs tab (98) or Advanced tab (Me).
   b. Make sure the disk or drive where your Project Files are located is available, click Add, then click Browse.
   c. Navigate to the drive and folder where your Project Files are located.
   d. Click the Files of type list arrow, then click All Files.
   e. Double-click Program Files, then double-click Accessories, double-click WordPad, then click Next.
   f. Click Start Menu in the Select Program Folder dialog box, click Next, click finish, then click OK.
   g. Display the Start button with the Wired Coffee Logo, then press [ESC].
   h. Open the Taskbar & Start Menu, then click the start Menu Programs tab (98) or Advanced tab (Me).
   i. Click Remove, locate and click Wired Coffee Logo in the list, click Remove, then click Yes to confirm the deletion if necessary.
   j. Close the dialog box

▶ Independent Challenges

1. A large law firm has retained you as a consultant. The firm just installed Windows 98 or Me, and its employees need to learn how to customize Windows to fit their needs. As you prepare your presentation, you customize the display so it is easier for employees to see. Make the following changes and make sure you change them back to the default settings or setup when you finish.

To complete this independent challenge:
   a. Open the Display Properties dialog box from the Control Panel.
   b. Change the background to Straw Mat.
   c. Set the screen saver for 1 minute so you can show employees how it works without waiting too long.
   d. On the Appearance tab, set the Scheme to High contrast black (extra large).

Practice

e. Save the scheme as *Demo*, then apply the changes.

f. Print the screen. (Press [Print Screen] to make a copy of the screen, open Paint, click Edit on the menu bar, click Paste to paste the screen into Paint, then click Yes to paste the large image, if necessary. Click File on the menu bar, click Print, then click OK.)

g. Delete the scheme Demo, then select the Windows Standard scheme.

h. Set the screen saver for 5 minutes.

2. As owner of a small optical laboratory, you are trying to abide by the Americans with Disabilities Act, which states that employers should make every reasonable effort to accommodate workers with disabilities. One worker is visually impaired. Customize the Windows desktop for this employee so that it is easier to work in, desktop items are easier to see and read, and desktop colors strongly contrast with each other but are still easy on the eyes. Save this custom configuration so that this employee can use it when necessary.

To complete this independent challenge:

a. Open the Display Properties dialog box from the Control Panel.

b. Change the desktop color to red.

c. Change the font size for the menu to 12.

d. Change the size and color of the text in the title bar for the Active Window to 24 and light blue (the second color in the fifth row).

e. Change the font style for the message box to boldface.

f. Save the custom configuration as *Visible*.

g. Apply the scheme.

h. Print the screen. (See Independent Challenge 1, Step f, for screen printing instructions.)

i. Delete the scheme Visible.

j. Select the Windows Standard scheme.

3. As system administrator of a small computer network for a chain of specialty book stores, you want to make sure all the computers run efficiently. To accomplish this goal, you want to set up a scheduled task to clean the hard disk drives of all the computers on a weekly basis.

To complete this independent challenge:

a. Open the Scheduled Tasks window.

b. Schedule the Disk Cleanup program as a task.

c. Schedule the task for a weekly time period.

d. Set the time one minute ahead of the current time.

e. When the Disk Cleanup program appears, print the screen. (See Independent Challenge 1, Step f, for screen printing instructions.)

f. Delete the Disk Cleanup scheduled task.

4. As owner of Lew's Office Supply, you need to make your business computers easier for your employees to use. One way to do that is to add programs to the Start menu. Your employees use WordPad and Paint almost exclusively, and they also use the same documents quite often.

To complete this independent challenge:

a. Add a WordPad shortcut to the Start menu. (*Hint*: Select WordPad.exe located in the Accessories folder within the Program Files folder.)

b. Add a Paint shortcut to the Start menu. (*Hint*: Select MSpaint.exe located in the same place as WordPad.)

c. Create a memo to employees about the upcoming company picnic using WordPad, then save the memo as *Company Picnic Memo* in the drive and folder where your Project Files are located.

d. Close the memo and WordPad.

e. Add the Company Picnic Memo file to the Start menu.

f. Open the Company Picnic Memo from the Start menu.

g. Print the screen. (See Independent Challenge 1, Step f, for screen printing instructions.)

h. Remove all the shortcuts you created.

Windows 98 and Me | **Practice**

▶ Visual Workshop

Re-create the screen shown in Figure E-23, which displays the Windows desktop, then print the screen. (See Independent Challenge 1, Step f, for screen printing instructions.) You don't have to change the Log Off name on the Start menu.

FIGURE E-23

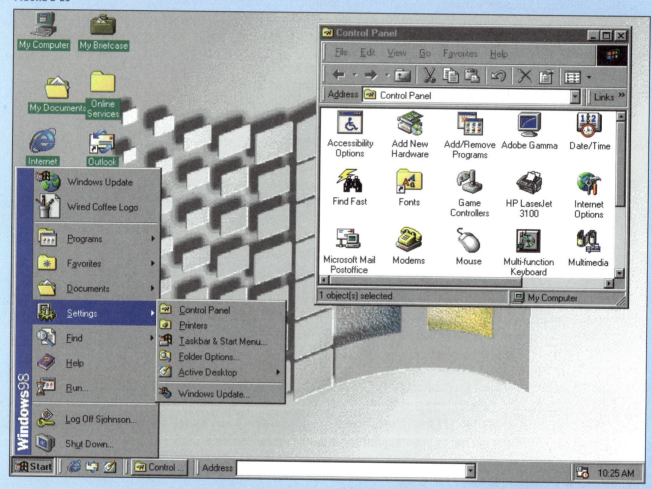

Windows 98 and Me

Exploring
the Internet with Microsoft Internet Explorer

Objectives

- ▶ Understand Web browsers
- ▶ Start Internet Explorer
- ▶ Explore the browser window
- ▶ Open a Web page and follow links
- ▶ Add a Web page to the Favorites list
- ▶ Make a Web page available offline
- ▶ Change your home page and add a link button
- ▶ Search the Web
- ▶ Preview and Print a Web page

A valuable component included with Windows is Microsoft Internet Explorer 5.5, a software program that helps you access the World Wide Web. In this unit, you learn about the benefits of the World Wide Web, examine the basic features of Internet Explorer 5.5, and access Web pages. This unit requires a connection to the Internet. If your computer is not connected to the Internet, check with your instructor or technical support person to see if it's possible for you to connect. If not, simply read the lessons to learn about using Internet Explorer. Wired Coffee Company is a growing business that wants to take advantage of Internet technology. John uses Internet Explorer to open the company Web page and find information related to the coffee business.

Understanding Web Browsers

The Internet is a worldwide collection of more than 40 million computers linked together to share information. The Internet's physical structure includes telephone lines, cables, satellites, and other telecommunications media, as depicted in Figure F-1. Using the Internet, computer users can share many types of information, including text, graphics, sounds, videos, and computer programs. The **World Wide Web** (also known as the Web or WWW) is a part of the Internet that consists of Web sites located on different computers around the world. A **Web site** contains Web pages linked together to make searching for information on the Internet easier. **Web pages** are documents that contain highlighted words, phrases, and graphics, called **hyperlinks** (or simply **links**) that open other Web pages when you click them. Some Web pages contain frames. A **frame** is a separate window within a Web page. Frames let you see more than one Web page at a time. Figure F-2 shows a sample Web page. **Web browsers** are software programs that you use to "browse the Web," or access and display Web pages. Browsers make the Web easy to navigate by providing a graphical, point-and-click environment. This unit features Internet Explorer 5.5, a popular browser from Microsoft that comes with Windows 98 and Me. Netscape Communicator is another popular browser. John realizes that there are many uses for Internet Explorer in his company.

Display Web pages from all over the world
John can look at Web pages for business purposes, such as checking the pages of other coffee companies to see how they market their products.

Display Web content on your desktop
John can make his desktop look and work like a Web page. John can display Web content, such as the Microsoft Investor Ticker, ESPN SportsZone, Expedia Maps Address Finder, or MSNBC Weather Map, directly on his desktop and have the content updated automatically.

Use links to move from one Web page to another
John can click text or graphical links (which appear as either underlined text or as graphics) to move from one Web page to another, investigating different sources for information. Because a Web page can contain links to any location on the Internet, you can jump to Web pages all over the world.

Play audio and video clips
John can click links that play audio and video clips, such as the sound of coffee grinding or a video of workers picking coffee beans. He can also play continuous audio and video broadcasts through radio and television stations over the Internet.

Search the Web for information
John can use search programs that allow him to look for information about any topic throughout the world.

Make favorite Web pages available offline
John can create a list of his favorite Web pages to make it easy for him to return to them at a later time. He can also make a Web page available offline. When he makes a Web page available offline, he can read its content when his computer is not connected to the Internet.

Print the text and graphics on Web pages
If John finds some information or images that he wants to print, he can easily print all or part of the Web page, including the graphics.

FIGURE F-1: Structure of the Internet

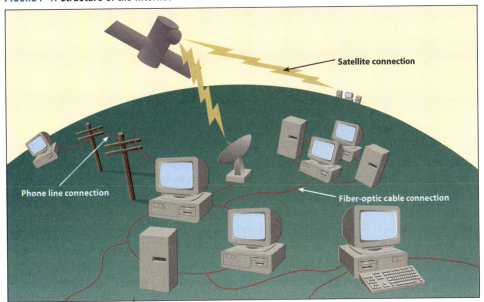

FIGURE F-2: Sample World Wide Web page

The history of the Internet and World Wide Web

The Internet has its roots in the Advanced Research Projects Agency Network (ARPANET), which the United States Department of Defense started in 1969. In 1986, the National Science Foundation formed NSFNET, which replaced ARPANET. NSFNET expanded the foundation of the U.S. portion of the Internet with high-speed, long-distance data lines. In 1991, the U.S. Congress expanded the capacity and speed of the Internet further and opened it to commercial use. The Internet is now accessible in over 300 countries. The World Wide Web was developed in Switzerland in 1991 to make finding documents on the Internet easier. Software programs designed to access the Web (Web browsers) use "point-and-click" interfaces. The first such Web browser, Mosaic, was introduced at the University of Illinois in 1993. Recently, Microsoft Internet Explorer and Netscape Communicator became the two most popular Web browsers.

Starting Internet Explorer

Internet Explorer is a Web browser that you use to search the World Wide Web. (To use it, you also need a physical connection to the Internet.) When you install Windows 2000, an icon for Internet Explorer appears on the desktop and its button appears on the Quick Launch toolbar on the taskbar. You can also make your desktop look and work like a Web page. You can display a Web page or custom Web content directly on your desktop and have the content updated automatically. The specialized Web content, known as a **channel**, is designed to deliver content from the Internet to your computer. To display Web content on your desktop, simply right-click the desktop, point to Active Desktop, then click Show Web Content. Before John can take advantage of the many features of the World Wide Web, he must start Internet Explorer.

Steps

Trouble?
If your computer is not connected to the Internet, check with your instructor or technical person to see if it's possible for you to connect.

1. **Establish a connection to the Internet via the network or telephone**
   If you connect to the Internet through a network, follow your instructor's or technical support person's directions to establish your connection. If you connect by telephone, create a new connection using the Connection Wizard to establish your connection or use an existing Dial-Up Networking connection.

2. **Locate the Internet Explorer icon on your desktop**
   The icon probably appears on the left side of your screen, as shown in Figure F-3, but it doesn't matter where it is or even if it is not on your desktop. There are several different ways to start Internet Explorer, depending on your circumstances. If you have upgraded from Internet Explorer 4 or Windows 98, the desktop Channel Bar and the View Channels button on the Quick Launch toolbar are also available on the desktop.

Trouble?
If the Internet Explorer icon isn't on your desktop, click the Start button, point to Programs, then click Internet Explorer.

3. **Double-click or click the Launch Internet Explorer Browser button on the Quick Launch toolbar**
   Internet Explorer opens. If you connect to the Internet through a network, follow your instructor's or technical support person's directions to log on. If you connect to the Internet by telephone using a dial-up networking connection, you need to enter your user name and password. See your instructor or technical support person for this information.

4. **If necessary, enter your user name, press [Tab], enter your password, then click Connect**
   Upon completion of the dial-up connection, you connect to the Internet (unless an error message appears).

5. **If necessary, click the Maximize button to maximize the Internet Explorer window**
   Internet Explorer displays a Web page, as shown in Figure F-4. It's okay if the Web page on your screen is not the same as the one shown in Figure F-4. Later in this unit, you will learn how to change the Web page that appears when you first start Internet Explorer. Continue to the next lesson to view the various elements of the browser window.

▶ WINDOWS 98 AND ME F-4   EXPLORING THE INTERNET WITH MICROSOFT INTERNET EXPLORER

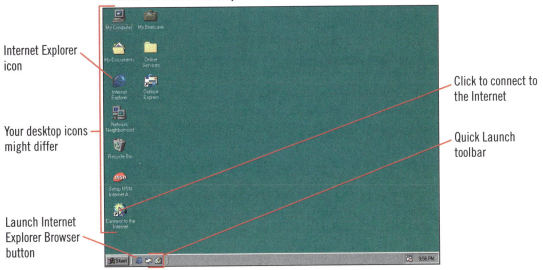

FIGURE F-3: Windows desktop

- Internet Explorer icon
- Your desktop icons might differ
- Launch Internet Explorer Browser button
- Click to connect to the Internet
- Quick Launch toolbar

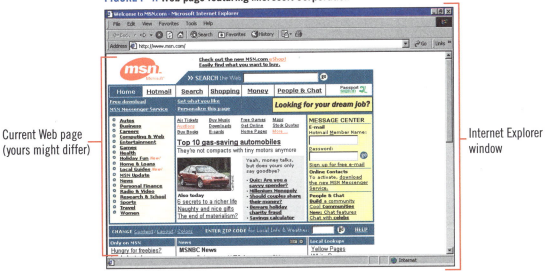

FIGURE F-4: Web page featuring Microsoft Corporation

- Current Web page (yours might differ)
- Internet Explorer window

Clues to Use

Connecting to the Internet

Sometimes connecting your computer to the Internet can be the most difficult part of getting started. The Connection Wizard simplifies the process, whether you want to set up a new connection using an existing account or you want to select an **Internet Service Provider (ISP)**—a company that provides Internet access for a fee—and set up a new account. You might need to obtain connection information from your ISP or your system administrator. To connect to the Internet using the Connection Wizard, double-click the Internet Connection Wizard icon on the desktop or click the Start button, point to Programs, point to Accessories, point to Communications, click Internet Connection Wizard, and then follow the step-by-step instructions. If you are on a network, you might need to use a **proxy server**, which provides a secure barrier between your network and the Internet and prevents other people from seeing confidential information on your network. To configure your computer to use a proxy server, click View on the menu bar, click Internet Options, click the Connections tab, and click LAN Settings. See your instructor or technical support person for setting details to connect to your network.

EXPLORING THE INTERNET WITH MICROSOFT INTERNET EXPLORER WINDOWS 98 AND ME F-5

Exploring the Browser Window

The elements of the Internet Explorer program window, shown in Figure F-5, allow you to view, print, and search for information on the Internet. Before exploring the Web, John decides to familiarize himself with the components of the browser window.

He notes the following features:

 The **title bar** at the top of the page displays the name of the Web page and the name of the browser you are using.

 The **menu bar** provides access to a variety of commands, much like other Windows programs.

 The **toolbar** provides buttons for easy access to the most commonly used commands in Internet Explorer. See Table F-1 for a description of each toolbar button. These button commands are also available on the menus.

 The **Address bar** displays the address of the current Web page or the contents of a local or network computer drive. The **Web address**, like a postal address, is a unique place on the Internet where you can locate a Web page. The Web address is also called the **URL**, which stands for **Uniform Resource Locator**.

 The **Links bar** displays link buttons to Web pages on the Internet or to documents on a local or network drive.

 The **status indicator** (the Internet Explorer logo) spins to indicate a new Web page is loading.

 The **document window** displays the current Web page or the contents of a local or network computer drive. You may need to scroll down the page to view its entire contents.

 The **vertical scroll bar** allows you to move up or down the current Web page. The **scroll box** indicates your relative position within the Web page.

 The **status bar** displays information about your connection progress with new Web pages that you open, including notification that you have connected to another site and the percentage of information transferred from that site. This bar also displays the locations of the links in the document window as you move your mouse pointer over them.

Getting help with Internet Explorer

If you are new to the Internet or to Internet Explorer, you can take a tour to learn how Internet Explorer can help you efficiently browse the Web. To take the tour, click Help on the menu bar, click Tour, then follow the step-by-step instructions. If you want information on a general topic or a specific task, you can find the information you are looking for in Microsoft Internet Explorer Help. To access Help, click Help on the menu bar, then click Contents and Index. The Microsoft Internet Explorer Help window appears and works in the same way the Windows 2000 Help does. If you need more help with Internet Explorer on the Web, you can probably find it by clicking Help on the menu bar, then clicking Online Support. You can also get tips on how to use Internet Explorer more effectively. To display a tip, click Help on the menu bar, then click Tip of the Day. A Tip pane appears at the bottom of the Internet Explorer window. Read the tip, then click the Next tip link to display another tip. Click the Close button in the Tip pane to close the pane.

FIGURE F-5: Elements of Internet Explorer program window

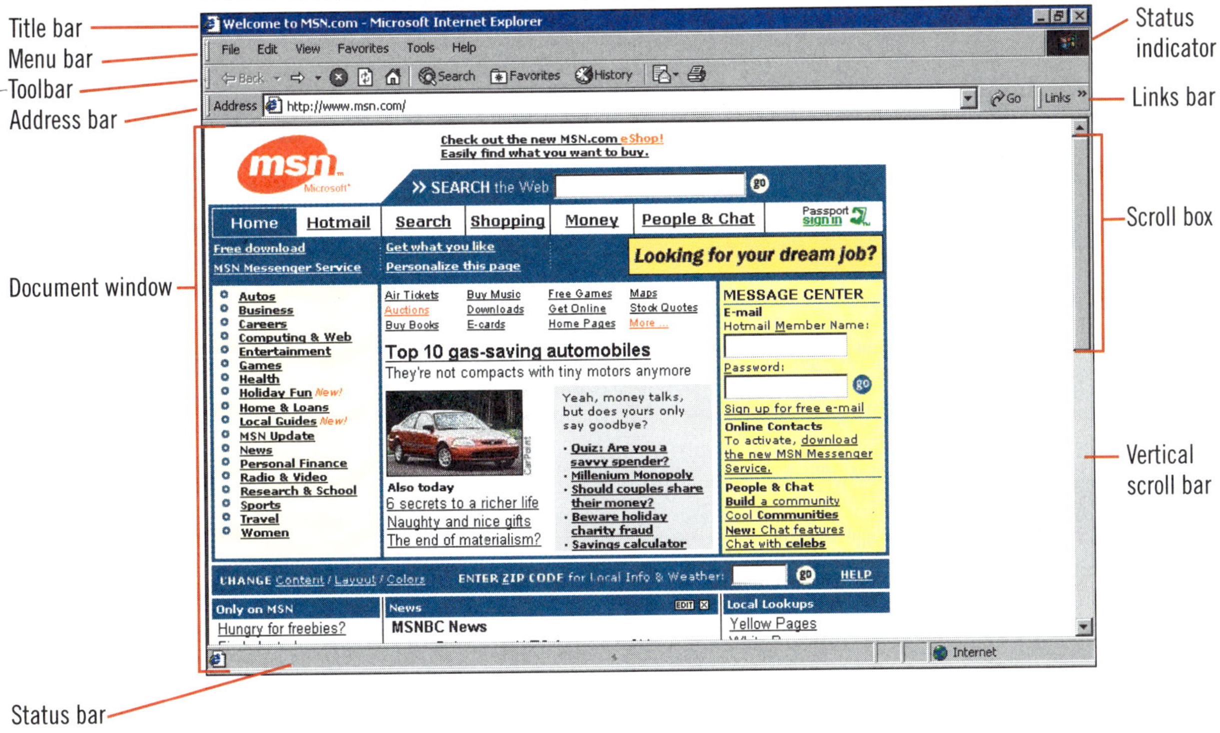

Callouts (left side): Title bar, Menu bar, Toolbar, Address bar, Document window, Status bar

Callouts (right side): Status indicator, Links bar, Scroll box, Vertical scroll bar

TABLE F-1: Internet Explorer toolbar buttons

button	name	description
←	Back	Opens the previous page
→	Forward	Opens the next page
⊗	Stop	Stops loading a page
↻	Refresh	Refreshes the contents of the current page
⌂	Home	Opens the Home page
🔍	Search	Opens the Search Bar
★	Favorites	Opens the Favorites list
🕒	History	Opens the History list
✉	Mail	Displays options for working with Mail and News
🖨	Print	Prints the current Web page
→	Go	Displays the current Web address

EXPLORING THE INTERNET WITH MICROSOFT INTERNET EXPLORER

Windows 98 and Me

Opening a Web Page and Following Links

You can open a Web page quickly and easily using the Address bar. If you change your mind, or the Web page takes too long to **download**, or open on the screen, you can click the Stop button on the toolbar. If you stop a Web page while it is downloading and the page doesn't completely open, you can click the Refresh button on the toolbar to update the screen. Often Web pages connect to each other through links that you can follow to obtain more information about a topic, as shown in Figure F-6. A link can move you to another location on the same Web page, or it can open a different Web page altogether. To follow a link, simply click the highlighted word, phrase, or graphic. (The cursor changes to the hand pointer when it is over a link.) John contracts with a Web development company to create a Web site for Wired Coffee. He wants to access the Web site and follow some of its links in order to give feedback to the developer. John knows that the URL for the Web page is http://www.course.com/illustrated/wired/.

Steps

> **Trouble?**
> If you receive an error message, type one of the URLs listed in Table F-2 instead to open a Web page, then follow a link.

1. Click anywhere in the Address bar

The current address is highlighted, and any text you type replaces the current address. If the current address isn't highlighted, select the entire address.

2. Type **www.course.com/illustrated/wired/**, then press **[Enter]** or click the **Go button** on the toolbar

Be sure to type the address exactly as it appears. When you enter a Web address, you don't have to type "http://" in the Address bar. Internet Explorer inserts it for you. The status bar displays the connection process. After downloading for a few seconds, the Web page appears in the document window.

> **QuickTip**
> You can browse folders on your hard disk drive and run programs from the Address bar. Click anywhere in the Address bar, then type the location of the folder or program. For example, typing "C:\My Documents\" opens the My Documents folder.

3. Locate the **menu link** on the main page, and move the mouse pointer over the link, as shown in Figure F-7

When you move the mouse pointer over a link, the mouse pointer changes to . This indicates that the text or graphic is a link. The address of the link appears in the Status bar.

4. Click the **menu link**

The status indicator spins as you access and open the new Web. The menu Web page appears in the document window.

5. Move the mouse pointer over the **Wired Coffee logo** (the image in the upper-left corner), then click it

The Wired Coffee Company page appears in the document window.

6. Click the **Back button** on the toolbar

The previous Web page appears in the document window.

7. Click the **Forward button** on the toolbar

The Company page appears in the document window again. You could have also clicked the Wired Coffee logo link to return to the Company page.

> **QuickTip**
> To expand the document window to fill the screen, click View on the menu bar, then click Full Screen. Press [F11] to return to the normal view.

8. Click the **Back button list arrow** on the toolbar, then click **Wired Coffee Home Page** or http://www.course.com/illustrated/wired

The Wired Coffee Home Page appears in the document window. Notice that when you have already visited a link, the color of the link changes.

FIGURE F-6: Web pages connected through links

Graphic hyperlink; click to jump to InfoZone Web page

FIGURE F-7: Wired Coffee Company Web page

Graphic hyperlink appears without any distinguishing marks

Web page address

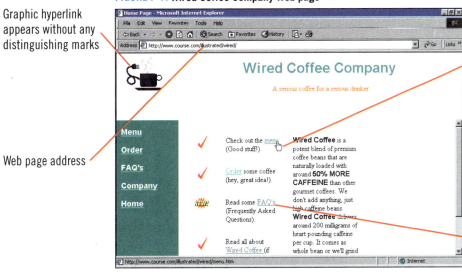

Mouse pointer changes to a hand when positioned over a link

Text hyperlinks appear in color with an underline (color on your screen may differ)

TABLE F-2: URLs of Web sites dealing with coffee

company name	url
Boyd Coffee Company	http://www.boyds.com
Peet's Coffee & Tea	http://www.peets.com
Seattle's Best Coffee	http://www.seabest.com
Starbucks Coffee	http://www.starbucks.com

Understanding a Web address

The address for a Web page is called a URL. Each Web page has a unique URL that begins with "http" (HyperText Transfer Protocol) followed by a colon, two slashes, and the name of the Web site. The Web site is the computer where the Web pages are located. At the end of the Web site name, another slash may appear, followed by one or more folder names and a filename. For example, in the address, http://www.course.com/illustrated/wired/wired_main.htm, the name of the Web site is *www.course.com*; folders at that site are called */illustrated/wired*; and within the wired folder is a file called *wired_main.htm*.

EXPLORING THE INTERNET WITH MICROSOFT INTERNET EXPLORER

Adding a Web Page to the Favorites List

Rather than memorizing URLs or keeping a handwritten list of Web pages you want to visit, you can use a feature called **Favorites** to store and organize the addresses. When you display a Web page in your document window that you want to display again at a later time, you can add the Web page to your Favorites list. Once you add the Web page to the Favorites list, you can return to the page by opening your Favorites list and selecting the link to the page you want. John wants to add the Wired Coffee Web page to his Favorites list.

Steps

> **QuickTip**
> To view Web pages offline, click File on the menu bar, then click Work Offline. If you want to access other Web pages, you need to reconnect to the Internet.

1. Click **Favorites** on the menu bar, then click **Add to Favorites**
   The Add Favorites dialog box opens, as shown in Figure F-8. You have the option to make the Web page available for offline viewing. When you make a Web page available for **offline viewing**, you copy the pages to your computer for later viewing, after you disconnect your Internet connection. This is helpful when you want to read a Web page without worrying about your connect time.

2. In the Name text box, select the current text, type **Wired Coffee Company**, then click **OK**
   You name the Web page "Wired Coffee Company" and add it to your Favorites list.

> **Trouble?**
> URLs may be case-sensitive, you must type them exactly as they appear, using upper-case and lowercase letters.

3. Click anywhere in the Address bar, type **www.course.com**, then press **[Enter]**
   When you type a Web address in the Address bar, a feature called **AutoComplete** suggests possible matches from previous entries you made for Web addresses. If a suggestion in the list matches the Web address you want to enter, click the suggestion from the Address bar list.

4. Click the **Favorites button** on the toolbar
   The Explorer Bar opens on the left side of the document window and displays the Favorites list. The Favorites list contains several folders, including a Links folder, a Media folder, and individual favorite Web pages that come with Windows 98 or Me.

> **QuickTip**
> You can import favorites, known as bookmarks, from Netscape Navigator by clicking File on the menu bar, then clicking Import and Export.

5. Click **Wired Coffee Company** in the Favorites list
   The Wired Coffee Company Web page appears in the document window, as shown in Figure F-9. The Favorites list also includes folders to help you organize your Favorites list. You can click a folder icon in the Favorites list to display its contents.

6. Click the **Links folder** in the Favorites list
   The Favorites list in the Links folder expands and appears in the Explorer Bar, as shown in Figure F-10. To open a favorite in the Links folder, position the mouse pointer over the favorite you want to open (the mouse pointer changes to a hand and the favorite appears underlined), then click the mouse button.

> **QuickTip**
> To start Internet Explorer and open a favorite, click the Start button, point to Favorites, then click a favorite Web page.

7. Click the **Links folder** in the Favorites list again
   The Favorites list in the Links folder collapses to display the Links folder icon only. If you no longer use a favorite, you can delete it from the Favorites list, as described in the Clues to Use, "Organizing Favorites."

FIGURE F-8: Add Favorite dialog box

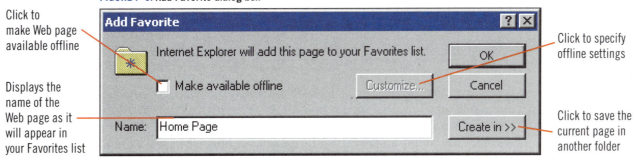

- Click to make Web page available offline
- Displays the name of the Web page as it will appear in your Favorites list
- Click to specify offline settings
- Click to save the current page in another folder

FIGURE F-9: Internet Explorer window with Favorites list

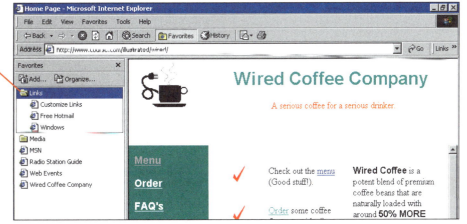

- Explorer Bar displays Favorites list
- Click to close Explorer Bar
- Individual Favorite Web pages
- Folders to help you organize your Favorites list
- Your Favorites list might differ

FIGURE F-10: Links folder with Favorites listed

- Click to display or collapse the Favorites list in the Links folder

Organizing favorites

If your list of favorites grows long, you can delete favorites you don't visit anymore or move favorites into folders. To delete and move your favorites, click the Favorites menu, click Organize Favorites, select one or more files from the Favorites list, then click the Delete or Move to Folder button. If you want to add a new folder to your Favorites list, click the Create Folder button, type the new folder name, then press [Enter]. If you prefer to use another name for a favorite, you can select the favorite you want to rename, click the Rename button, type the new name, then press [Enter]. When you finish making changes, you can click Close to exit.

EXPLORING THE INTERNET WITH MICROSOFT INTERNET EXPLORER

Making a Web Page Available Offline

When you make a Web page available offline, you can read its content when your computer is not connected to the network and Internet. For example, you can view Web pages on your laptop computer when you have no network or Internet connection. Or you might want to read Web pages at home but not want to tie up a phone line. When you make a Web page available offline, you save, or **synchronize**, the latest online version of your Web page on your hard disk drive for offline viewing. You can specify how much content you want available, such as an individual Web page or a Web page and all its links, and choose how you want to update that content on your computer. John wants to make the Wired Coffee Company Web site on the Favorites list available for offline viewing. After viewing the offline version of the Web site, John updates the offline version to make sure he has the latest data.

Steps

1. Click **Favorites** on the menu bar, then click **Organize Favorites**
   The Organize Favorites dialog box opens.

2. In the Favorites list, click **Wired Coffee Company**
   Status information about the Wired Coffee Company favorite appears in the Organize Favorites dialog box, as shown in Figure F-11.

3. Click the **Make available offline check box** to select it, then click **Close**
   You open the Synchronize dialog box and synchronize the Wired Coffee Company Web page; you save the latest version of your Web page on your hard disk drive for offline viewing.

4. Click **File** on the menu bar, then click **Work Offline**
   You disconnect Internet Explorer from the network and Internet.

5. Click the **Home button** on the toolbar, then click **Wired Coffee Company** in the Favorites list
   When you access the Wired Coffee Company Web site in offline mode, Internet Explorer displays the offline version of the Web page that is on your hard disk drive. You can view any offline Web page, but if you click a link to a Web page not available offline, Internet Explorer reconnects you to the network and Internet.

6. Click **File** on the menu bar, then click **Work Offline**
   When you re-establish the connection to the network and Internet, you can synchronize with the latest online version of the Wired Coffee Web page to update the offline version on your hard disk drive.

7. Click **Tools** on the menu bar, then click **Synchronize**
   The Items to Synchronize dialog box opens, as shown in Figure F-12. You can select which Web pages or files you want to synchronize and specify when and how you want them updated.

8. Click the **Wired Coffee Company check box** to select it if necessary, deselect all other check boxes, then click **Synchronize**
   You re-synchronize the Wired Coffee Company Web page, with the latest online version of the Web page on to your hard disk drive and ready for offline viewing.

9. Right-click **Wired Coffee Company** in the Favorites list, click **Delete**, click **Yes**, then click the **Close button** in the Explorer Bar
   You delete the Wired Coffee Company Web page from the Favorites list, and the Explorer Bar closes.

QuickTip
To make the current Web page available offline, click Favorites on the menu bar, click Add to Favorites, click the Make available offline check box to select it, click Custom, follow the wizard instructions, click Finish, then click OK.

QuickTip
When you choose to work offline, Internet Explorer starts in offline mode until you click File on the menu bar, then click Work Offline again to clear the check mark.

QuickTip
To specify a schedule for updating that page and how much content to download, click Properties. You can also click Setup to schedule updating when you log on to your computer and when your computer becomes idle, no activity.

FIGURE F-11: Organize Favorites dialog box

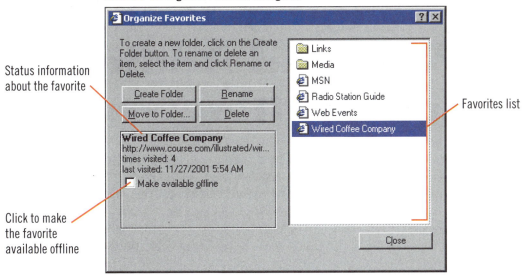

FIGURE F-12: Items to Synchronize dialog box

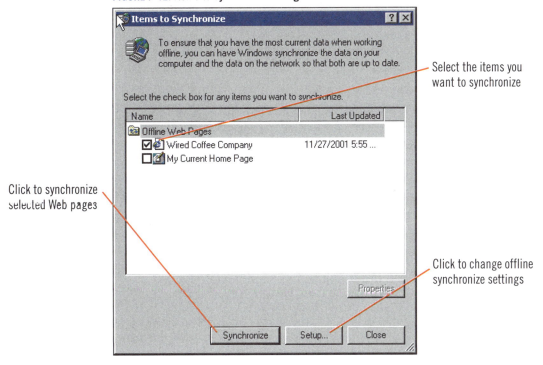

Saving a Web page

If you want to view a Web page offline, and you don't need to update its content, you can save the page on your computer. There are several ways you can save the Web page, from just saving the text to saving all of the graphics and text needed to display that page as it appears on the Web. To save a Web page, click File on the menu bar, then click Save As. Specify the drive and folder in which you want to save the file, type the name you want for the file, click the Save As Type list arrow, select the file format type you want, then click Save. When you save a complete Web page, Internet Explorer saves all the graphic and text elements in a folder.

Changing Your Home Page and Adding a Link Button

Your **home page** in Internet Explorer is the page that opens when you start the program. When you first install Internet Explorer, the default home page is the Microsoft Network (MSN) Web site. If you want a different page to appear when you start Internet Explorer (and whenever you click the Home button), you can change your home page. You can choose one of the millions of Web pages available through the Internet, or you can select a particular file on your hard drive. You can also change the Web pages associated with the buttons on the Links bar. John decides to change his home page to the Wired Coffee Web page and add a link button to the Links bar.

Steps

> **QuickTip**
>
> You change your home page back to http://www.msn.com in the Skills Review exercise at the end of this unit. If you want to change it back at any other time, type "www.msn.com" in the Address bar, press [Enter], then complete Steps 1 through 3 of this lesson.

1. Click **Tools** on the menu bar, click **Internet Options**, then click the **General tab** if necessary
   The Internet Options dialog box opens, as shown in Figure F-14. The Internet Options dialog box allows you to change a variety of Internet Explorer settings and preferences. See Table F-3 for a description of each tab.

2. In the Home page section, click **Use Current**
   The address of the Wired Coffee Company Web page appears in the Address text box.

3. Click **OK**
   You associate the Home button on the toolbar with the current Web page, Wired Coffee Company.

4. Click the **FAQ's link**, then click the **Home button** on the toolbar
   The home page appears in the document window.

> **QuickTip**
>
> You can move the Links bar by dragging it to a new location.

5. Double-click the word **Links** on the Links bar
   The Links bar opens and may hide the Address bar. The Links bar contains buttons with links to Web pages. You can drag a link on a page or a Web site address in the Address bar to a blank area on the Links bar to create a new Links button.

6. Drag the **Order link** on the main page to the left of the first button on the Links bar (the mouse pointer changes to a black bar to indicate the placement of the button), then release the mouse button
   A new link button appears on the Links bar with the name associated with the Web site, as shown in Figure F-13. You can delete or change the properties of a links button. Simply right-click the link button you want to change, then click the Delete or Properties command on the shortcut menu.

7. Click the **Order button** on the Links bar, then click the **Back button** on the toolbar

8. Right-click the **Order button** on the Links bar, click **Delete**, then click **Yes**
   The home page appears in the document window.

9. Position the mouse pointer over the word **Links**, then drag the **Links bar** to the right to hide it

FIGURE F-13: New button on Links bar

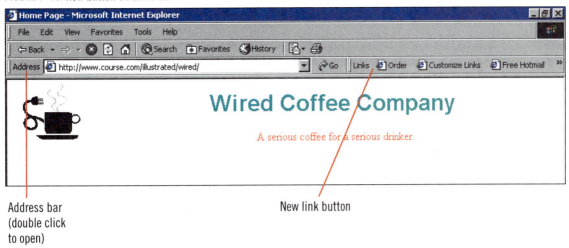

Address bar (double click to open)

New link button

TABLE F-3: Internet Options dialog box tabs

tab	allows you to
General	Change your home page, temporary file settings, and history settings
Security	Select security levels for different parts of the Internet
Content	Set up a rating system for Internet content and personal information for typing Web addresses and buying items over the Internet
Connections	Change connection settings (phone and network)
Programs	Choose which programs (Mail, News, and Internet call) you want to use with Internet Explorer
Advanced	Change individual settings for browsing, multimedia, security, printing, and searching

CLUES TO USE

Viewing and maintaining a History list

Sometimes you run across a great Web site and simply forget to add it to your Favorites list. With Internet Explorer there's no need to try to remember all the sites you visit. The History feature keeps track of where you've been by date, site, most visited, or order visited today. To view the History list, click the History button on the toolbar, and click a day or week in the Explorer Bar to expand the list of Web sites visited. Because the History list can grow to occupy a large amount of space on your hard drive, it's important that you control the length of time you retain Web sites in the list. Internet Explorer deletes the History list periodically, based on the settings you specify in the General tab of the Internet Options dialog box, as shown in Figure F-14.

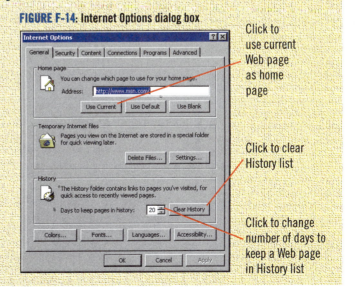

FIGURE F-14: Internet Options dialog box

Click to use current Web page as home page

Click to clear History list

Click to change number of days to keep a Web page in History list

EXPLORING THE INTERNET WITH MICROSOFT INTERNET EXPLORER

Searching the Web

You can find all kinds of information on the Web. The best way to find information is to use a search engine. A **search engine** is a program you access through a Web site and use to search through a collection of Internet information to find what you want. Many search engines are available on the Web, such as Yahoo! and Excite. When performing a search, the search engine compares the words or phrases, known as **keywords**, you submit with words the search engine finds on various Web sites on the Internet. If it finds your keywords in the stored database, it lists the matched sites on a Web page. (These matched sites are sometimes called **hits**.) The company that manages the search engine determines what information its database stores, so search results of different search engines vary. ✎ John wants to search for other coffee-related Web sites to check out the competition.

QuickTip
To customize the search options, click the Customize button in the Explorer Bar, click the option button to use the Search Assistant or one search engine, select the search options you want, then click OK or Update.

1. **Click the Search button 🔍 on the toolbar**
   A search engine appears in the Explorer Bar, as shown in Figure F-15. In this case, the search engine is MSN Web Search; your search engine might differ. If you prefer another search engine, you can choose the search engine you want to use from the custom search options.

2. **Click the Find a web page option button in the Explorer Bar if necessary**
   You can select search options to find a personal or business address, display a list of links to previous searches, and find a map for a specific address. Each search option requires different search criteria, which is information related to what you want to find. To search for a Web page containing the information you want, you need to enter a keyword or words (a word or phrase that best describes what you want to retrieve) in the search text box. The more specific your search criteria, the better list of matches you receive from the search engine.

3. **In the Find a Web page containing text box, type coffee imports**
   Now you're ready to start the search.

QuickTip
To search for other items using a search engine, such as a file, computer, or person, click the Start button, point to Find (98) or Search (Me), then click Files or Folders, Computers, or People.

4. **Click Search in the Explorer Bar**
   The search engine retrieves and displays a list of Web sites that match your criteria, as shown in Figure F-16. The total number of Web sites found is listed at the top. The search results appear in order of decreasing relevance. The percentage next to each Web site indicates the degree of relevance. If the search results return too many hits, you should narrow the search by adding more keywords. As you add more keywords, the search engine finds fewer Web pages that contain all of those words. See Table F-4 for other techniques to narrow a search.

QuickTip
To perform a new search, click the New button in the Explorer Bar.

5. **Click any link to a Web site in the list of matches**
   The Web site that you open appears in the right pane of the document window. You can follow links to other pages on this Web site or jump to other Web sites. When you finish, close the Explorer Bar.

6. **Click Close button in the Explorer Bar**
   The Explorer Bar closes.

7. **Click the Home button 🏠 on the toolbar**
   John returns to the Wired Coffee Company home page.

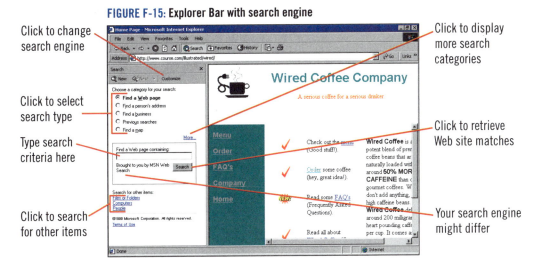

FIGURE F-15: Explorer Bar with search engine

- Click to change search engine
- Click to select search type
- Type search criteria here
- Click to search for other items
- Click to display more search categories
- Click to retrieve Web site matches
- Your search engine might differ

FIGURE F-16: Search engine results

Search results; your list might differ (scroll down to see entire list)

TABLE F-4: Techniques to narrow a search

technique	example
Use descriptive, specific words	Beaches surfing pacific
Use plain English phrases	Surfing beaches on the pacific ocean
Place exact phrases and proper names in quotes	"Sunset beach"
Use a + sign between words your results must contain	Surf + beach
Use a - sign between words your results should not contain	Surf + beach - Atlantic
Use AND to find results containing all words	Surf AND sea AND sand
Use OR to find results containing at least one word	Surf OR beach

CLUES TO USE

Searching for people on the Web

Internet Explorer includes several directory services to help you find people you know who may have access to the Internet. (Figure F-17 shows one service, Bigfoot.) To find a person on the Internet, click the Start button, point to Find (98) or Search (Me), click For People, select the directory service you want to use, type the person's name, and click Find Now. Each directory service accesses different databases on the Internet, so if you don't find the person using the first service, try a different directory service.

FIGURE F-17: Find People dialog box

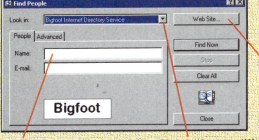

- Click to open Web site for selected directory service
- Enter name or e-mail address of person you want to find here
- Click to choose a different directory service

EXPLORING THE INTERNET WITH MICROSOFT INTERNET EXPLORER

Windows 98 and Me

Previewing and Printing a Web Page

Web pages are designed for viewing on a computer screen, but you can also print all or part of one. Before you print, you should verify that the page looks the way you want. You save time, money, and paper by avoiding duplicate or wasteful printing. Print Preview shows you exactly how your Web page will look on the printed page. This is especially helpful when you have multiple pages to print. When you are ready to print, Internet Explorer provides many options for printing Web pages. For Web pages with frames, you can print the page just as you see it, or you can elect to print a particular frame or all frames. You can even use special Page Setup options to include the date, time, or window title on the printed page. You can also choose to print the Web addresses from the links contained on a Web page. John previews and prints a Web page and then exits Internet Explorer.

Steps

1. **Click File on the menu bar, then click Print Preview**
   The Print Preview window opens, as shown in Figure F-18.

2. **Click the Zoom In button on the Print Preview toolbar**
   The entire page appears in the Print Preview window.

> **QuickTip**
> You can also click the Print button on the toolbar to print the current page directly or click File on the menu bar, then click Print to open the Print dialog box.

3. **Click the Print button on the Print Preview toolbar**
   The Print dialog box opens, as shown in Figure F-19.

4. **In the Select Printer box, select the printer you want to use**

5. **Click the Pages option button**
   This option prints the pages specified, in this case, pages 1 to 1. The Print dialog box also gives you several options to print the frames. You can print the Web page as laid out on the screen, only the selected frame, or all frames individually.

6. **Click the As laid out on screen option button, if necessary**
   Instead of writing links on a Web page, you can automatically print the Web site addresses for each link.

> **QuickTip**
> You do not need to save the page before you exit, because you only view documents with Internet Explorer; you do not create or change documents.

7. **Click the Print table of links check box to select it, then click OK**
   The Print Preview window closes, and the Web page prints on the selected printer.

8. **Click the Close button in the Internet Explorer window**
   The Internet Explorer window closes. If you connected to the Internet by telephone, a disconnect dialog box opens. If you connected to the Internet through a network, follow your instructor's or technical support person's directions to close your connection.

> **Trouble?**
> If you connected by telephone, you can right-click the Connect Icon on the right side of the taskbar, then click Disconnect.

9. **If the disconnect dialog box opens, click Disconnect**

FIGURE F-18: Previewing a Web page

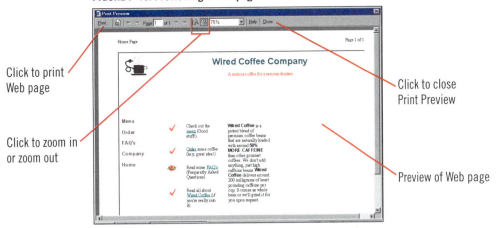

FIGURE F-19: Printing a Web page

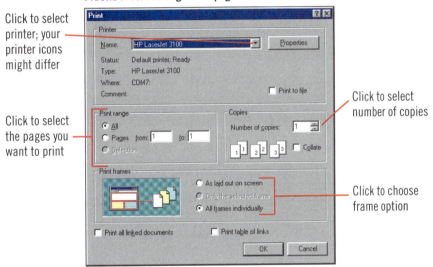

Setting up the page format

When you print a Web page, you can use the Page Setup dialog box to control the printing of text and graphics on a page. The Page Setup dialog box, shown in Figure F-20, specifies the printer properties for page size, orientation, and paper source; in most cases, you won't want to change them. From the Page Setup dialog box, you can also change header and footer information. In the Headers and Footers text boxes, you can type text to appear as a header and footer of a Web page you print. In these text boxes, you can also use variables to substitute information about the current page, and you can combine text and codes. For example, if you type "Page &p of &P" in the Header text box, the current page number and the total number of pages prints at the top of each printed page. Check Internet Explorer Help for a complete list of header and footer codes.

FIGURE F-20: Page Setup dialog box

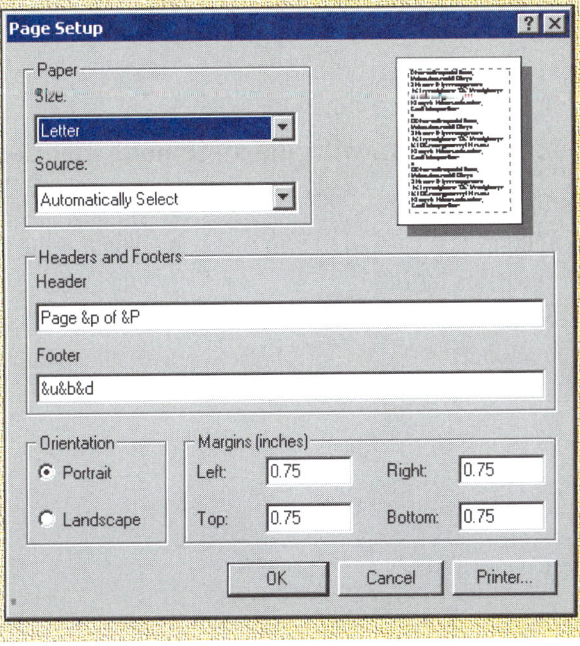

EXPLORING THE INTERNET WITH MICROSOFT INTERNET EXPLORER

Practice

Windows 98 and Me

▶ Concepts Review

Label each element of the screen shown in Figure F-21.

FIGURE F-21

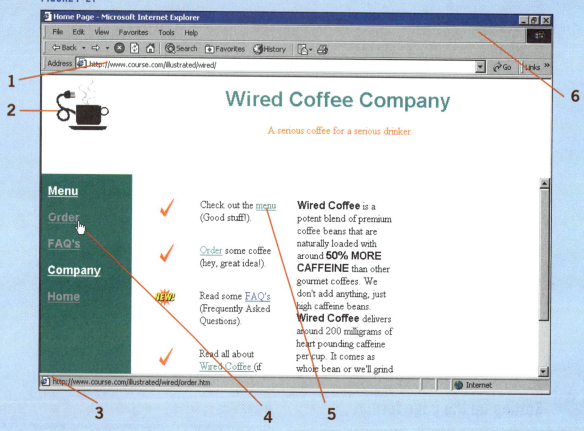

Match each term with the statement that describes its function.

7. Address bar
8. Toolbar
9. Favorites button
10. Status indicator
11. Back button

a. Spins as Internet Explorer loads a page
b. Displays the URL for the current page
c. Provides shortcuts for options on the menu bar
d. Displays a list of selected Web pages and folders to organize them
e. Displays the previously viewed page

Practice

Select the best answers from the lists of choices.

12. Software programs used to access and display Web pages are called:
    a. Web sites.
    b. Search engines.
    c. Web utilities.
    d. Web browsers.

13. If you want to save the name and URL of a Web page in Internet Explorer and return to it later, you can add it to a list called:
    a. Favorites.
    b. Bookmarks.
    c. Home pages.
    d. Preferences.

14. An international telecommunications network that consists of linked documents is called the:
    a. NSFNET.
    b. Netscape Communicator.
    c. Internet Explorer.
    d. World Wide Web.

15. In Internet Explorer, where are the buttons that perform common functions such as moving to a previous Web page?
    a. Address bar
    b. Toolbar
    c. Status bar
    d. Menu bar

16. Which of the following is a valid URL?
    a. http:/www.usf.edu/
    b. htp://www.usf.edu/
    c. htp:/ww.usf.edu/
    d. http//www.usf.edu/

17. Underlined words that you click to jump to another Web page are called:
    a. Explorers.
    b. Favorites.
    c. Web browsers.
    d. Hyperlinks.

18. The URL of the current Web page appears in the:
    a. Title bar.
    b. Document window.
    c. Address bar.
    d. Status bar.

Skills Review

1. **Start Internet Explorer.**
   a. Connect to the Internet.
   b. Start Internet Explorer.

2. **Explore the browser window.**
   a. Identify the toolbar, menu bar, Address bar, Links bar, status bar, status indicator, URL, document window, and scroll bars.
   b. In the toolbar, identify icons for searching, viewing favorites, viewing history, viewing Internet Explorer in full screen, and moving to the previous page.

3. **Open a Web page and follow links.**
   a. Click in the Address bar, type **www.cnet.com**, then press [Enter].
   b. Explore the Web site by using the scroll bars, toolbar, and hyperlinks.
   c. Click in the Address bar, type **www.sportsline.com**, then press [Enter].
   d. Follow the links to investigate the content.

Windows 98 and Me | Practice

4. Add a Web page to the Favorites list.
   a. Click in the Address bar, type www.loc.gov, then press [Enter].
   b. Click Favorites on the menu bar, then click Add to Favorites.
   c. Click OK.
   d. Click the Favorites button.
   e. Click the Home button.
   f. Click the link Library of Congress Home Page in the Favorites list.

5. Make a Web page available offline.
   a. Click Favorites on the menu bar, then click Organize Favorites.
   b. In the Favorites list, click Library of Congress.
   c. Click the Make available offline check box to select it, then click Close.
   d. Click File on the menu bar, then click Work Offline.
   e. Click Library of Congress Home Page in the Favorites list.
   f. Click File on the menu bar, then click Work Offline.
   g. Click Tools on the menu bar, then click Synchronize.
   h. Click the Library of Congress Home Page check to select it if necessary, then deselect all other check boxes.
   i. Click Synchronize.
   j. Right-click Library of Congress Home Page in the Favorites list, click Delete, then click Yes.
   k. Click the Close button in the Favorites list.

6. Change your home page and add a link button.
   a. Click in the Address bar, type www.msn.com, then press [Enter].
   b. Click View on the menu bar, then click Internet Options.
   c. Click the General tab.
   d. Click Use Current.
   e. Click OK.
   f. Click the Back button.
   g. Click the Home button.

7. Search the Web.
   a. Click the Search button.
   b. Click the Find a Web page option button.
   c. Type **job computer training** in the search text box.
   d. Click the Search button.
   e. Click a link to a Web site from the matches list.
   f. Click the Close button in the Explorer Bar.
   g. Click the Home button.

8. Preview and print a Web page.
   a. Click File on the menu bar, then click Print Preview.
   b. Click the Zoom In button on the Print Preview toolbar.
   c. Click the Print button on the Print Preview toolbar.
   d. In the Select Printer box, click a printer.
   e. Click the Pages option button. (Use the range 1 to 1.)
   f. Click OK.
   g. Click the Close button to exit Internet Explorer.
   h. Click Yes to disconnect, if necessary.

Practice

▶ **Independent Challenges**

1. You will soon graduate from college with a degree in business management. Before entering the workforce, you want to make sure that you are up-to-date on all advances in the field. You decide that checking the Web would provide the most current information. In addition, you can look for companies with employment opportunities.
   To complete this independent challenge:

   a. Use Internet Explorer to investigate the All Business Network at http://www.all-biz.com/.
   b. When you find a promising site, print the page.

2. You leave tomorrow for a business trip to France. You want to make sure that you take the right clothes for the weather and decide that the best place to check France's weather might be the Web.
   To complete this independent challenge:

   a. Access one or two of the following weather sites.
The Weather Channel	http://www.weather.com/
World Weather Guide	http://www.weatherlabs.com
CNN Weather	http://www.cnn.com/WEATHER/

   b. Print at least two reports on the Paris weather

3. Your boss wants to buy a new desktop computer (as opposed to a laptop). He assigns you the task of investigating the options. You decide that looking on the Web would be more expedient than visiting computer stores in the area.
   To complete this independent challenge:

   a. Visit the following Web sites:
IBM	http://www.ibm.com/
Apple	http://www.apple.com/
Dell	http://www.dell.com/

   b. Print a page from each of the two that you think offer the best deal.

4. During the summer, you want to travel to national parks in the United States. Use one of the search engines available through your Web browser to find Web sites with maps of the national parks. Visit four or five sites from the match list and print a page from the three that you think offer the best maps and related information for park visitors.

Windows 98 and Me | Practice

▶ Visual Workshop

Re-create the screen shown in Figure F-22, which displays the document window with a search engine and a Web site. Your search results might differ. (*Hint*: Use the Customize button to change search engines.) Print the Web page and then print the screen. (Press [Print Screen] to make a copy of the screen, open Paint, click Edit on the menu bar, click Paste to paste the screen into Paint, then click Yes to paste the large image if necessary. Click File on the menu bar, click Print, then click OK in the Print dialog box.)

FIGURE F-22

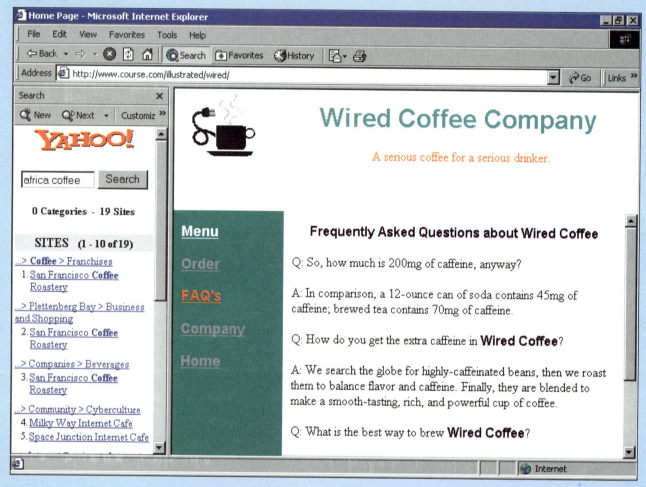

Windows 98 and Me

Exchanging
Mail and News

Objectives

- Start Outlook Express
- Explore the Outlook Express window
- Add a contact to the Address Book
- Compose and send e-mail
- Retrieve, read, and respond to e-mail
- Manage e-mail messages
- Select a news server
- View and subscribe to a newsgroup
- Read and post a news message

 If you are not connected to the Internet, you cannot work through the steps in this unit; however, you can read the lessons without completing the steps to learn what you can accomplish using Outlook Express.

Windows 98 and Me includes Microsoft Outlook Express, a powerful program for managing **electronic mail** (known as e-mail). With an Internet connection and Microsoft Outlook Express, you can exchange e-mail messages with anyone on the Internet and join any number of **newsgroups**, collections of e-mail messages on related topics posted by individuals to specified Internet locations. In this unit John Casey, owner of the Wired Coffee Company, uses Outlook Express to send and receive e-mail messages and join a newsgroup about the coffee industry.

Starting Outlook Express

Unit G — Windows 98 and Me

Outlook Express puts the world of online communication on your desktop. Whether you want to exchange e-mail with colleagues and friends or join newsgroups to trade ideas and information, the tools you need are here. When you install Windows 98 or Me, a button for Outlook Express appears on the Quick Launch toolbar, located on the taskbar. If your computer is not connected to the Internet or you have no e-mail account, check with your instructor or technical support person to see if it's possible for you to connect or set up an e-mail account. John wants to use Outlook Express to exchange e-mail with his employees.

Steps

1. **If necessary, establish a connection to the Internet via the network or telephone**

   If you connect to the Internet through a network, follow your instructor's or technical support person's directions to establish your connection. If you connect by telephone, create a new connection using the Connection Wizard to establish your connection, or use an existing dial-up networking connection.

2. **Click the Launch Outlook Express button on the Quick Launch toolbar, as shown in Figure G-1**

   The Outlook Express window opens and displays the Outlook Express Start Page, as shown in Figure G-2. If you connect to the Internet through a network, follow your instructor's or technical support person's directions to log on. If you connect to the Internet by telephone using a dial-up networking connection, you might need to enter your user name and password. See your instructor or technical support person for this information.

   > **Trouble?**
   > If a Browse For Folder dialog box opens, click OK to accept the default folder where Outlook Express should store your messages, then continue.

3. **If necessary, type your user name, press [Tab], type your password, then click Connect**

   Upon completion of the dial-up connection, you are connected to the Internet (unless an error message appears). When you start Outlook Express for the first time, the Internet Connection Wizard opens, asking you about your e-mail account set-up information. See your instructor or technical support person for this information.

4. **If necessary, enter the information required by the Internet Connection Wizard; type your name, click Next, type your e-mail address, click Next, type the name of the incoming mail server, type the name of the outgoing server, click Next, type your e-mail account name, type your password, click Next, then click Finish**

   Set up your mail account.

   > **QuickTip**
   > To modify or add an account, click Tools on the menu bar, click Accounts, click an account and click Properties, or click Add, click an account type, and follow the wizard instructions.

5. **If necessary, click the Maximize button to maximize the Outlook Express window**

FIGURE G-1: Windows desktop

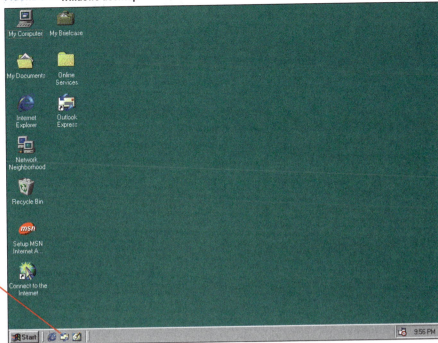

Launch Outlook Express button

FIGURE G-2: Outlook Express window

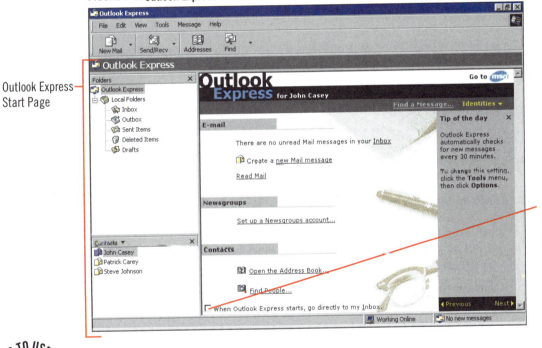

Outlook Express Start Page

Click to display Inbox when you start Outlook Express

Starting Outlook Express from your Web browser

You can set Outlook Express as your default e-mail program, so that whenever you click an e-mail link on a Web page or choose the mail command in your Web browser, Outlook Express opens. Likewise, you can set Outlook Express as your default news reader, so that when you click a newsgroup link on a Web page or choose the news reader command in your Web browser, Outlook Express opens. To set Outlook Express as your default e-mail or newsgroup program, start Internet Explorer, click Tools on the menu bar, click Internet Options, click the Programs tab, click either the E-mail or Newsgroups list arrow, click Outlook Express, then click OK.

EXCHANGING MAIL AND NEWS WINDOWS 98 AND ME G-3

Exploring the Outlook Express Window

After you start Outlook Express, the Outlook Express window displays the Outlook Express Start Page, as shown in Figure G-3. The **Outlook Express Start Page** displays tools that you can use to read e-mail, set up a newsgroup account, read newsgroup messages, compose e-mail messages, enter and edit Address Book information, and find people on the Internet. Before reading his e-mail, John decides to familiarize himself with the components of the Outlook Express window.

Details

He notes the following features:

 The **title bar** at the top of the window displays the name of the program.

 The **menu bar** provides access to a variety of commands, much like other Windows programs.

 The **toolbar** provides icons, or buttons, for easy access to the most commonly used commands. See Table G-1 for a description of each toolbar button. These commands are also available on menus.

 The **Go to MSN link** opens your default Web browser program and displays the MSN Web page.

 The **Folders list** displays folders where Outlook Express stores e-mail messages. You can also use folders to organize your e-mail messages.

 The **Contacts list** displays the contact names in the Address Book.

 The **new Mail message link** opens the New Message dialog box where you can compose and send e-mail messages.

 The **Read Mail link** jumps to the Inbox where you can read and reply to incoming e-mail messages.

 The **Set up a Newsgroups account link,** which creates a newsgroup account (appears instead of the **Read News link** if you have not set up a newsgroup account).

 The **Read News link** connects to newsgroups that you can view and subscribe to.

 The **Open the Address Book link** opens the Address Book where you can enter and edit your contacts list.

 The **Find People link** opens the Find People dialog box where you can search for people on the Internet or in your Address Book.

 The **Tip of the day** on the right side of the window displays an Outlook Express tip; click Next and Previous to move between the tips.

 The **status bar** displays information about your Internet connection with a mail or news group server.

FIGURE G-3: Outlook Express window with Start Page

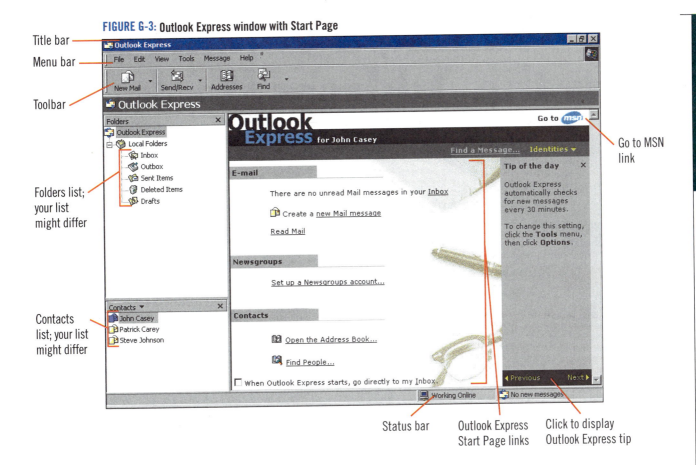

TABLE G-1: Outlook Express Start Page toolbar buttons

button	description
	Opens the e-mail message composition window
	Sends e-mail messages and checks for new messages
	Opens the Address Book
	Finds e-mail messages, text in an e-mail message, or people on the Internet

Getting help in Outlook Express

If you need help connecting to the Internet to get mail or learning how to use Outlook Express features, you can get help from several different sources. To get Outlook Express Help, you can use the online Help system that comes with the program or view Outlook Express Web sites on the Internet. To open Outlook Express online Help, click Help on the menu bar, then click Contents and Index. To learn more about Outlook Express from Web sites on the Internet, click Help on the menu bar, point to Microsoft on the Web, then click Product News. Internet Explorer starts and displays the Outlook Express Web site.

EXCHANGING MAIL AND NEWS

Adding a Contact to the Address Book

A **contact** is a person or company that you communicate with. One contact can have several mailing addresses, phone numbers, e-mail addresses, or Web sites. You can store this information in the **Address Book**, along with other detailed information—such as the contact's title, street address, phone number, and personal Web page addresses. When you want to create a new contact or edit an existing one, you use the Properties dialog box to enter or change contact information. You can organize your contacts into **contact groups**, which are groups of related people you communicate with regularly, or into folders. One contact group might be your family members or people at work. John wants to add a new employee to his Address Book.

Steps

1. **Click the Open the Address Book link on the Outlook Express Start Page**
   The Address Book window opens, as shown in Figure G-4, displaying the current contacts in the Address Book. Your list of contacts might differ or be empty. The Address Book toolbar is above the list of contacts. See Table G-2 for a description of each toolbar button. These commands are also available on the menus.

   > **QuickTip**
   > You can also click the Address Book button on the toolbar to open the Address Book.

2. **Click the New button on the Address Book toolbar, then click New Contact**
   The New button allows you to create new contacts, contact groups, and folders to organize contacts. The Properties dialog box opens, displaying the Name tab with empty text boxes. See Table G-3 for a description of each tab in the Properties dialog box.

   > **QuickTip**
   > To create a contact group, click the New button on the toolbar, click New Group, type a group name, click Select Members, double-click names from the Address Book, click OK, then click OK again.

3. **Type Shawn in the First text box, press [Tab] twice to move to the Last name text box, then type Brooks**
   The complete name of the new contact appears in the Display box; this is the name that will appear in the list of contacts unless you click the Display list arrow and choose a different name.

4. **Click the E-Mail Addresses text box, type shawnbrooks@course.com, then click Add**
   The e-mail address appears in the box below the E-Mail Addresses text box, as shown in Figure G-5. E-mail addresses are not case-sensitive (capitalization doesn't matter) and cannot contain spaces.

   > **QuickTip**
   > To modify an e-mail address, select it, then click Edit. To delete an e-mail address no longer in use, select it, then click Remove.

5. **Click OK**
   The Properties dialog box closes, and you return to the Address Book. Instead of opening the Properties dialog box every time you want to see a more complete listing of a contact's information, you can position the mouse pointer over a contact in the Address Book to display a ScreenTip summary of the contact's information.

6. **Position the mouse pointer over Shawn Brooks in the Address Book**
   A ScreenTip summary appears on the screen. You can move the mouse pointer to remove the ScreenTip or wait. To edit a contact, simply double-click anywhere on the contact's entry in the Address Book.

   > **QuickTip**
   > To print a phone list or business cards, click the Print button on the toolbar, click a print option, then click Print.

7. **Double-click Shawn Brooks**
   The Shawn Brooks Properties dialog box opens and displays the selected contact's information. You can use any of the tabs in this dialog box to add to or change the contact information.

8. **Click the Business tab, click the Phone text box, type 925-555-3084, then click OK**
   Shawn's business phone number appears in the Address Book.

9. **Click the Close button in the Address Book window**

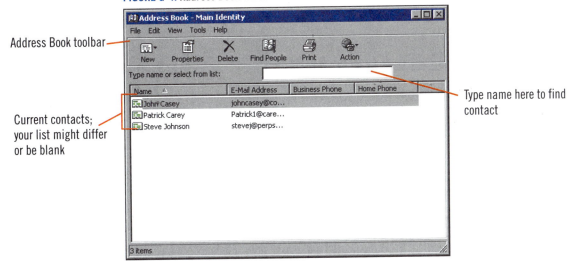

FIGURE G-4: Address Book window

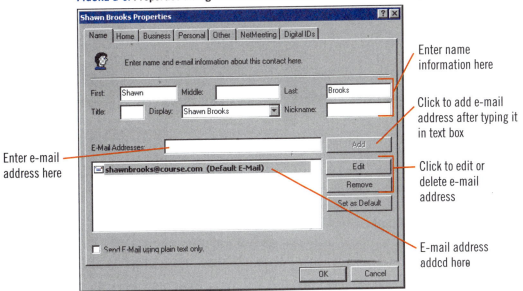

FIGURE G-5: Properties dialog box with new contract

TABLE G-2: Address Book Toolbar Buttons

button	description	button	description
	Creates a new contact, group, or folder		Finds people on the Internet
	Opens property information for the selected contact		Opens the Print dialog box
	Deletes the selected contact		Sends mail, dials a connection, or places an Internet call

TABLE G-3: New contact Properties dialog box tabs

tab	description	tab	description
Name	Enter name and e-mail information	Other	Enter notes about contact
Home	Enter information related to the contact's home	NetMeeting	Add and modify e-mail conferencing addresses and servers
Business	Enter business-related information	Digital Ids	Add, remove, and view security identification numbers for the contact
Personal	Enter personal information		

EXCHANGING MAIL AND NEWS

Composing and Sending E-mail

Unit G — Windows 98 and Me

E-mail is quickly becoming the primary form of written communication for many people. E-mail messages follow a standard memo format with fields for the sender, recipient, date, and subject of the message. To send an e-mail message, you need to enter the recipient's e-mail address, type a subject, and then type the message itself. You can send the same message to more than one individual, to a contact group, or to a combination of individuals and groups. You can personalize your e-mail messages (and newsgroup messages) with built-in stationery, or you can design your own. ➤ John wants to send an e-mail message to the new employee whose contact information he added to the Address Book in the previous lesson.

Steps

QuickTip
To create a new message without stationery, you can click the New Mail button on the toolbar, click the new Mail message link in the Outlook Express window, or double-click a name in the Contacts list.

1. **Click the New Mail button list arrow on the toolbar, click Clear Day or another available stationery, such as Ivy, then click the Maximize button**
   The New Message window opens and is maximized, as shown in Figure G-6, displaying the Clear Day stationery in the message box.

2. **Click To next to the To text box**
   The Select Recipients dialog box opens, as shown in Figure G-7, displaying the contacts from the Address Book.

QuickTip
To remove a name from the Message recipients list, click the person's name in the Message recipients list box, then press [Delete].

3. **In the list of contacts, click the down scroll arrow if necessary, click Shawn Brooks, then click To**
   The contact's name, Shawn Brooks, appears in the Message recipients list box. You can also add additional recipients to this list, select another recipient and click the Cc (carbon copy) button to send a copy of your e-mail message to that person, or click the Bcc (blind carbon copy) button to send a copy of your e-mail message to another person whose name will not appear in the e-mail message.

4. **Click OK**
   Shawn's name appears in the To text box. Shawn's e-mail address is associated with the name selected even though it does not appear. John includes a subject title.

5. **Click the Subject text box, then type Welcome aboard!**
   The message title bar changes from New Message to the subject text, "Welcome aboard!"

QuickTip
To save an incomplete message, click the Save button on the toolbar. You save the e-mail message with the name of the subject and place it in the Drafts folder.

6. **Click the text box at the bottom of the message window**
   You activate the Formatting toolbar, just below the Subject text box. The Formatting toolbar works just like the Formatting toolbar in WordPad or other Windows programs. You can use it to change the format of your message text at any time.

7. **Type Dear Shawn:, press [Enter] twice, type I would like to welcome you to the Wired Coffee Company. We are excited that you have joined our team. Wired Coffee is a growing company, and I believe your contributions will make a big difference. Please come to a luncheon for new employees this Thursday at 12:30 in the company cafe., press [Enter] twice, then type John**

QuickTip
If you don't want to send the e-mail message right now, click File on the menu bar, then click Send Later. This places the e-mail message in the Outbox but does not send it.

8. **Click the Send button on the toolbar, then click OK in the Information box, if necessary**
   The New Message window closes; the e-mail message is placed temporarily in the Outbox, a folder for storing outgoing messages; and then the e-mail is sent automatically to the recipient. A copy of the outgoing message remains in the Sent Items folder so you can reference the message later.

▶ WINDOWS 98 AND ME G-8 EXCHANGING MAIL AND NEWS

FIGURE G-6: New Message window with Clear Day stationery

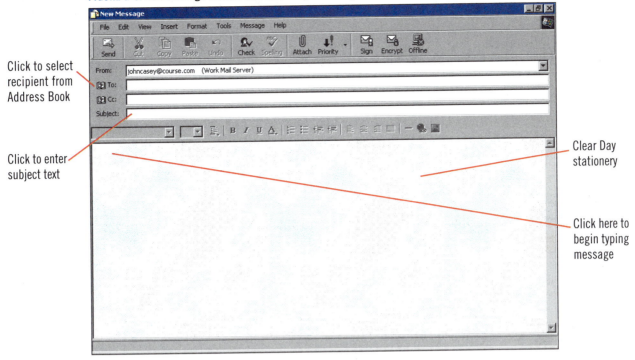

FIGURE G-7: Selecting recipients for e-mail message

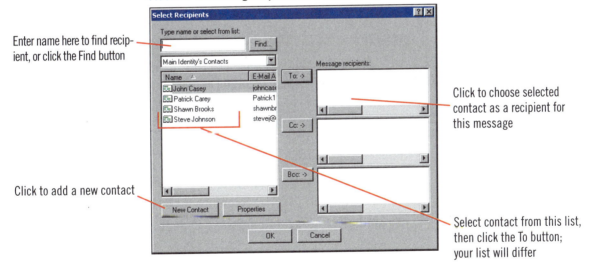

Attaching a file to an e-mail message

You can easily share files using e-mail. You can send a file, such as a picture or a document, by attaching it to an e-mail message. Upon receiving the e-mail, the recipient can open the file in the program that created it or save it on disk. For example, suppose that you are working on a report that you created using WordPad and that a colleague working in another part of the country needs to present the report today. After you finish the report, you can attach the report file to an e-mail message and send the message to your colleague, who can then open, edit, and print the report. To attach a file to an e-mail message, create the message, click the Attach button on the toolbar, navigate to the drive and folder location of the file you want to attach, select the file, then click Attach.

EXCHANGING MAIL AND NEWS

Retrieving, Reading, and Responding to E-mail

You can retrieve your e-mail manually or set Outlook Express to retrieve your messages automatically. New messages appear in the Inbox along with any messages you haven't yet stored elsewhere or deleted. One or more **message flags** may appear next to a message to indicate that the message has a certain priority, that a file is attached to it, and whether or not it has been read. See Table G-4 for a description of the message flags. John forwards an e-mail message he received from Shawn Brooks to another person at the company.

Steps

QuickTip
To check automatically for messages every few minutes, click Tools on the menu bar, click Options, then click the Check for messages option.

1. **Click the Send/Recv button on the toolbar**
   An information box displays the progress of the e-mail messages you are sending and receiving. After you send or receive your e-mail messages, the dialog box closes. When you receive new e-mail, the Inbox folder name in the Folders list is boldfaced, indicating that it contains unread messages, and a number in parentheses indicates the number of newly received e-mail messages in the folder.

QuickTip
To display the Inbox when you start Outlook Express, click the When Outlook Express starts, go directly to my Inbox check box on the Outlook Express Start Page.

2. **In the Folders list, click Inbox**
   The Inbox folder opens, as shown in Figure G-8. The **preview pane** displays the messages in your Inbox. The **display pane** displays the e-mail message selected in the preview pane. You have not opened e-mail messages in the preview pane with boldfaced subject or heading text.

3. **Click the message you received from Shawn Brooks**

Trouble?
If you didn't receive a message from Shawn Brooks, click the Send/Recv button on the toolbar again. It may take a few minutes for the message to arrive.

4. **Double-click the message you received from Shawn Brooks in the preview pane, then click the Maximize button in the message window**
   When you receive a short message, you can quickly read it by clicking the message and then reading the text in the display pane. Longer messages, like the one from Shawn Brooks, are easier to open and read in a full window. After reading a message, you can reply to the author, reply to all recipients, forward the message to another person, or simply close or delete the message. John forwards the message to his human resources administrator to ask her to add Shawn Brooks to the list of luncheon attendees. You forward the message to your instructor or technical support person or to someone else whose e-mail address you know.

5. **Click the Forward button on the message toolbar**
   The Forward Message window opens, as shown in Figure G-9, displaying the original e-mail message you sent. At the top of the message box, you can add additional text to the message.

6. **Click in the upper-left corner of the message box, then type Please add Shawn Brooks to Thursday's luncheon guest list.**

Trouble?
If you don't know an e-mail address to send the forwarded message to, click the Close button in the message window, then continue to the next lesson.

7. **Click the To text box, type the e-mail address of your instructor, technical support person, or someone else you know, then click the Send button on the toolbar**
   You send the e-mail message.

8. **Click the Address Book button on the toolbar, click Shawn Brooks, click the Delete button, click Yes, then click the Close button**
   You delete Shawn from John's Address Book.

WINDOWS 98 AND ME G-10 EXCHANGING MAIL AND NEWS

FIGURE G-8: Outlook Express window with Inbox

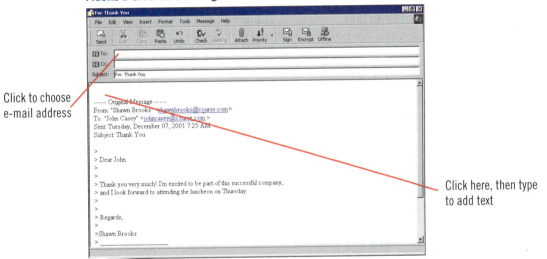

- Contents of highlighted folder in preview pane
- Contacts list; your list might differ
- Your list of messages will differ
- Preview pane
- Selected e-mail message in the display pane

FIGURE G-9: Forward Message window

- Click to choose e-mail address
- Click here, then type to add text

TABLE G-4: Mail message flag icons

icon	description	icon	description
✉	Unread message; message heading text appears bold	❗	Sender marked message as high priority
✉	Read message	↓	Sender marked message as low priority
📎	One or more files attached to message		

Printing e-mail messages and contacts

You can print your e-mail messages from any folder at any time using Outlook Express. To print an e-mail message, open the message, then click the Print button 🖨 on the toolbar. You can also open the Address Book and print contact information in a variety of formats, such as Memo, Business Card, and Phone List. The Memo style prints all the information you have for a contact with descriptive titles. The Business Card style prints the contact information without descriptive titles. The Phone List style prints all the phone numbers for a contact or for all your contacts. To print contact information, open the Address Book, select a specific contact (if desired), click 🖨 on the toolbar, select a print range, print style, and the number of copies you want to print, then click Print.

EXCHANGING MAIL AND NEWS

Managing E-mail Messages

A common problem with using e-mail is an overcrowded Inbox. To keep your Inbox organized, you should move messages you want to save to other folders and subfolders, delete messages you no longer want, and create new folders as you need them. Storing incoming messages in other folders and deleting unwanted messages makes it easier to see the new messages you receive and to keep track of messages to which you have already responded. John wants to create a new folder for his important messages in the Local Folders location, move a message from the Inbox to the new folder, and then delete the messages he no longer needs.

Steps

1. Click **File** on the menu bar, point to **New**, then click **Folder**
   The Create Folder dialog box opens, displaying the list of folders contained in the Outlook Express folder, as shown in Figure G-10.

2. Type **Important**, then click **Local Folders** in the Folders list
   You name the new folder Important, and it will appear in the Folders list under Local Folders. To create a subfolder (a folder in a folder), you select one of the folders in the Folders list under Local folders. The Folders list works like the left pane of Windows Explorer. When you create a subfolder, a plus sign (+) appears next to the name of the folder that contains the subfolder.

3. Click **OK**
   The new folder, Important, appears in the Folders list under Local Folders.

   > **QuickTip**
   > To block all messages from a sender, click a message from the sender, click Message on the menu bar, then click Block Sender.

4. In the preview pane of the Inbox, right-click the **message you received from Shawn Brooks**
   A pop-up menu appears, displaying commands, such as move, copy, delete, print, and add sender to Address Book, to help you manage your e-mail messages.

5. Click **Move To Folder** on the pop-up menu
   The Move dialog box opens, allowing you to specify the folder where you want to move the selected message.

   > **QuickTip**
   > To move a message to a folder, drag the message from the preview pane to the folder in the Folders list.

6. Click the **Important folder**, then click **OK**

7. In the Folders list, click the **Important folder**
   The e-mail message you just moved appears in the preview and display panes, as shown in Figure G-11.

   > **QuickTip**
   > To sort messages by sender, subject, date, priority or flag, click a header in the preview pane.

8. In the Folders list, right-click the **Important folder**, click **Delete**, then click **Yes**
   You place the Important folder in the Deleted Items folder. The Delete Items folder works just like the Recycle Bin. The folder temporarily stores deleted messages until you automatically or manually delete them.

9. In the Folders list, right-click the **Deleted Items folder**, click **Empty 'Deleted Items' Folder**, then click **Yes**
   You permanently delete the Important folder and all of its contents.

FIGURE G-10: Create Folder dialog box

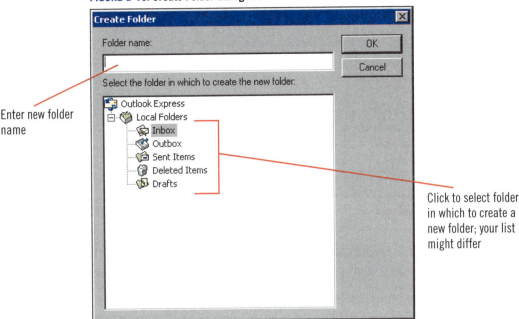

Enter new folder name

Click to select folder in which to create a new folder; your list might differ

FIGURE G-11: Important folder

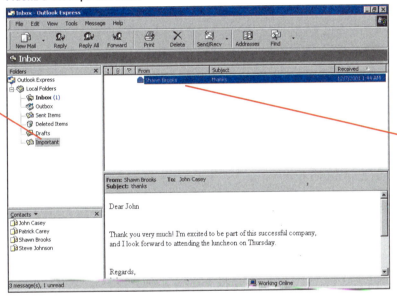

Click to display contents of folder

Right-click to display a pop-up menu of file management commands

Diverting incoming e-mail to folders

Outlook Express can direct incoming messages that meet criteria to other folders in the Folders list rather than to your Inbox. Let's say that your friend loves sending you funny e-mail, but you often don't have time to read it right away. You can set message rules to store any messages you receive from your friend in a different folder so they won't clutter your Inbox. When you are ready to read the messages, you simply open the folder and access the messages just as you would messages in the Inbox. To set criteria for incoming messages, click Tools on the menu bar, point to Message Rules, then click Mail. If the New Mail Rule dialog box opens, no previous message rules exist. Otherwise, the Message Rules dialog box opens; click New to create a new message rule. The New Mail Rule dialog box opens. Select the conditions for your rule, select the actions for your rule, click any undefined value (such as the e-mail address you want to divert and the folder where you want to store the diverted messages) and provide information, type a name to identify the rule, then click OK.

EXCHANGING MAIL AND NEWS WINDOWS 98 AND ME G-13

Windows 98 and Me

Selecting a News Server

A newsgroup is an electronic forum where people from around the world with a common interest can share ideas, ask and answer questions, and comment on and discuss any subject. You can find newsgroups on almost any topic, from the serious to the lighthearted, from educational to controversial, from business to social. Before you can participate in a newsgroup, you must select a news server. A **news server** is a computer located on the Internet, which stores newsgroup messages, also called **articles**, on different topics. Each news server contains several newsgroups from which to choose. The Internet Connection Wizard walks you through the process of selecting a news server. This wizard also appears the first time you use Outlook Express News. To complete the wizard process and the steps in this lesson, you need to get the name of the news server you want to use from your instructor, technical support person, or Internet service provider (ISP), and possibly an account name and password. John wants to add a news server account so he can access coffee-related newsgroups.

Steps

Trouble?
If you have not already selected a news server, the Internet Connection Wizard opens. Skip to Step 4 to complete the wizard. If you already have a news server, continue to Step 2.

QuickTip
To add a new e-mail account, click Add, click Mail, then follow the Internet Connection Wizard instructions.

QuickTip
To change a news server name, right-click the news server in the Folders list, click Properties, type a name in the News Accounts text box, then click OK.

1. In the Folders list, click Outlook Express, then click the **Read News link** or click the **Set up a Newsgroups account link** in the Outlook Express Start Page

2. Click **Tools** on the menu bar, click **Accounts**, then click the **News tab**
   The Internet Accounts dialog box opens, as shown in Figure G-12, displaying the News tab with your list of available news servers. Using the Internet Accounts dialog box, you can add, remove, and view properties for news servers, mail servers, and directory services.

3. Click **Add**, then click **News**
   The Internet Connection Wizard dialog box opens.

4. Type your **name**, if necessary, then click **Next**
   The name you enter appears in messages you post to a newsgroup.

5. Type your **e-mail address**, if necessary, then click **Next**
   Individuals participating in the newsgroup need to know your e-mail address so they can reply to your news messages, either by posting another news message or by sending you an e-mail message.

6. Type the **name of the news server** provided by your instructor, technical support person, or ISP, as shown in Figure G-13, then click **Next**

7. Click **Finish**, click **Close** if the Internet Accounts dialog box opens, then click **No** to download a list of available newsgroups
   The news server name appears in the Folders list, as shown in Figure G-14. You view a list of available newsgroups in the next lesson.

FIGURE G-12: Internet Accounts dialog box

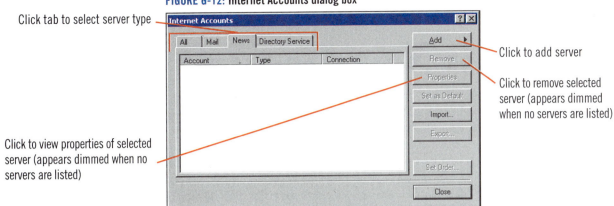

Click tab to select server type

Click to add server

Click to remove selected server (appears dimmed when no servers are listed)

Click to view properties of selected server (appears dimmed when no servers are listed)

FIGURE G-13: Internet Connection Wizard dialog box

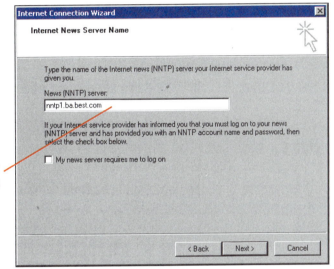

Enter news server here; your news server probably differs from this one

FIGURE G-14: Outlook Express window with news servers

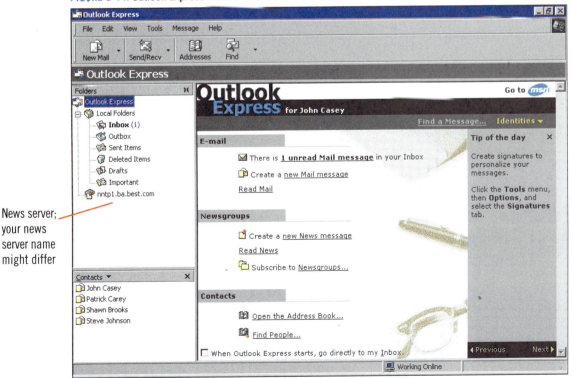

News server; your news server name might differ

EXCHANGING MAIL AND NEWS

Viewing and Subscribing to a Newsgroup

When you add a news server account to Outlook Express, it retrieves a list of newsgroups available on that server. Often this list is quite lengthy. Rather than scroll through the entire list looking for a particular topic, you can have Outlook Express search the list for that topic. Similarly, you can search all the messages you retrieve from a newsgroup for a particular message. Once you select a newsgroup, you can merely view its contents, or, if you expect to return to the newsgroup often, you can subscribe to it. Subscribing to a newsgroup places a link to the group in the news server folder in your Outlook Express Folders list, providing easy access to the newsgroup. ✒ John wants to find and subscribe to a newsgroup for coffee drinkers, so he can keep track of what people want from a coffee company.

Steps

1. Click the **Read News link** in the Outlook Express Start Page, then click **Yes** if necessary, to view a list of available newsgroups
   The Newsgroups Subscriptions dialog box opens, as shown in Figure G-15, displaying news servers on the left (if more than one exists) and related newsgroups on the right.

2. In the News server list, click the **news server you added in the previous lesson** if necessary
   A list of the newsgroups you subscribe to appears in the preview pane. Your list might be empty.

   > **QuickTip**
   > To subscribe to a newsgroup, double-click it in the Newsgroup Subscriptions dialog box.

3. Type **coffee** in the Display Newsgroups which contain text box
   Newsgroups related to coffee appear in the News groups list box, as shown in Figure G-16.

4. Scroll if necessary, click the newsgroup **rec.food.drink.coffee** (if available), or click a different newsgroup from your list, then click **Go To**
   The newsgroup name you choose appears selected in the Folders list, and the newsgroup messages appear in the preview pane of the Outlook Express window, as shown in Figure G-17. John thinks this newsgroup looks promising, so he decides to subscribe to it.

   > **QuickTip**
   > To download new newsgroup messages, click the newsgroup in the Folders list, then click Synchronize Account.

5. Right-click the **newsgroup name** in the Folders list, then click **Subscribe**
   The number of newsgroup messages appears next to the newsgroup name in the Folders list. The icon next to the newsgroup changes from gray to color to indicate the subscription is complete.

Filtering unwanted newsgroup messages

After you become familiar with a newsgroup, you might decide that you don't want to retrieve messages from a particular person, about a specific subject, of a certain length, or older than a certain number of days. This is called filtering newsgroup messages. To filter unwanted messages, click Tools on the menu bar, point to Message Rules, then click News. If the New News Rule dialog box opens, no previous message rules exist. Otherwise, the Message Rules dialog box opens; click New to create a new message rule. The New News Rule dialog box opens. Select the conditions for your rule, select the actions for your rule, click any undefined value (such as the e-mail address you want to divert and the folder where you want to store the unwanted messages), provide the information, type a name for the rule, then click OK.

FIGURE G-15: Newsgroup dialog box

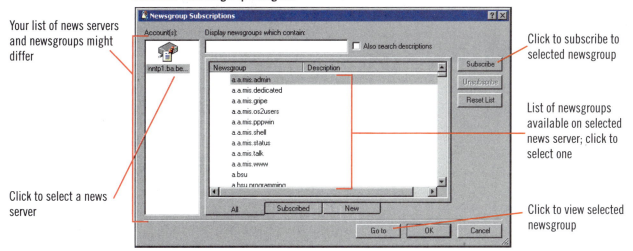

Your list of news servers and newsgroups might differ

Click to select a news server

Click to subscribe to selected newsgroup

List of newsgroups available on selected news server; click to select one

Click to view selected newsgroup

FIGURE G-16: List of newsgroups relating to coffee

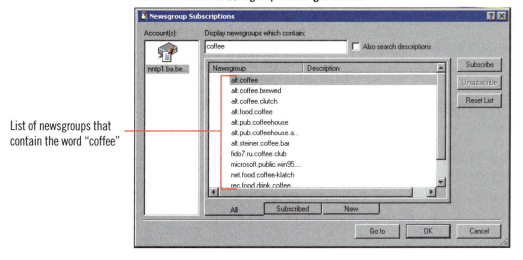

List of newsgroups that contain the word "coffee"

FIGURE G-17: Outlook Express window with newsgroup

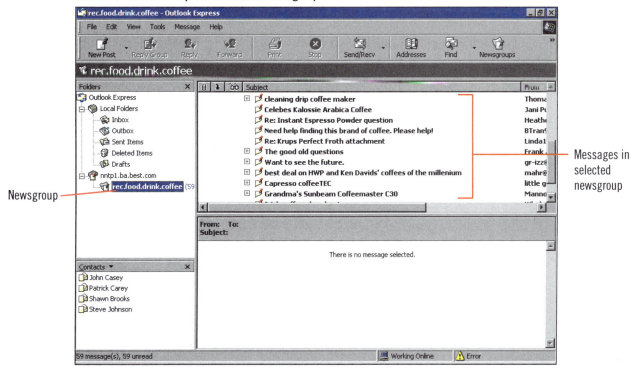

Newsgroup

Messages in selected newsgroup

Reading and Posting News Messages

After retrieving new newsgroup messages, you can read them. Newsgroup messages appear in the preview pane, just as e-mail messages do. To view a newsgroup message in the display pane, click the title of the message in the preview pane. If a plus sign (+) in a box appears to the left of a newsgroup message, then the message contains a conversation thread. A **conversation thread** consists of the original message on a particular topic along with any responses that include the original message. To read the responses, click the + to display the message titles, and then click the title of the message you want to read. John decides to read some of the messages in the newsgroup. When he finishes, he restores his news server settings by unsubscribing from this newsgroup and removing the news server from the Folders list.

Steps

Trouble?
If a newsgroup message has no +, click a message without a +, then skip to Step 3.

1. Click a **newsgroup message** in the preview pane with a **+** to the left of the title, then read the message in the display pane
   The newsgroup message appears in the display pane.

2. Click the **+** next to the newsgroup message
   The titles of the responses to the original message appear under the original newsgroup message, as shown in Figure G-18.

QuickTip
To view only unread messages, click View on the menu bar, point to Current View, then click Hide Read Messages.

3. Click **each reply message under the original message**, and read the reply
   As you read each message, you can choose to compose a new message, send a reply message to everyone viewing the newsgroup (known as posting), send a reply message to the author's private e-mail address (rather than posting it on the newsgroup), or forward the message to another person.

4. After reading the last reply message, click the **Reply Group button** on the toolbar, then click the **Maximize button** if necessary

QuickTip
To see the exchange of messages and replies, click a message in the thread, click Message on the menu bar, then click Watch Conversation.

5. Type a response to the newsgroup message, as shown in Figure G-19

6. Click the **Send button** on the toolbar, then click **OK**
   Your reply message appears in the preview pane along with the other replies to the original message. Everyone viewing the newsgroup can download and read your response.

7. Right-click the **newsgroup** in the Folders list, click **Unsubscribe**, then click **OK** (if necessary, click No to subscribe to the Newsgroup, and click No to view a list of newsgroups)

8. Right-click the **news server** in the Folders list, click **Remove Account**, then click **Yes**

9. Click **File** on the menu bar, click **Exit**, then click **Yes** if necessary to disconnect from the Internet

FIGURE G-18: Reading a newsgroup message

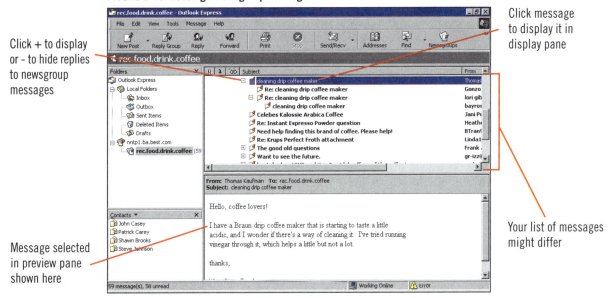

- Click + to display or − to hide replies to newsgroup messages
- Click message to display it in display pane
- Your list of messages might differ
- Message selected in preview pane shown here

FIGURE G-19: Posting a newsgroup message

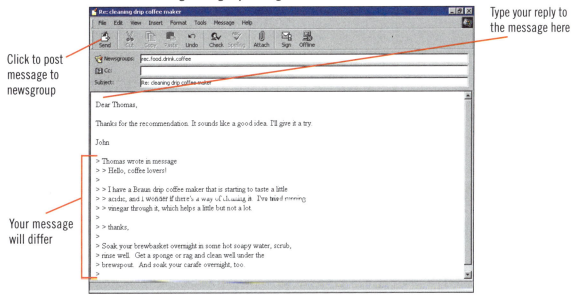

- Click to post message to newsgroup
- Type your reply to the message here
- Your message will differ

Deleting old news messages

Your hard drive stores newsgroup messages, so you should delete unneeded messages to free disk space. Outlook Express gives several clean-up options to help you optimize your hard drive space. You can delete entire messages (titles and bodies), compress messages, remove just the message bodies (leaving the title headers), or reset the information stored for selected messages, which allows you to refresh messages (download again). To clean up files on your local hard drive, select a news server in the Folders list, click Tools on the menu bar, click Options, then click the Maintenance tab. You can select any of the clean-up options to delete or compress news messages at a specified time, or click Clean Up Now, then click the button for the clean-up option you want to perform now.

EXCHANGING MAIL AND NEWS

Windows 98 and Me

Practice

▶ Concepts Review

Label each element of the screen shown in Figure G-20.

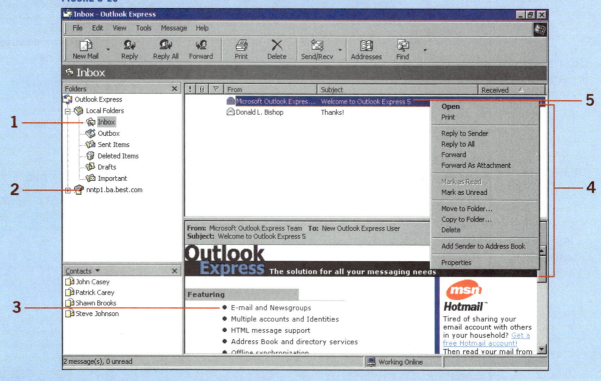

FIGURE G-20

Match each term with the statement that describes its function.

6. Message flag
7. Outlook Express Start Page
8. Message Rules
9. Outlook Express window
10. News server

a. A computer on the Internet that stores articles
b. Displays e-mail and newsgroups
c. An icon that indicates e-mail to folders
d. Diverts selected incoming e-mail status
e. Jumps to folders and opens tools

Select the best answers from the lists of choices.

11. The location that allows you to jump to folders and open tools is called the:
   a. Outlook Express window.
   b. Outlook Express Start Page.
   c. Folders list.
   d. Outlook Express Link Page.

12. To compose a message, you can:
   a. Click the new Mail message link.
   b. Click New Mail button on the toolbar.
   c. Click Message on the menu bar, then click New Message.
   d. All of the above.

▶ WINDOWS 98 AND ME G-20   EXCHANGING MAIL AND NEWS

Practice

13. **A contact is a:**
    a. Person you communicate with.
    b. Mailing address.
    c. Newsgroup.
    d. Program.
14. **When you click the Send button on the toolbar in the New Message window, you first send an e-mail message to the:**
    a. E-mail address.
    b. Outbox.
    c. Internet.
    d. Cc and Bcc addresses.
15. ✉ **indicates that the message has:**
    a. Not been read.
    b. Been read.
    c. One or more files attached to it.
    d. Been marked as low priority by the sender.

▶ Skills Review

1. **Start Outlook Express and explore the Outlook Express window.**
   a. Connect to the Internet.
   b. Click the Launch Outlook Express button on the Quick Launch toolbar.
   c. Identify the title bar, menu bar, toolbar, Internet Explorer link, Folders list, Read Mail link, Read News link, new Mail message link, Open the Address Book link, Find People link, and status bar.
   d. On the toolbar, identify icons for opening the Address Book, sending and receiving e-mail messages, composing a message, and finding a message.
   e. If necessary, enter your user name and password, then click Connect.
2. **Add a contact to the Address Book.**
   a. Click the Address Book button.
   b. Click the New button, then click New Contact.
   c. Type **John** in the First name text box, press [Tab] twice, then type **Asher**.
   d. Click in the E-Mail Addresses text box, then type **JohnA@course.com**.
   e. Click Add, then click OK.
   f. Click the Close button.
3. **Compose and send e-mail.**
   a. Click the New Mail button, then click the Maximize button if necessary.
   b. Click the To button.
   c. Click the name John Asher.
   d. Click To, then click OK.
   e. Click the Subject text box, then type **Financial Update Request**.
   f. Press [Tab] to move to the message window, then type **John: Please send 2001 year-end financial report ASAP. Thanks**.
   g. Click the Send button.
4. **Retrieve, read, and respond to e-mail.**
   a. Click the Send/Recv button. It may take a few minutes before you receive a message from John Asher.
   b. In the Folders list, click Inbox.
   c. Click the message you just received from John Asher.
   d. Click the Forward Message button, then click the Maximize button if necessary.
   e. Click the To text box, then enter your e-mail address.

Windows 98 and Me | Practice

    f. Enter a response in the message window.
    g. Click the Send button.
5. **Manage e-mail messages.**
    a. Click File on the menu bar, point to New, then click Folder.
    b. Type **Archive**.
    c. Click Local Folders in the Folders list, then click OK.
    d. Right-click the message received from John Asher, then click Move To Folder on the shortcut menu.
    e. Click Archive, then click OK.
    f. In the Folders list, click the Archive folder.
    g. Right-click the message received from John Asher, then click Delete on the shortcut menu.
    h. Right-click the Archive folder, click Delete, then click Yes.
    i. Click the Address Book button.
    j. Click John Asher, click the Delete button, then click Yes.
    k. Click the Close button.
6. **Select a news server.**
    a. In the Folders list, click Outlook Express.
    b. Click the Read News link or the Set up a Newsgroup account link.
    c. If the Internet Connection Wizard appears, skip to Step e. Otherwise, click Tools on the menu bar, click Accounts, then click News tab.
    d. Click Add, then click News.
    e. Type your name, then click Next.
    f. Type your e-mail address, then click Next.
    g. Type the name of a news server (see your instructor, technical support person, or ISP for a name), then click Next.
    h. Click Finish, click Close if necessary, then click No.
7. **View and subscribe to a newsgroup.**
    a. Click the Read News link, then click Yes if necessary.
    b. In the News server list, click the news server you just added (if available).
    c. Type **caffeine**. (If no items appear, type **tea** or **chocolate**.)
    d. Click a newsgroup.
    e. Click Go To.
    f. Right-click the newsgroup in the Folders list, then click Subscribe.
8. **Read and post a news message.**
    a. Click a newsgroup message with a +.
    b. Click the + next to the newsgroup message.
    c. Click and read each reply.
    d. Click the Reply Group button, then type a response.
    e. Click the Send button, then click OK.
    f. Right-click the newsgroup in the Folders list, click Unsubscribe, then click OK.
    g. Right-click the news server in the Folders list, click Remove Account, then click Yes.
    h. Click File on the menu bar, click Exit, then click Yes if necessary to disconnect.

▶ Independent Challenges

1. You are a new lawyer at Bellig & Associates. You have a computer with Windows 2000 and Outlook Express. Because e-mail is an important method of communication at the law firm, you want to start Outlook Express, open the Address Book, and enter colleagues' e-mail addresses.

    To complete this independent challenge:
    a. Start Outlook Express, then open the Address Book.

Practice

   b. Enter the following names and e-mail addresses:
      Greg Bellig   gregb@bellig_law.com
      Jacob Bellig   jacobb@bellig_law.com
      Jarod Higgins   jarodh@bellig_law.com
   c. Print the Address Book in both the Business Card and Memo styles.
   d. Delete the names and e-mail addresses you just entered in the Address Book.

2. As president of Auto Metals, you just negotiated a deal to export metal auto parts to an assembly plant in China. Your lawyer, Josh Higgins, drew up a preliminary contract. You want to send Josh an e-mail indicating the terms of the deal so he can finish the contract. When Josh responds, move the e-mail into the Legal folder.

STOP If you do not have a connection to the Internet, ask your instructor or technical support person for help completing this challenge.

To complete this independent challenge:
   a. Open a New Message window using the stationery called Technical.
   b. Type **jhiggins@course.com** in the To text box in the message window, and type **China Deal Contract** in the Subject text box.
   c. Enter the following message:
      Dear Josh,
      I have completed the negotiations with the assembly plant. Please modify the following terms in the contract:
      1. All parts shall be inspected before shipping.
      2. Ship 10,000 units a month for 3 years with an option for 2 more years.
      Sincerely yours,
      [your name]
   d. Send the e-mail.
   e. Print the e-mail you receive from Josh Higgins.
   f. Create a new folder called Legal, then move the e-mail message you received from Josh Higgins to the new folder.
   g. Delete the Legal folder.

3. You are a legal assistant at a law firm specializing in international law. Your boss asks you to research international contracts with China. You decide to start your research with newsgroups on the Internet.

To complete this independent challenge:
   a. Select a news server. (See your instructor, technical support person, or ISP to obtain a news server.)
   b. Subscribe to a newsgroup about China, then read several newsgroup messages and replies.
   c. Reply to a message, then post a new message.
   d. Print the newsgroup messages, including the original message and replies.
   e. Unsubscribe to the newsgroup, then remove the newsgroup server.

4. You like to play sports, watch sports, read about sports, and talk about sports all the time, so you decide to join a sports newsgroup.

To complete this independent challenge:
   a. Select a news server. (See your instructor, technical support person, or ISP to obtain a news server.)
   b. Subscribe to a newsgroup about sports, then read several newsgroup messages and replies.
   c. Reply to a message, then post a new message.
   d. Print the newsgroup messages, including the original message and replies.
   e. Unsubscribe to the newsgroup, then remove the newsgroup server.

Windows 98 and Me | **Practice**

▶ Visual Workshop

Re-create the screen shown in Figure G-21, which displays the Outlook Express window with a message that has been sent. Print the Outlook Express window. (To print the screen, press [Print Screen], open Paint, click File on the menu bar, click Paste to paste the screen into Paint, then click Yes to paste the large image if necessary. Click File on the menu bar, click Print, then click Print in the Print dialog box.)

FIGURE G-21

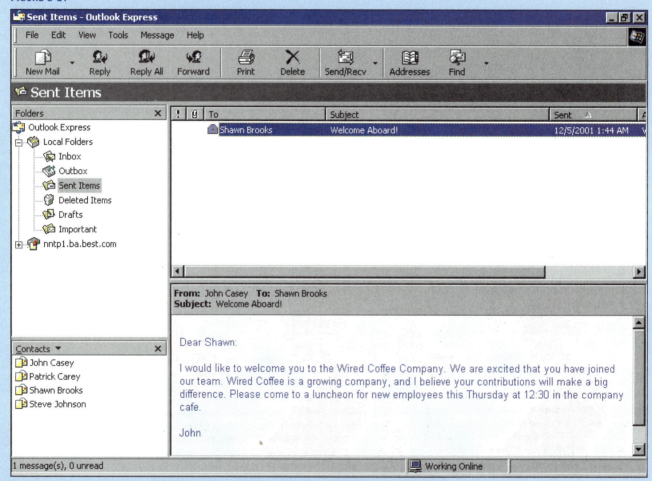

Windows 98 and Me

Managing
Shared Files Using a Network

Objectives

- ▶ Understand network services
- ▶ Examine network computer properties
- ▶ Open and view a network
- ▶ Create a shared folder
- ▶ Map a network drive
- ▶ Copy and move shared files
- ▶ Open and edit a shared file
- ▶ Disconnect a network drive

 If you are not connected to a network, you can not work through the steps in this unit; however, you can read the lessons without completing the steps to learn what is possible in a network environment.

Windows 98 includes **Network Neighborhood** and Windows Me includes My **Network Places**, a powerful tool for managing files and folders across a network. A **network** is a system of two or more computers connected together to share resources. Network Neighborhood (98) or My Network Places (Me) is integrated with Windows Explorer, allowing you to view the entire network and to share files and folders with people from other parts of the network. In this unit John Casey uses network tools to manage files and folders for use by multiple users on the Wired Coffee Company network.

Windows 98 and Me

Understanding Network Services

Windows is a secure, reliable network operating system that allows people using many different computers to share programs, files, folders, and printers that are stored on computers other than their own. A single computer, called a **server**, can be designated to store these resources. Other computers on the network, called **clients** or **workstations**, can access the resources on the server instead of having to store them. You can share resources using two or more client computers, or you can designate one computer to serve specifically as the server. If the network computers are close together, the network is called a **local area network**, or **LAN**. If the computers are spread over a wider area, the network is called a **wide area network**, or **WAN**. To connect multiple computers at a central location, you can use a **hub**. When data arrives at one port of the hub, it is copied to the other ports so that all connected network devices see the data. **File sharing** allows many people to work on the same files without needing to create or store multiple copies. John realizes there are many benefits to using the Wired Coffee network to manage files and folders:

 Share central resources through client/server networking

Windows provides the option of using a setup called **client/server networking**. Under this arrangement, a single computer is designated as a server, allowing access to resources for any qualified user. Client/server networking provides all users on a network a central location for accessing shared files. Figure H-1 shows an example of a typical network configuration.

 Share resources through peer-to-peer networking

The Windows network operating system also offers a network configuration called peer-to-peer networking. **Peer-to-peer networking** enables two or more computers to link together without designating a central server. In this configuration, any computer user can access resources stored on any other computer, as long as those resources aren't restricted. Peer-to-peer networking allows individual computer users to share files and other resources, such as a printer, with other users on the network. Using peer-to-peer networking, you can transfer files from one computer directly to another without having to access a server.

 Share resources through network and dial-up connections

Windows provides connectivity between your computer and a network, another computer, or the Internet using Network and Dial-up Connections. **Network and Dial-up Connections** enables you to access network resources, whether you are physically connected using a direct cable or remotely connected using a modem. You can connect securely to a network over the Internet using a **Virtual Private Network** connection. You can also connect your computer to another computer or network by having another computer call your computer. For example, you can enable your home computer to access your office computer.

 Grant permission to share designated files and folders on your machine with other users

Windows provides support for security, so that even though your computer is connected to a network, you can designate which resources on your computer you want to share with others on the network. Before being able to take advantage of any resources on your computer, other users must be granted the required permission.

 Map drives on your machine that let you share the resources of another client or server

If you have rights to share resources on another computer, Windows includes a method for connecting automatically to the other computer. You can add a drive letter to your computer that is automatically linked to the shared folder on the other computer every time you log on.

FIGURE H-1: Typical client/server network

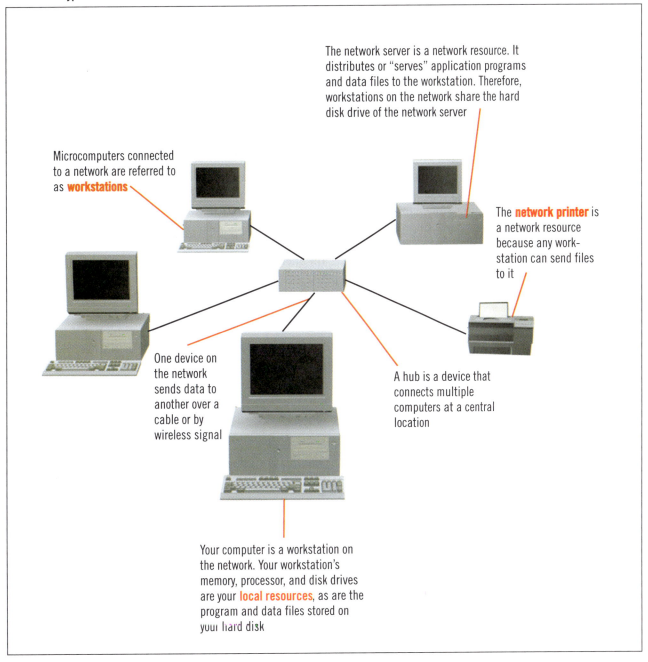

File permission properties

Every file in the Windows file system includes **permissions** for each user, or settings that designate what each user can and cannot do to each file. Two basic types of file permissions are available for users: read and full. **Read permission** allows the user to open and view the file but not to make changes that can be saved in the file. When you open a read-only file, the words "Read Only" appear in the title bar. You can makes changes, but an error message appears when you try to save the file. You can save the file with a new name in a different location (and have full access to it). **Full permission** allows the user to edit and save changes to the file (or "write") and execute programs on server or client computers. Qualified users or system administrators use file permissions and passwords to control who can access any specific area of the network. In this way, the network remains secure against unauthorized use.

Examining Network Computer Properties

Names and locations identify computers on networks. The computer's name refers to the individual machine, whereas the computer's location refers to how the machine is grouped together with other computers. In a peer-to-peer network, individual computers are often organized into workgroups. A **workgroup** is a group of computers that performs common tasks or belongs to users who share common duties and interests. In a client/server network, individual computers are often grouped into domains. A **domain** is a collection of computers that the person managing the network creates to group together computers used for the same tasks and to simplify the set up and maintenance of the network. The difference between a domain and a workgroup is that the network administrator defines the domains that exist on the network and controls access to computers within those domains. In a workgroup, each user determines who has access to his or her computer. Computers anywhere on the network can be located easily through the naming hierarchy and can be addressed individually by name. You can find the name and workgroup or domain of a computer on the network by examining the network computer properties. John decides to check the properties of his network computer.

QuickTip
To display network properties, you can also double-click the Network icon in the Control Panel.

1. Right-click the **Network Neighborhood icon** (98) or **My Network Places icon** (Me) on the desktop, then click **Properties**
   The network dialog box for your network computer opens with the Configuration tab in front, as shown in Figure H-2.

2. Click **File and Print Sharing**
   The File and Print Sharing dialog box opens. Before you can use your computer on a network, you need to make sure the file and print sharing option is selected.

3. Click the **I want to be able to give others access to my files check box** to select it, if necessary
   Now you can share files on your computer with other users on the network. If you are working in a lab, check with your administrator before setting up your computer for networking.

4. Click **OK**
   The network dialog box opens.

5. Click the **Identification tab**
   The Identification tab appears, displaying the network computer name at the top, as shown in Figure H-3. The domain or workgroup name appears below the network computer name. In this case, the network computer name is JOHNCASEY and the workgroup name is NETONE.

6. Click **Cancel**
   The network dialog box closes.

FIGURE H-2: Configuration tab in the Network dialog box

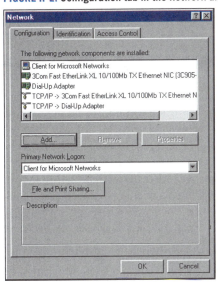

FIGURE H-3: Identification tab in the Network dialog box

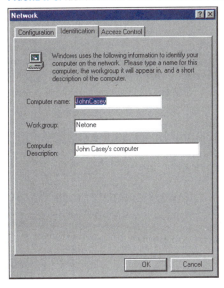

Viewing network properties

A computer that uses a Windows network must be configured so that other machines on the network recognize it. On a small network, you might be responsible for configuring your computer or that responsibility might fall to the network administrator. You can view and modify some of the network settings for your computer using the Network and Dial-up Connections dialog box. In the Control Panel, double-click the network icon to display the network settings. The network dialog box opens displaying the configuration tab. The network configuration consists of four components: adapter, protocol, service, and binding. The **adapter** is a device that connects your computer to the network. Adapters are usually cards, called **network interface cards**, or **NICs**, inserted in a slot in the back of your computer. To display the name of your NIC, click the Local Area Connection icon in the Network and Dial-up Connections window. **Protocol** is the language that the computer uses to communicate with other computers on the network. The **service** allows you to share your computer resources, such as files and printers, with other networked computers. A **binding** is a connection that enables communications among the adapters, protocols, and services installed in Windows. Understanding which components are installed on your computer helps you understand the capabilities and limitations of your computer on the network.

Opening and Viewing a Network

The key to managing files and folders in a network environment is understanding the structure of your particular network. Most networks consist of multiple types of computers and operating systems. Network Neighborhood (98) and My Network Places (Me) let you view the entire network or just your part of the network to give you access to the servers, domains, and workgroups on the network. The Entire Network window allows you to view a list of servers not in your workgroup and to view other network domains. If you want to add a server to your workgroup, you can use the Add Network Place Wizard (Me) to help you through the process. John uses Windows networking to see where his computer fits with all the others on his network.

QuickTip
To search for a computer on the network (Me), double-click the My Network Places icon, click Search on the toolbar, type the name of the computer you want to find, then click Search Now.

1. **Double-click the Network Neighborhood icon (98) or My Network Places (Me) on the desktop, then click the Maximize button in the window if necessary**
   The icon is usually right below the My Computer icon on the desktop. The Windows networking window opens, as shown in Figure H-4, and displays icons for all of the active computers in John's immediate network (including an icon for his own computer) and an icon for the Entire Network. John's immediate network is currently running server and client computers.

2. **Double-click the Entire Network icon if available (if not, skip to Step 4)**
   Windows networking displays the various segments and computers connected to John's network, as shown in Figure H-5. If you are on a large network, you might have other choices that display more segments of the network.

3. **Click the Back button on the toolbar**
   The Network window again displays the active computers in John's immediate neighborhood. John decides to view the contents of a computer connected to his network.

4. **Double-click a network computer icon in your immediate network**
   The computer connected to your network opens and displays the contents of the drive or folder.

5. **Click on the toolbar**
   The Network window again displays the active computers in John's immediate neighborhood.

▶ WINDOWS 98 AND ME H-6   MANAGING SHARED FILES USING A NETWORK

FIGURE H-4: My Network Places Windows (Me)

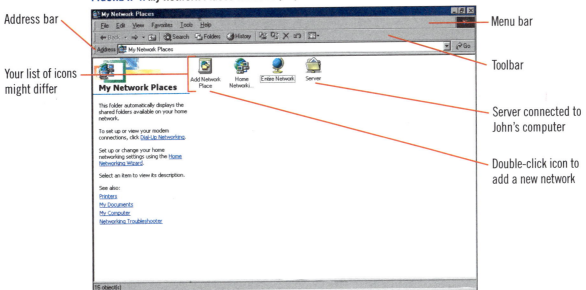

FIGURE H-5: Entire Network window

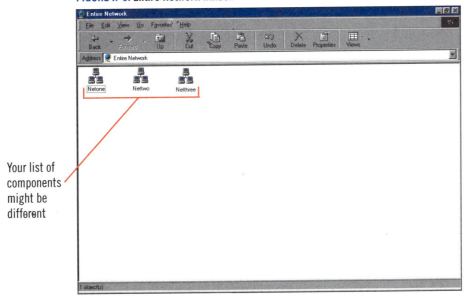

Setting up a network at home

If you have more than one computer in your home, you can use Home Networking (Me) to share files, printers, and an Internet connection among your computers. The Home Networking Wizard helps you to set up Home Networking on computers in your home. Before you can use the Home Networking Wizard, you need to assemble, connect, and install the following network components: two or more computers for a network, the cables or media used to connect your computers, a network interface card or NIC to physically connect your computer to the network, the Windows networking software needed to enable your devices to communicate with each other, an optional Internet connection, which includes the hardware and wiring necessary to access the Internet, and an optional hub, which connects multiple computers at a central location. You may already have many of these components installed. To set up a home network, double-click the My Network Places icon, double-click the Home Networking icon, then follow the step-by-step Wizard instructions to access the Internet connection, enter computer and workgroup names, select file and printer sharing options, and create a Home Networking Setup disk.

MANAGING SHARED FILES USING A NETWORK

Creating a Shared Folder

To create a shared folder, you use many of the file management skills you learned with Windows Explorer. You must first decide where you will put the new folder. If you are working at your own computer, you might create the shared folder in a subfolder within your My Documents folder. Otherwise, you may have to ask your instructor or technical support person for permission to create a folder in another location, or you can simply follow the steps without actually creating a folder. If you are not working in a network environment, you may not be able to complete these steps. In this case, simply read the steps without completing them. ➤ John has decided to create a shared folder called Sales on his computer that will allow employees from anywhere on the network to add information to Sales files.

Steps

1. **Click the Address list arrow on the Address bar**
   The window displays the desktop and drives of your computer. You can now work with the files and folders from your computer and still have the option of connecting to various other parts of the network.

2. **Click Hard Disk (C:)** (or the name and drive letter assigned to your hard drive), then double-click the **My Documents folder** (98 or Me) or click the **My Documents link** in the left pane (Me)
   The window displays the contents of the My Documents folder on your hard drive.

3. **Right-click** anywhere in the My Documents window (except on a file or folder), point to **New**, then click **Folder**
   A new folder, named New Folder, appears in the window.

4. **Type Sales, then press [Enter]**
   The folder is now named Sales.

   Trouble?
   If the Sharing command is not available, double-click the Network icon in the Control Panel, click File and Print Sharing, then click the I want to be able to give others access to my files check box.

5. **Click File on the menu bar, then click Sharing**
   The Sales Properties dialog box opens. The Sales Properties dialog box is where you adjust the settings to allow other users access to the files in your shared folder. The Sharing tab allows you to designate the kind of access you want other users to have for the folder you just created.

6. **Click the Shared As option button**
   Figure H-6 shows the sharing information about the Sales folder. The sharing tab includes a text box for entering the shared name of the folder. Unless you have a very good reason for naming it differently, it's best to make the shared name the same as the folder name. Keeping the names consistent helps to avoid confusion. By default, Windows automatically enters the name of the folder as the shared name and sets the file permission to read-only. John wants to give full access to other users with some password protection.

7. **Click the Full option button**
   John wants to add password protection to the Sales folder.

8. **Click the Full Access Password text box**, then type **Beans**

9. **Click OK** to close the Sales Properties dialog box
   The Password Confirmation dialog box opens, asking you to retype the password.

10. **Type Beans, then click OK**
    Anyone with the right password can now access the Sales folder, shown in Figure H-7, from anywhere on the network. The 📁 icon, a folder with a hand underneath, indicates the folder is a shared folder.

▶ WINDOWS 98 AND ME H-8   **MANAGING SHARED FILES USING A NETWORK**

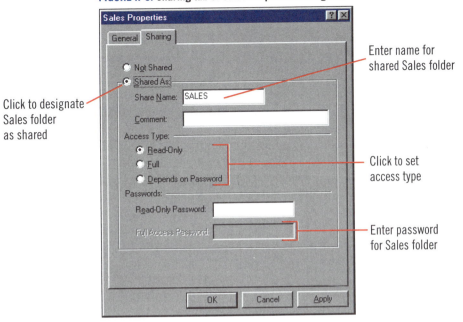

FIGURE H-6: Sharing tab of Sales Properties dialog box

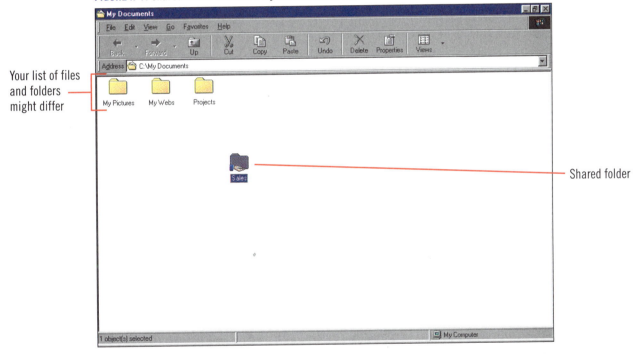

FIGURE H-7: Shared folder within the My Documents folder

Password protection

With Windows, you can use passwords to control access to your computer, the network, and specific files and folders. You can set different passwords and varying degrees of access for the different drives, folders, and files. You can also manage your files and printers from a remote computer and set password protection to limit access. To set or change password protection in Windows, open the Control Panel and double-click the Passwords icon. You can also use the Power Management (98) or Power Options (Me) utility in the Control Panel to password protect your computer when it's in Sleep mode or use the Display utility to password protect files when it's in screen saver mode.

MANAGING SHARED FILES USING A NETWORK

Mapping a Network Drive

Windows networking enables you to connect your computer to other computers on the network quite easily. If you connect to a network location frequently, you might want to designate a drive letter on your computer as a direct connection to a shared drive or folder on another computer. Instead of spending unnecessary time opening Network Neighborhood (98) or My Network Places (Me) and the shared drive or folder each time you want to access it, you can create a direct connection, called **mapping** a drive, to the network location for quick and easy access. At John's request, the network administrator creates a shared folder called Wired Coffee on the computer named Server. Now John uses Network Neighborhood or My Network Places to map a drive letter from his computer to that folder so that he can easily move files to this central location for others to share. To complete these steps, you need to map to a network computer and a folder specified by your instructor or technical support person.

Steps

Trouble?
Before beginning, ask your instructor which networked computer you can map onto your computer. If you do not have a networked computer available, read the steps without completing them.

1. **Click the Address list arrow, then click Network Neighborhood (98) or My Network Places (Me) (scroll down if necessary)**
   Windows networking shows all the active computers in your immediate network.

2. **Double-click the networked computer icon supplied by your instructor or technical support person**
   John opens the networked computer called Server. The window for the networked computer opens and displays the folders available for file sharing, as shown in Figure H-8. Your available folders might differ from those shown in Figure H-8.

QuickTip
If you already know the network path for the drive you want to map, right-click the Network Neighborhood icon (98) or the My Network Places icon (Me), click Map Network Drive, enter the network path in the Path text box, then click OK.

3. **Click the shared Wired Coffee folder** (or the folder specified by your instructor or technical support person) to select it, click File on the menu bar, then click **Map Network Drive**
   The Map Network Drive dialog box opens, as shown in Figure H-9. By default, the Map Network Drive dialog box highlights the next available drive letter. The network path is automatically entered by Windows networking.

4. **If you want to use a different drive letter, click the Drive list arrow, then click the drive letter you want to use**
   John decides that the default choice is okay, but he also wants to reconnect to the drive every time he logs on.

Trouble?
If your mapped drives do not automatically reconnect when you log on, make sure your user name and password are the same for all the networks to which you connect.

5. **If not already checked, click the Reconnect at logon check box, then click OK**
   The Map Network Drive dialog box closes, and Windows networking maps a drive connecting your computer to the shared Wired Coffee folder (or to the shared folder specified by your instructor or technical support person). When the connection is complete, a window appears for the newly mapped drive, allowing you to view the files within the mapped drive, as shown in Figure H-10. John can now easily copy folders and files from his floppy disk into the shared folder.

6. **Click the Close button in the mapped drive window**

7. **Click the Back button list arrow on the toolbar, then click Network Neighborhood (98) or My Network Place (Me)**
   The Windows networking window displays the active computers in your immediate network.

MANAGING SHARED FILES USING A NETWORK

FIGURE H-8: Server computer icon window

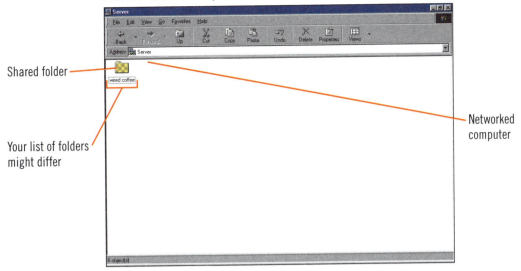

- Shared folder
- Your list of folders might differ
- Networked computer

FIGURE H-9: Map Network Drive dialog box

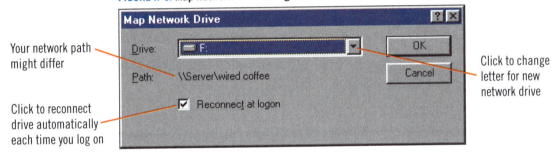

- Your network path might differ
- Click to reconnect drive automatically each time you log on
- Click to change letter for new network drive

FIGURE H-10: Wired Coffee folder window

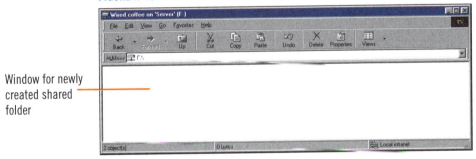

- Window for newly created shared folder

CLUES TO USE

Creating a network or dial-up connection

Dial-up Connections provide connectivity between your computer and a network, another computer, or the Internet. With Dial-up Networking, you can establish a Virtual Private Network connection through the Internet, a direct computer connection, or a dial-up connection. To establish any one of these connection types, click the Start button on the taskbar, point to Programs, point to Accessories, point to Communications, click Dial-up Networking, double-click Make New Connection, click Next, click the connection option you want, and then follow the instructions in the Network Connection Wizard. To connect to the network, double-click the connection icon in the Dial-up Networking window. If you want to connect to your computer from another computer, you need to grant incoming connection access to your computer. This means your computer running Windows Me can operate as a remote access server, or dial-up network server. To grant incoming connection access rights to your computer, open Dial-up Connections, click Connections on the menu bar, click Dial-Up Server, click the Allow caller access option button, set a password, then click OK.

MANAGING SHARED FILES USING A NETWORK

Copying and Moving Shared Files

Windows 98 and Me

Once you create shared folders and map your network drives, copying and moving shared files and folders in Windows is as easy as managing files on your own computer. The only difference is data transfer can take longer over a network than it does on your local computer. You can copy and move files using any of the Windows file management tools: Network Neighborhood (98) or My Network Places (Me), My Computer, or Windows Explorer. Network Neighborhood and My Network Places work just like My Computer. John wants to copy files from his floppy disk into the shared Sales folder on his hard drive to make them accessible to the other users on his network. He also needs to move a file from the shared Sales folder to the Wired Coffee folder on the network drive (F:) to make it accessible to another department. Since he's copying files to several locations, John uses Windows Explorer to drag and drop the files.

Steps

Trouble?
If you are using a Project Disk, make a copy of the disk before you use it and insert the copy into your disk drive. See your instructor or technical support person for assistance.

1. Make sure a copy of the disk or drive where your Project Files are located is available

2. In the Windows networking window, click the **Address list arrow**, click the drive where your Project Files are located, then double-click the folder where your Project Files are located
   The Windows networking window displays the contents of your Project Files.

3. Right-click the **Wired Coffee folder**, click **Explore**, then click the **Sales folder** in the Explorer Bar
   Windows Explorer opens, displaying the available folders and drives in the left pane, as shown in Figure H-11. You can now copy or move files easily from your computer to anywhere on the network. Next John copies the files named Coffee Prices, Customer Profile, and Suppliers to the shared Sales folder he created on Drive C.

Trouble?
If you click the shared Sales folder by mistake, click the Sales folder on the floppy disk, then go to Step 5.

4. In the Explorer Bar, click the **+** next to the My Documents folder to display the shared Sales folder (the one with a hand), as shown in Figure H-12, but do not click the folder

5. Click **Edit** on the menu bar, click **Select All**, then drag the files from the right pane to the shared **Sales folder** in the Explorer Bar
   This copies files to the shared Sales folder on the hard drive. The employees who have access to John's computer can now share the files.

6. In the Explorer Bar, click the shared **Sales folder**, then click the **down scroll arrow** in the Explorer Bar until you can see the icon representing the mapped network folder
   Windows Explorer lists the contents of the Sales folder, as shown in Figure H-12.

7. Right-click and drag the **Suppliers file** to the mapped networked folder in the Explorer Bar, then click **Move Here**
   The Suppliers file is now in the networked folder.

8. Click the **mapped network folder** in the Explorer Bar to view the Suppliers file, then click the **Close button** in both windows

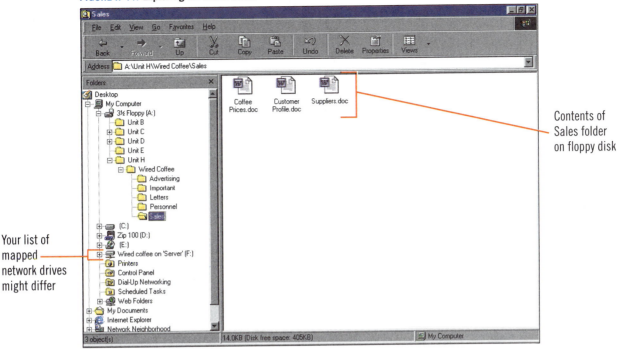

FIGURE H-11: Exploring the Sales folder

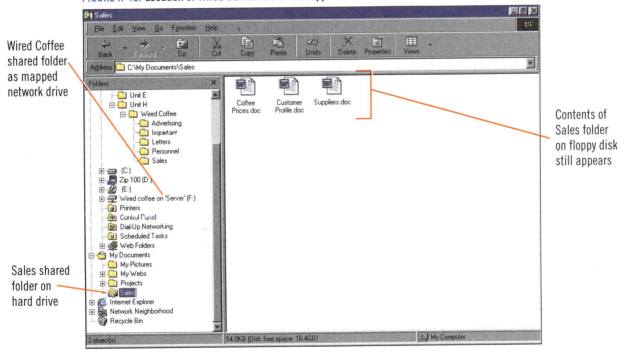

FIGURE H-12: Location of Wired Coffee folder on mapped network drive (F:)

Clues To Use

Network traffic

Large networks can serve hundreds of users simultaneously. Like water flowing through pipes, only a certain amount of data can pass through the wires connecting the individual computers at any given time. If the amount of network traffic is sufficiently heavy, then the flow of data might slow considerably, causing file operations such as opening, saving, and copying to take longer to complete.

MANAGING SHARED FILES USING A NETWORK   WINDOWS 98 AND ME H-13

Opening and Editing a Shared File

Working with shared files on a network is a simple task with Windows. Once you map all the necessary drives to your network folders, you can use network files in any program from your computer. For example, you can use WordPad to edit text files or Paint to create a graphic. You might also be able to use programs installed on the server specifically for the use of individual clients. (Ask your system administrator about available options.) John uses WordPad to make corrections in the Suppliers file that he placed in the Wired Coffee folder on the server.

Steps

1. Click the **Start button** on the taskbar, point to **Programs**, point to **Accessories**, then click **WordPad**
   The WordPad window opens.

2. Click **File** on the menu bar, click **Open**, then click the **Look in list arrow**
   The Open dialog box opens, as shown in Figure H-13, displaying the Look in list with local and networked drives. From here you can open files located on all drives and folders, including the drives mapped to the network.

3. Click the **icon** for the mapped network drive to the Wired Coffee shared folder
   A list of files stored in the networked folder appears in the Open dialog box, as shown in Figure H-14.

4. Click **Suppliers**, then click **Open**
   The file named Suppliers opens. John wants to add another supplier to the list.

5. Click the bottom of the list, then type **Homegrown USA Coffee**

6. Click the **Save button** on the toolbar
   WordPad saves the changes to the file Suppliers.

7. Click the **Close button** in the WordPad window

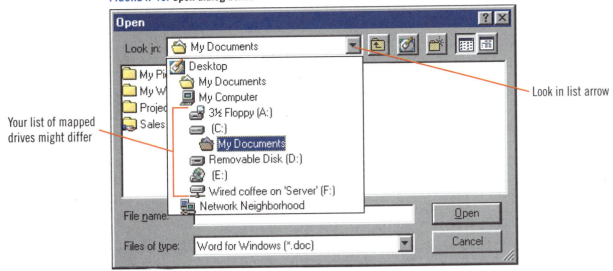

FIGURE H-13: Open dialog boxes

- Your list of mapped drives might differ
- Look in list arrow

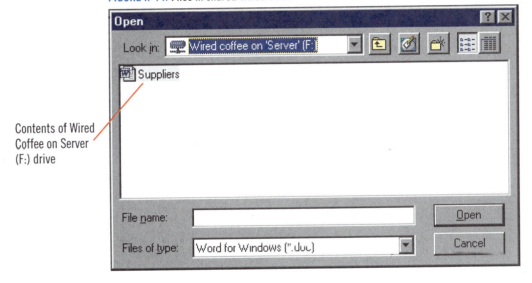

FIGURE H-14: Files in shared Wired Coffee folder

- Contents of Wired Coffee on Server (F:) drive

Opening read-only files

If you have read-only access to a folder, you can open a file from the folder, but you cannot make any changes to the file. When you open a read-only file, the words "Read Only" appear in the title bar. You can makes changes to the file, but an error message appears when you try to save it. However, if you like, you can save the file with a new name in a different location and have full access to the file.

Disconnecting a Network Drive

Windows 98 and Me

Usually, you map a network drive to reconnect automatically every time you log on. However, sometimes you might find it necessary to disconnect a mapped drive manually. Your system administrator might add new hard drives to the server, or she might reorganize the directory structure of the network, making the network path for the mapped drive incorrect. When this occurs, Windows makes the process of disconnecting a mapped drive very easy. The system administrator informs John that a network reorganization will take place over the weekend. To prepare for the reorganization, John cleans up his hard drive and the mapped drive. Then he disconnects the drive mapped to (F:) until he finds out what changes have been made.

Steps

1. Double-click the **My Computer icon** on the desktop, then double-click the **mapped drive**
   The contents of the mapped drive appear. John wants to delete the Suppliers file.

2. Right-click the **Suppliers file**, click **Delete**, then click **Yes** to confirm the deletion

3. Click the **Back button** on the toolbar

4. Double-click the **hard drive** with the shared Sales folder, then double-click the **My Documents folder**
   John wants to delete the shared folder.

5. Right-click the shared **Sales folder**, then click **Delete**
   The Confirm Folder Delete dialog box opens. John confirms the deletion.

6. Click **Yes**, click **Yes** again, then click the **Close button** in the My Documents window
   After cleaning up his hard drive and the mapped drive, John disconnects the mapped drive.

QuickTip
To disconnect a network drive in Windows Explorer, right-click the mapped network drive in the left pane, then click Disconnect.

7. Right-click the **Network Neighborhood icon** (98) or **My Network Places icon** (Me) on the desktop
   A pop-up menu appears, as shown in Figure H-15. This menu provides several options for working in a network environment. See Table H-1 for a description of the options available on this menu.

8. Click **Disconnect Network Drive** on the pop-up menu
   The Disconnect Network Drive dialog box appears, as shown in Figure H-16. The dialog box lists all the network drives that you have mapped from your computer. You should check with your system administrator or instructor before actually disconnecting a drive. To quit without actually disconnecting a drive, click Cancel. John wants to disconnect the drive he mapped.

9. To disconnect the drive you mapped, click the **mapped drive** with the Wired Coffee folder, click **OK**, then click **Yes**, if necessary, to respond to the warning message
   Windows disconnects the drive you selected and closes the Disconnect Network Drive dialog box.

Network paths
The path to a shared network directory is like the path to a file on a hard or floppy disk. For example, the path to the Suppliers file on your Project Files Disk is A:\Wired Coffee\Sales\Suppliers. Network paths replace the drive designation with the host computer name, as in \\Server\Wired Coffee. In either case, the path tells the computer where to look for the files you need.

FIGURE H-15: Pop-up menu for Network Neighborhood

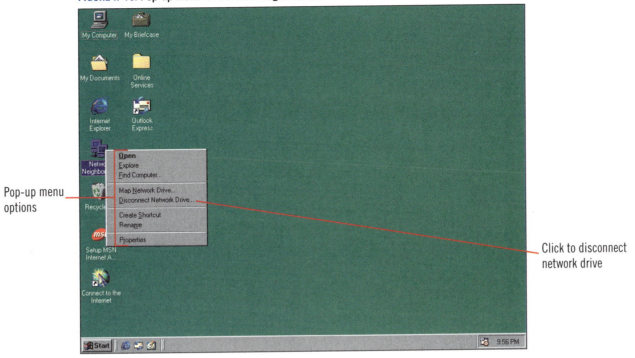

Pop-up menu options

Click to disconnect network drive

FIGURE H-16: Disconnect Network Drive dialog box

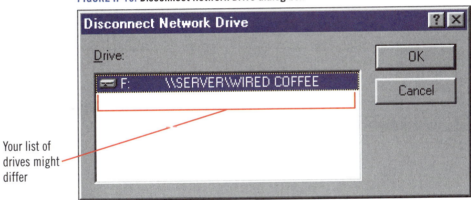

Your list of drives might differ

TABLE H-1: Pop-up menu commands for Network Neighborhood or My Network Places

option	function
Open	Starts Network Neighborhood (98) or My Network Places (Me)
Explore	Opens Windows Explorer in order to copy and move files or folders from one folder to another, whether on your local computer or the network
Find Computer (98) or Search for Computer (Me)	Finds a computer whose name you know but not its location
Map Network Drive	Maps a drive from your computer to a shared directory on another computer
Disconnect Network Drive	Disconnects a drive on your computer from a shared directory on another computer
Create Shortcut	Creates a shortcut to Network Neighborhood (98) or My Network Places (Me)
Rename	Renames the Network Neighborhood icon (98) or My Network Places icon (Me)
Properties	Views the properties of your network

MANAGING SHARED FILES USING A NETWORK

Windows 98 and Me Practice

▶ Concepts Review

Label each element of the screen shown in Figure H-17.

FIGURE H-17

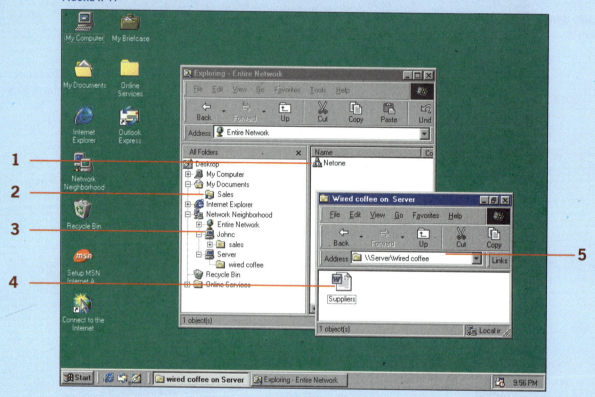

Match each term with the statement that describes its function.

6. Shared folder
7. File permissions
8. Entire Network icon
9. Network path
10. Disconnect Network Drive command

a. Determines who can read, write, or execute files
b. A location where multiple users can access the same files
c. Displays all workgroups and computers attached to a network
d. The address for an individual computer on a network
e. Removes a mapped drive from the local computer

Practice

Select the best answers from the following lists of choices.

11. **The Windows 98 network management tool that allows you to inspect the configuration of your network is called:**
    a. Windows Explorer.
    b. My Computer.
    c. Network Neighborhood.
    d. My Network Places.

12. **To disconnect a network drive:**
    a. Double-click the drive letter in Network Neighborhood (98) or My Network Places (Me).
    b. Highlight the drive letter, click File on the menu bar, then click Delete.
    c. Click the drive letter, then drag it to the Recycle bin.
    d. Right-click the Network Neighborhood icon (98) or My Network Places icon (Me), then click Disconnect Network Drive.

13. **When you highlight a drive letter in Network Neighborhood (98) or My Network Places (Me), click File on the menu bar, then click Explore:**
    a. My Computer starts, allowing you to manage files and folders.
    b. Network Neighborhood (98) or My Network Places (98) displays the entire network.
    c. Windows Explorer starts, allowing you to manage files and folders.
    d. File Manager starts, allowing you to manage files and folders.

14. **When you map a networked drive:**
    a. Windows networking displays a graphic showing the entire structure of the network.
    b. You can use the shared files and folders of another computer on the network.
    c. The computer you are using is attached to the network.
    d. Windows networking adds your computer to the network path.

15. **If the file permissions for a shared folder are set to read-only:**
    a. No one can read the files in the folder.
    b. You can edit the file and save your changes.
    c. Everyone can read the files but not write to the files.
    d. Everyone can execute files but not write to the files.

Windows 98 and Me | **Practice**

▶ Skills Review

1. **Examine network computer properties.**
   a. Right-click your network computer icon.
   b. Click Properties.
   c. View the network properties.
   d. Click OK.

2. **Open and view a network.**
   a. Double-click the Network Neighborhood icon (98) or My Network Places (Me).
   b. Double-click the Entire Network icon.
   c. Click the Back button.
   d. Double-click the network icon in your immediate network.
   e. Click the Back button.

3. **Create a shared folder.**
   a. Click the Address list arrow, click your computer's hard drive, then double-click the My Documents folder (98 or Me) or click the My Documents link (Me).
   b. Right-click in the My Documents window, point to New, then click Folder.
   c. Name the new folder *Memos*, then press [Enter].
   d. Click File on the menu bar, then click Sharing.
   e. Click the Shared As option button.
   f. Click the Read-Only option button.
   g. Click OK.

4. **Map a network drive.**
   a. Click the Address list arrow, then click Network Neighborhood (98) or My Network Places (Me).
   b. Double-click the icon for the computer to which you want to map.
   c. Click the shared folder to which you want to map.
   d. Click File on the menu bar, then click Map Network Drive.
   e. Click the Reconnect at logon check box.
   f. Click OK.
   g. Click the Close button.

5. **Copy and move shared files.**
   a. Make sure a copy of the disk or drive where your Project Files are located is available.
   b. Click the Address list arrow, click the drive where your Project Files are located, then double-click the folder where your Project Files are located.
   c. Click the Wired Coffee folder.
   d. Click File on the menu bar, then click Explore.
   e. Click the Letters folder in the Explorer Bar.
   f. Click the + next to the My Documents folder.
   g. Click Edit on the menu bar, then click Select All.
   h. Drag all the files to the shared Memos folder you created in the My Documents folder.
   i. Click the shared Memos folder in the Explorer Bar.
   j. Right-drag the IRS Letter file to the mapped networked folder in the Explorer Bar, then click Move Here.
   k. Click the mapped networked folder in the Explorer Bar to view the file.
   l. Click the Close buttons in both windows.

Practice

6. **Open and edit a shared file.**
   a. Start WordPad.
   b. Open the IRS Letter file from the shared Memos folder on your hard drive.
   c. Change the month in the body of the letter from **April 25** to **May 10**.
   d. Save the file, print it, then close the file and WordPad.

7. **Disconnect a network drive.**
   a. Double-click the My Computer icon, then double-click the mapped drive.
   b. Click the IRS Letter File, press [Delete], then click Yes.
   c. Click the Address list arrow, then click My Documents.
   d. Right-click the shared Memos folder, then click Delete.
   e. Click Yes, then click Yes again to confirm the deletion.
   f. Click the Close button.
   g. Right-click the My Network Places icon.
   h. Click Disconnect Network Drive.
   i. Select the drive you mapped in Step 4.
   j. Click OK, then click Yes if necessary.

▶ Independent Challenges

1. As the new clerk at Holly's (a craft store), you are asked to create a list of suppliers' names. Your task is to enter the supplier information in a new file and place that file in two places for others to use. You must create a shared folder on your computer to store the file, then map a drive to a network folder that will also contain the file.

If you are not connected to a network, ask your instructor or technical support person for help in completing this independent challenge. If you are working in a lab environment, you may not be able to create a shared folder. If so, do not create a shared folder; use the folder supplied by your instructor instead.

To complete this independent challenge:
   a. Right-click the Network Neighborhood icon (98) or My Network Places icon (Me), then click Explore.
   b. Open the My Documents folder.
   c. Create a shared folder called *Suppliers* with read-only permissions.
   d. Open WordPad and enter the following information in a new document:

Name	Address	City & State
Baskets & Things	101 Hopyard Road	Chicago, IL
Frames R Us	1934 Hummingbird Lane	Los Angeles, CA
Season's	125 34th Street	New York, NY

   e. Save the file as *Supplier List* in the newly created Suppliers folder.
   f. Print the Supplier List file.
   g. Map a drive to a shared folder on another computer to which you have permission.
   h. Create a *US Suppliers* folder on that drive.
   i. Copy the Supplier List file from the Suppliers folder on the local computer to the US Suppliers folder on the mapped drive.
   j. Print the Screen. (Press [Print Screen] to make a copy of the screen, open Paint, click Edit on the menu bar, click Paste to paste the screen into Paint, then click Yes to paste the large image if necessary. Click File on the menu bar, click Print, then click OK.)
   k. Delete the Suppliers folder on your hard drive and the US Suppliers folder on the mapped drive.
   l. Disconnect the network drive you mapped, and delete the shared folder you created.

MANAGING SHARED FILES USING A NETWORK

Windows 98 and Me — Practice

2. As president of your company, you decide to increase the pay rates of two of your employees, Jessica Thielen and Debbie Cabral. You use WordPad to write a memo that you can edit and use for both employees. After completing the memos, you print the documents for the employees. You also want to copy the documents to the company server so they can be stored in the employees' folders.

To complete this independent challenge:

a. Create a *Memos* folder on the drive and in the folder where your Project Files are located.
b. Open WordPad and type the following memo in a new document:

Dear Jessica,
Your service to this company is greatly appreciated. To show my appreciation to such an outstanding employee as yourself, I have decided to give you a 10% raise in salary. The raise will go into effect with the next pay period.
Sincerely yours,
[your name here]

c. Use the Save As command to name the document *Thielen Raise* and save it in the Memos folder, then print the document.
d. Change *Dear Jessica* to *Dear Debbie* in the Thielen Raise memo.
e. Save the file as *Cabral Raise* in the Memos folder, and print the document.
f. Close the file and close WordPad.
g. Map a drive to a shared folder on another computer to which you have permission.
h. Create a folder called *Thielen* on the mapped drive, and copy the Thielen Raise file from your Student Disk into the Thielen folder.
i. Create a shared folder called *Cabral* on the mapped drive, and copy the Cabral Raise file into the Cabral folder.
j. Print the screen. (See Independent Challenge 1, Step j for screen printing instructions.)
k. Delete the Thielen and Cabral shared folders on the mapped drive.
l. Disconnect the network drive you mapped.

3. You are system administrator for your company's computer network. During peak usage of the network, you want to monitor who is on the network. You use the Properties command in the Network Neighborhood (98) or My Network Places (Me) to learn who is connected to the network.

To complete this independent challenge:

a. Open Network Neighborhood (98) or My Network Places (Me).
b. Display the network identification for two connected computers to learn their names and domain.
c. Print the screen for the network identification for the connected computers. (See Independent Challenge 1, Step j for screen printing instructions.)
d. Map two drives to a shared folder on another computer to which you have permission.
e. Display the network identification for the mapped drives.
f. Print the screen for the network identification for the mapped drives (See Independent Challenge 1, Step j for screen printing instructions.)
g. Disconnect the network drives you mapped.

Practice

4. The system administrator for your network calls and informs you that he needs to make some changes to the directory structure. He advises you to move any files you put on the server recently and to disconnect any mapped drives. To complete this independent challenge:
   a. Map a drive to a shared folder on another computer to which you have permission, and copy two files from your Project Files to this mapped drive.
   b. Using Network Neighborhood (98) or My Network Places (Me), create a shared folder on your local hard disk called *Network Files*.
   c. Move the files from the folder on the network drive to the shared Network Files folder on the local hard disk.
   d. Print the screen. (See Independent Challenge 1, Step j for screen printing instructions.)
   e. Disconnect the mapped drive from the network.
   f. Delete the shared folder on your local hard drive.

Windows 98 and Me | Practice

▶ Visual Workshop

Re-create the screen shown in Figure H-18, which displays the files on a local hard drive and files on a network drive. Print the screen. (See Independent Challenge 1, Step j for screen printing instructions.)

FIGURE H-18

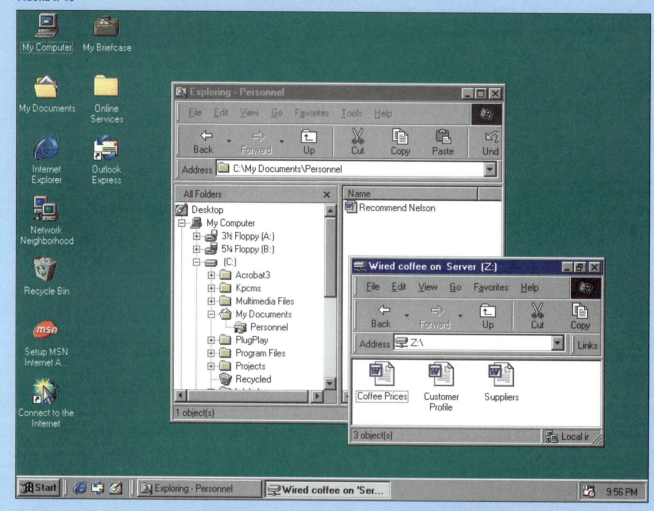

Glossary

Windows 98 and Me

Accessibility Wizard Helps you configure Windows for your vision, hearing, and mobility needs.

Accessories Built-in programs that come with Windows 98.

Active window The window you are currently using.

Active Desktop The screen that appears when you first start Windows 98 or Me, providing access to your computer's programs and files and to the Internet.

Active Desktop items Elements you can place on the desktop to access or display information from the Internet.

Active program The program that is open. The title bar changes from gray to blue.

Adapter A device that connects your computer to the network.

Address bar Displays the address of the current Web page or the contents of a local or network computer drive.

Address Book Stores mailing addresses, phone numbers, e-mail addresses, or Web sites, along with contact's title, street address, phone number, and personal Web page addresses.

Applications *See* programs.

Articles Another name for newsgroup messages.

Auto hide A feature that helps you automatically hide the taskbar.

Back up To save files to another location in case you have computer trouble and lose files.

Background The primary surface on which icons and windows appear; you can customize its appearance using the Display Properties dialog box.

Binding A connection that enables communications among the adapters, protocols, and services installed in Windows.

Bitmapped character A character that consists of small dots organized to form a letter.

Browser A software program used to access and open Web pages.

Bullet mark An indicator that shows an option is enabled.

Cascading menu A list of commands from a menu item with an arrow next to it. Pointing to the arrow displays a submenu from which you can choose additional commands.

Center A form of paragraph alignment in which the lines of text are centered between the left and right margins.

Channel A specialized Web page designed to deliver Internet content from a specific channel, such as Disney, MSNBC, or the Microsoft Network to your computer.

Check mark An indicator that shows a feature is enabled.

Clicking The act of pressing a mouse button once and releasing it.

Client/server networking A network setup that provides all users on network a central location for accessing shared files.

Clients Other computers on the network can access the resources on the server instead of having to store them.

Clipboard A temporary storage space on a hard drive that contains information that has been cut or copied.

Collection Organized clips for use in different movie projects.

Command A directive that provides access to a program's features.

Contact A person or company that with whom you communicate.

Contact groups A group of contacts that you can organize together.

Contacts list Displays the contact names in the Address Book.

Windows 98 and Me Glossary

Context-sensitive help Help that relates to the task you are currently working on.

Control Panel A central location for changing Windows settings. A window containing various programs that allow you to specify how your computer looks and performs.

Conversation thread Consists of the original message on a particular topic along with any responses that include the original message.

Copied A copy is placed in the Clipboard to be pasted in another location, but the text also remains in its original place in the document.

Cut To remove information from a file and place it on the Clipboard, usually to be pasted in another location.

Defragment A feature that allows you to rewrite the files on your disk to contiguous blocks rather than in random blocks.

Delete A file or folder that is removed from the disk.

Dialog box A window that appears to request information; many dialog boxes have options you must choose before Windows or a program can carry out a command.

Disk label A name you assign to a hard or floppy disk using the Properties dialog box.

Display pane The bottom pane of Outlook Express that displays the e-mail message selected in the preview pane. *See also* preview pane.

Document window Displays the current Web page or the contents of a local or network computer drive or the current document. The work area of the WordPad window.

Document A file created using a word-processing program such as WordPad.

Domain A collection of computers that the person managing the network creates, to group together computers used for the same tasks and to simplify the set-up and maintenance of the network.

Double-clicking Clicking the mouse button twice.

Download The process by which you access and display a Web page from the Internet.

Dragging Moving items or text to a new location using the mouse button.

Edit Changing the contents of a document without re-creating it.

Electronic mail (e-mail) A system used to send and receive messages electronically.

Explorer Bar The pane on the left side of the screen that displays all drives and folders on the computer.

Favorites Stores and organizes the most frequented Web addresses.

File An electronic collection of information that has a unique name, distinguishing it from other files.

File hierarchy A logical structure for files and folders that mimics how you would organize files and folders in a filing cabinet.

File management The process of organizing and keeping track of files and folders.

File sharing Allows many people to work on the same files without needing to create or store multiple copies.

Find People link Opens the Find People dialog box where you can search for people on the Internet or in your Address Book.

First-line indent marker The top triangle that controls where the first line of the paragraph begins.

Folder A collection of files and/or other folders that helps you organize your disks.

Folders list Displays folders where Outlook Express stores e-mail messages. You can also use folders to organize your e-mail messages.

Font The design of letters, numbers, and other characters. For example, Times New Roman.

Format Bar A tool bar in WordPad that contains formatting buttons.

Format To change the appearance of information but not the actual content.

Glossary

Frame A separate window within a Web page.

Full permission Allows the user to edit and save changes to the file and execute programs on server or client computers.

Go to MSN link Opens your default Web browser program and displays the MSN Web page.

Graphical user interface (GUI) Pronounced "gooey"—an environment made up of meaningful symbols, words, and windows in which you can control the basic operation of a computer and the programs that run on it.

Hanging indent marker A paragraph format in which the first line of a paragraph starts farther to the left than the subsequent lines.

Hard copy A paper document that you can share with others or review as a work in progress.

Highlight When an item is shaded differently indicating it is selected. *See also* Select.

Hits The result of an Internet search that, when clicked, opens a Web page or category.

Home page The page that opens every time you start Internet Explorer.

Hub Used to connect multiple computers at a central location.

Hyperlinks (links) Highlighted text or graphics in a Web page that open other Web pages when you click them.

Icons Graphical representations of computer elements such as files and programs.

Insertion point A blinking vertical line that appears in the work area of the WordPad window, indicating where new text will appear when you type.

Internet A communications system that connects computers and computer networks located around the world using telephone lines, cables, satellites and other telecommunications media.

Internet Service Provider (ISP) A company that provides Internet access.

Keywords A word or phrase you submit to a search engine to find various Web sites on the Internet. *See also* Search engine.

Left indent marker The small square under the bottom triangle that allows you to move the first-line indent marker and the left indent marker simultaneously.

Links bar Displays link buttons to Web pages on the Internet or to documents on a local or network drive.

Local area network (LAN) A network of computers close together that can share resources using two or more client computers.

Mapping A direct connection to the network location for quick and easy access.

Margin The extra white space around the edge of a document.

Maximize To enlarge a window so it fills the entire screen.

Menu A list of available commands in a program.

Menu bar A bar at the top of a window that organizes commands into groups of related operations.

Message flags An icon associated with an e-mail message that helps you determine the status or priority of the message.

Minimize To reduce the size of a window. Located in the upper-right corner of a window.

Mouse A hand-held input device that you roll across a flat surface (such as a desk or a mousepad). *See also* Mouse Pointer.

Mouse buttons The two buttons (right and left) on the mouse used to make selections and commands.

Mouse pointer The arrow-shaped cursor on the screen that follows the movement of the mouse. The shape changes depending on the program and the task being executed. *See also* Mouse.

Multi-tasking Working with more than one Windows program at a time.

Windows 98 and Me Glossary

Navigating Repositioning the insertion point in a document.

Network A system of two or more computers connected together to share resources.

Network and Dial-up Connections Enable access to network resources, whether you are physically connected using a direct cable or remotely connected using a modem.

Network interface cards (NICs) A type of adapter, cards are inserted in a slot in the back of your computer, that connect your computer to the network.

Network Neighborhood An icon on the Windows 98 desktop that lists the computers on the network and helps manage files and folders across the network.

Network Places An icon on the Windows Me desktop that lists the computers on the network and helps manage files and folders across the network.

New Mail message link Opens the New Message dialog box where you can compose and send e-mail messages.

News server A computer located on the Internet, which stores newsgroup messages.

Newsgroups A collection of e-mail messages on related topics posted by individuals to specified Internet locations.

Open the Address Book link Opens the Address Book where you can enter and edit your contacts list.

Open Type font Based on a mathematical equation that creates letters with smooth curves and sharp corners.

Operating system A computer program that controls the basic operation of your computer and the programs you run on it. Windows 98 is an example of an operating system.

Outlook Express Start Page Displays tools that you can use to read e-mail, set up a newsgroup account, read newsgroup messages, compose e-mail messages, enter and edit Address Book information, and find people on the Internet.

Pane Part of a window that divides it into two or more sections.

Pattern A design that will display as your desktop background.

Peer-to-peer networking A network setup that enables two or more computers to link together without designating a central server.

Personalized Menus Keeps track of which programs you use and hides the programs you have not used recently.

Point A unit of measurement (1/72nd inch) used to specify the size of text.

Pointing Positioning the mouse pointer over an icon or over any specific item on the screen.

Pop-up menu Right-clicking an item on the desktop displays this menu.

Power scheme A predefined collection of power usage settings.

Preview pane Displays the messages in your Inbox.

Print Preview A layout and formatting of a document you can view before printing.

Printout A paper document that you can share with others or review as a work in progress.

Program button Located on the taskbar, represents any window that is minimized but still running.

Programs Task-oriented software you use to accomplish specific tasks, such as word processing, managing files on your computer, and performing calculations.

Properties The characteristics of a specific element (such as the mouse, keyboard, or desktop) that you can customize.

Protocol A language that the computer uses to communicate with other computers on the network.

Proxy server An Internet connection option that provides a secure barrier between your network and the Internet and prevents other people from seeing confidential information on your network.

Quick Launch toolbar A toolbar located next to the Start button on the taskbar that contains buttons to start Internet-related programs and show the desktop.

Glossary

Random Access Memory (RAM) A temporary storage space whose contents are erased when you turn off the computer.

Read Mail link Jumps to the Inbox where you can read and reply to incoming e-mail messages.

Read News link Connects to newsgroups that you can view and subscribe to.

Read permission Allows the user to open and view the file but not to make changes that can be saved in the file.

Recycle Bin A temporary storage area for deleted files that is located on your desktop.

Restore button Returns a window to its previous size.

Right indent marker The triangle on the right side of the ruler that controls where the right edge of the paragraph ends.

Right-clicking Clicking the right mouse button.

Scheme A predefined combination of settings that assures visual coordination of all items.

Screen font A font that consists of bitmapped characters. *See also* Bitmapped character.

Screen saver A moving pattern that fills your screen after your computer has not been used for a specified amount of time.

ScreenTip A description of a toolbar button that appears on your screen when your position the mouse pointer over the button.

Scroll bar A bar that appears at the bottom and/or right edge of a Window whose contents are not entirely visible; Each scroll bar contains a scroll box and two scroll arrows. You click the arrows or drag the box in the scrollbar in the direction you want the window to move.

Scroll box A box located in the vertical and horizontal scroll bars that indicates your relative position in a window. *See also* Scroll bar.

Search engine A program you access through a Web site and use to search through a collection of information found on the Internet.

Select The act of clicking an item, such as an icon, indicates that you have it to perform some future operation on it.

Server A single computer designated to store and share resources, such as programs, files, and folders, with other users on a network.

Service Allows sharing your computer resources, such as files and printers, with other networked computers.

Set up a Newsgroups account link Creates a newsgroup account.

Shortcut A link that you can place in any location that gives you instant access to a particular file, folder, or program on your hard disk or on a network.

Shut down The action you perform when you are finished working with Windows. After you perfrom this action, it is safe to turn off your computer.

Skin The Media player's appearance.

Start button Located on the taskbar used to start programs, find and open files, access Windows Help and more.

Status bar A bar at the bottom of the Word window that indicates the current page number and section number, the total number of pages in the document, and the vertical position (in inches)of the insertion point.

Status indicator The Internet Explorer logo that spins to indicate a new Web page is loading.

Streaming media The Windows Media Player delivers continuous video, live broadcasts, sound, and music playback.

Stretch A Display properties option that displays the wallpaper picture or pattern enlarged across the desktop screen.

Submenu An arrow next to a menu item indicating a list of commands for that menu item.

Synchronize Latest online version of your Web page on your hard disk drive for offline viewing.

Tabs Located at the top of the dialog box separate options into related categories.

Windows 98 and Me — Glossary

Task Scheduler A tool that enables you to schedule tasks to run regularly, at a time convenient for you.

Taskbar A strip at the bottom of the screen that contains the Start button, Quick Launch toolbar, and shows which programs are running.

Thumbnails Miniature views or large icons.

Tile Displays the wallpaper picture or pattern consecutively across the screen.

Tip of the day Displays an Outlook Express tip.

Title bar Located at the top of the window and displays the name of the program and contains the name of the file.

Toggle A button that acts as an on/off switch.

Toolbar Provides buttons for easy access to the most commonly used commands.

TrueType font Based on a mathematical equation that creates letters with smooth curves and sharp corners.

Uniform Resource Locator (URL) A Web page's address.

Vertical scroll bar Allows you to move up or down the current page.

Virtual Private Network A secure connection to a network over the Internet.

Wallpaper A picture that serves as your desktop's background.

Web address A unique address on the Internet where you can locate a Web page. *See also* URL.

Web browsers Software programs that you use to "browse the Web," or access and display Web pages.

Web pages Documents that contain highlighted words, phrases, and graphics that open other Web pages when you click them.

Web site Contains Web pages linked together to make looking for information on the Internet easier.

Wide area network (WAN) A network of computers that is spread over a wide area.

Windows Help A book stored on your computer, complete with an index and a table of contents to make finding information easier.

Windows Media Player A built-in accessory that allows you to play video, sound, and mixed-media files.

Windows Movie Maker Allows you to create your own movies from a variety of sources.

Windows program Software designed to run on computers using the Windows operating system.

Window Rectangular frame on your screen that can contain several icons, the contents of a file, or other usable data.

Wizard A series of dialog boxes that walk you through the steps of customizing a folder.

WordPad A Windows word-processing program.

Wordwrap A feature that automatically places text that won't fit on one line onto the next line.

Workgroup A group of computers that performs common tasks or belong to users who share common duties and interests.

Workstations Other computers on the network that can access the resources on the server instead of having to store them.

World Wide Web (Web or WWW) Part of the Internet that consists of Web sites located on different computers around the world.

Index

3½ Floppy (A:) Properties dialog box, C-16
3D flying Objects screen saver, E-4

▶A

Accessibility Wizard, A-13
accessories, B-1
Accessories (Me) command, B-2, D-2, E-14, H-14
accessories or features, installing, E-15
Accessories submenu, B-2
accounts, adding or modifying, G-2
Accounts command, G-2, G-14
actions, undoing, B-8, B-10, D-14
Active Desktop, A-2
  Adding Web item, E-3
  customizing, E-2
  elements, A-3
  Web content, E-2
Active Desktop command, E-2
Active Desktop Gallery, E-3
Active Desktop items, enabling/disabling, E-2
active program, B-12
adapters, H-5
Ad Campaign file, C-12
Add Favorite dialog box, F-10
Add Network Place Wizard (Me), H-6
Add New Hardware dialog box, E-15
Add/Remove Program icon, E-15
Add/Remove Programs utility, E-15
  setup tab, C-9
  Windows Setup tab, E-7
Address Bar, C-4, D-2, H-8
Address Book, G-6, G-8
Address Book toolbar, G-6–G-7
Add Scheduled Task icon, E-14
Add to Favorites command, F-10
advanced search, D-11
Advertising folder, C-3, C-6, C-12, C-14, D-12
Advertising window, C-12
AM Coffee sound, B-18
AM Coffee sound clip, B-16

applications, A-1
Arial (True Type or Open Type) window, E-10
ARPANET (Advanced Research Projects Agency Network), F-3
Arrange Icons command, C-8, D-14
articles, G-14
asterisk (*) wildcard character, D-10
attaching files to e-mail, G-9
Auto Arrange command, C-8
Auto hide feature, E-16

▶B

Back button, C-6
backing up files, C-16–C-17
[Backspace] key, B-6
binding, H-5
bitmapped characters, E-10
Block Sender command, G-12
boldface text, B-8
Boyd Coffee Company Web site, F-9
Browse dialog box, E-18
Browse For Folder dialog box, G-2
browsers, A-7, F-2
bullet mark, A-10
business cards, printing, G-6
Business Card style, G-11
Business Letters folder, C-2–C-3, D-4
By Date command, C-8
By Name command, C-8, D-14
By Size command, C-8
By Type command, C-8

▶C

cascading menus, A-6
Catalog Pages folder, D-8, D-12
Catalog Text folder, D-8
centering
  objects, B-12
  text, B-8

Channel Bar, F-4
channels, F-4
check box dialog boxes, A-15
check mark, A-10
Clear Day stationery, G-8
clicking, A-4–A-5
clients, H-2
client/server networking, H-2
Clipboard, B-6
Clipboard Viewer, B-6
Close button, A-18
closing pop-up menus, A-4
Coffee Cup collection, B-18
Coffee Cup video, B-18
Coffee Cup video clip, B-16
Coffee Meltdown movie, B-18
Coffee Menu file, B-4, B-8
collections, B-18
color on desktop, E-6
command, A-10
command button dialog boxes, A-15
commands
  followed by ellipsis (...), A-14
  Start menu, A-6
Compressed Folder command, C-9
compressing
  drives, C-16
  files and folders, C-9
Confirm File Delete dialog box, C-14
Confirm Folder Delete dialog box, H-16
Connection Wizard, F-5
Connect to the Internet, A-3
contact groups, G-6
contacts, G-6, G-8, G-11
context-sensitive help, A-16–A-17
Control Panel, A-6, E-4
  Add New Hardware icon, E-15
  Date/Time icon, E-8
  Desktop Themes icon, E-7
  Fonts icon, E-10
  Maximize button, A-8

Index

Network icon, H-4
Regional Settings icon, E-8
Restore button, A-8
title bar, A-8
Control Panel command, E-2, E-4
Control Panel toolbar, A-10, A-12
Control Panel window, A-8, E-12
conversation threads, G-18
Copy command, B-12–B-13, C-11, C-15
Copy [Ctrl][C] keyboard shortcut, B-13
Copy Here command, C-11, D-12
copying
    data between programs, B-12
    files, C-10–C-11
    files to folder, D-12
    Project Disk, C-4
    selections, B-12
    shared files, H-12
    text, B-6
Course Web site, F-8
Create Folder dialog box, G-12
Create Shortcut command, C-14–C-15, H-17
Current View command, G-18
Customize my Desktop command, E-2
Customize this Folder command, D-16
Customize this Folder dialog box, D-16
Customize this Folder Wizard, D-16–D-17
customizing
    Active Desktop, E-2
    folders, D-16
    Start menu, E-18
    taskbar, E-16
    toolbars, A-10
    Windows Explorer, D-6
    World Wide Web search, F-16
Custom Settings dialog box (98), E-2
Cut command, B-13, C-11, C-15
Cut [Ctrl][X] keyboard shortcut, B-13
cutting
    files, C-10
    text, B-6

▶ D

damaged files, C-17
data, copying between programs, B-12
date, E-8
Date/Time Properties dialog box, E-8
default tab stops, B-7
defragmenting disks, C-16–C-17
Delete command, C-13–C-16
Deleted Items folder, G-12
[Delete] key, C-13, D-14
deleting
    character to left, B-6
    e-mail, G-12
    files, C-2, C-12–C-13
    folders, C-2, C-12
    newsgroup messages, G-19
    scheduled tasks, E-14
    schemes, D-6
    shortcuts, C-14
desktop, A-2, A-6
    accessing Internet, A-7
    background, E-4
    changing scheme, E-6
    Channel Bar, F-4
    color, E-6
    customizing, E-2
    desktop themes, E-7
    displaying Web content, F-4
    Internet Explorer icon, F-4
    listing icons, D-2
    patterns, E-4
    rearranging icons, A-4
    resizing, C-14, E-9
    themes, E-7
Details view, C-6
dialog boxes, A-14–A-15, A-17
Dial-up Connections, H-11
Dial-up Networking, H-11
Dial-up Networking window, H-11
disconnecting network drive, H-16
Disconnect Network Drive command, H-16–H-16
Disconnect Network Drive dialog box, H-16
disk label, C-16
disks, defragmenting, C-16–C-17
Display icon, E-4
Display Properties dialog box, E-2
    Appearance tab, E-6
    Background tab, E-4
    Color list arrow, E-6
    Delete, D-6
    Desktop, E-6
    Display list arrow (98), E-4
    Item list arrow, E-6
    Picture Display list arrow (Me), E-4
    Scheme list arrow, E-6
    Screen Area slider, E-9
    Screen Saver list arrow, D-6, E-4
    Screen Saver tab, D-6, E-4
    Settings tab, E-9
    Show Web content on my Active Desktop check box, E-2
    View my Active Desktop as web page check box (98), E-2
    Wallpaper section, E-4
    Windows Standard (extra large), E-6
documents
    margins, B-14
    navigating, B-6
    new, B-4
    opening and saving, B-4
    paragraph tabs, B-7
    printing, B-14
    Print Preview feature, B-14
    saving with new name, B-4
    storing, B-4
Documents command, A-6
document window, B-4
domains, H-4
double-clicking, A-4–A-5, A-14
downloading
    media file, B-17
    newsgroup messages, G-16
    Web pages, F-8
down scroll arrow, A-12
dragging, A-4–A-5, C-10
drawing tools, B-10
drives
    compressing, C-16
    listing, D-2

▶ E

editing text, B-6
electronic mail, G-1

e-mail, G-1
   attaching files to, G-9
   automatically checking for, G-10
   blocking, G-12
   composing, G-8
   contacts, G-11
   deleting, G-12
   diverting incoming to folders, G-13
   flag icons, G-11
   formatting, G-8
   managing, G-12
   message flags, G-10
   new message without stationery, G-8
   organizing, G-12
   reading, G-10
   removing name from Message recipients list, G-8
   responding, G-10
   retrieving, G-10
   saving, G-8
   sending, G-8
   sorting, G-12
   waiting to send, G-8
emptying Recycle Bin, C-12
Empty Recycle Bin command, C-12, D-14
Entire Network icon, H-6
Excite, F-16
Explore command, C-15, H-17
Explorer Bar, D-2
   Business Letters folder, D-6
   Close button, D-6, F-16
   collapsing and expanding folders, D-4
   Desktop icon, D-2
   Move Here button, D-14, H-12
   My Computer icon, D-2
   New button, F-16
   Recycle bin icon, D-14
   Search button, F-16
   Wired Coffee folder, D-8
Explorer Bar command, D-6
Exploring Your Computer category, A-16

▶ **F**
Favorites, F-10–F-11

Favorites command, A-6–A-7, F-10
File and Print Sharing dialog box, H-4
file hierarchy, C-2–C-4, D-4
   moving up and down, C-6
   viewing, D-2
file management, C-1–C-2
files, A-1
   advanced search, D-11
   attaching to e-mail, G-9
   backing up, C-16–C-17
   compressing, C-9
   copying, C-10–C-11
   copying to folder, D-12
   cutting, C-10
   damaged, C-17
   deleting, C-2, C-12–C-13
   Details view, C-6, D-6
   dragging, C-10
   finding, C-2, D-10, D-13
   full name of, D-6
   Large Icons view, C-6
   moving, C-10–C-12
   moving to folder, D-12
   naming, B-5
   opening, D-4
   organizing, C-3
   password protection, H-9
   permissions, H-3
   renaming, D-8
   restoring, C-12–C-13
   restoring deleted, D-14
   saving, B-5
   selecting non consecutive, D-12
   sending, C-10
   shortcuts, C-2, C-14
   sorting, C-8, D-6
   unknown type, C-2
   viewing, C-4, C-6, D-4
file sharing, H-2
Files or Folders (98) command, D-10
filtering newsgroup messages, G-16
Filter Keys, A-13
Find: All Files window (98), D-10–D-11
Find: Files names Catalog window (98), D-10
Find (98) command, A-6, C-15, D-10, F-16–F-17

Find Computer (98) command, H-17
finding
   files, C-2, D-10, D-13
   folders, D-13
Find People dialog box, F-17
Find program, D-10
first-line indent marker, B-9
floppy disks
   amount of space used, C-16
   checking information, C-16
   disk label, C-16
   formatting, C-4
   saving files to, B-5
   viewing contents, D-2
   viewing folders, D-4
Folder command, H-8
Folder Options (98) command, E-2
Folder Options dialog box (Me), D-3, E-2
Folder Options icon (Me), E-2
folders, C-1
   background picture, D-16
   compressing, C-9
   copying and moving files to, D-12
   creation of, C-8, D-8
   customizing, D-16
   deleting, C-2, C-12
   Details view, D-6
   dragging, C-10
   finding, D-13
   listing, D-2
   moving, C-10, C-12
   naming, C-8, D-8
   new, C-2
   organizing, C-2–C-3
   recently visited, C-6
   renaming, C-8, D-8
   restoring, C-12
   Screen tip, D-6
   selecting non consecutive, D-12
   sending, C-10
   shortcuts, C-2, C-14
   sorting, C-8, D-6
   viewing, C-4, C-6
Folders button, D-10
fonts, B-8, E-10

Index

Fonts command, B-8
Fonts toolbar, E-10–E-11
Fonts window, E-10
Format Bar buttons, B-8–B-9
Format command, C-4
formatting
    e-mail, G-8
    floppy disks, C-4
    Web pages, F-19
Formatting toolbar, G-8
Forward button, C-6
frames, F-2
full permission, H-3
Full Screen command, F-8

▶ G

Getting Started with Windows Desktop Update topic, A-16
Getting Started with Windows Me category, A-16
GUI (graphical user interface), A-1

▶ H

hanging indent marker, B-9
hard disks
    checking information, C-16
    disk label, C-16
    displaying contents, D-2
    saving files to, B-5
hardware, adding, E-15
Help
    categories, A-16
    dialog boxes, A-17
    Internet Explorer, F-6
    Outlook Express, G-5
    Windows 98, A-16
    Windows Me, A-16
Help command, A-6
Help dialog box, A-16
Hibernate (Me) option, A-18
hibernation, E-12
Hide Read Messages command, G-18
Hide Variations command, E-10
hiding taskbar, E-16
High Contrast, A-13
highlighted text, B-4

History folder, D-13
hits, F-16
Home Networking (Me), H-7
Home Networking Setup disk, H-7
Home Networking Wizard, H-7
home networks, H-7
home pages, changing, F-14
horizontal scroll bar, A-12
HTTP (Hyper Text Transfer Protocol), F-9
hubs, H-2
hyperlinks, F-2

▶ I

icons, A-1
    dragging, A-4
    listing desktop, D-2
    My Computer window, C-4
    rearranging, A-4
    smaller, A-10
images, C-7, D-17
Important folder, C-8, C-10, G-12
Import command, B-18, B-19
Inbox, G-10, G-12
indenting paragraphs, B-9
insertion point, B-6
installing
    accessory or feature, E-15
    fonts, E-10
Install New Font command, E-10
Internet, A-2
    accessing from desktop, A-7
    connecting to, F-4–F-5
    frequently visited places, A-7
    mouse, A-5
    playing media, B-17
Internet Accounts dialog box, G-14
Internet Connection Wizard, G-2, G-14
Internet Explorer, A-3, A-7, F-2–F-3
    Address bar, F-8
    Auto Complete, F-10
    expanding document window, F-8
    Favorites, F-10
    help, F-6
    Help window, F-6
    History list, F-15

    home page, F-14
    Links bar, F-6
    offline mode, F-12
    Online Support, F-6
    opening folders or documents, F-8
    organizing Favorites, F-11
    Print Preview, F-18
    saving Web pages, F-13
    scroll box, F-6
    searching for people, F-17
    starting, F-4
    status bar, F-6, F-8
    tips, F-6
    toolbar buttons, F-7
    tour, F-6
    vertical scroll bar, F-6
Internet Explorer window, F-4, F-6
Internet Options command, F-14
Internet Options dialog box, F-14–F-15
ISP (Internet Service Provider), F-5
italic text, B-8
Items to Synchronize dialog box, F-12
It's now safe to turn off your computer message, A-18

▶ L

LANs (local area networks), H-2
Large Icons view, C-6
Launch Outlook Express button, G-2
Learning more about Windows Me, A-16
left indent marker, B-9
left mouse button, A-4
Letters folder, C-2–C-3
links, F-2, F-8
Links bar, F-14
Links folder, F-10
list box dialog boxes, A-15
live broadcasts, B-17
logging off, A-19
Log Off command, A-6, A-19

▶ M

Mail Order Catalog file, D-12
manual tab stops, B-7
Map Network Drive command, H-10, H-17

Index

Map Network Drive dialog box, H-10
mapping network drive, H-10
margins, B-14
maximizing windows, A-8
media, playing from Internet, B-17
media files, downloading, B-17
Memo style, G-11
menu bar, A-10
menus, A-10–A-11
message flags, G-10
Message Rules command, G-13, G-16
Message Rules dialog box, G-13, G-16
message toolbar, G-10
minimizing windows, A-8
mixed-media file, B-16
modifying scheduled tasks, E-14
Mosaic, F-3
mouse, A-4–A-5, A-12, A-14
mouse buttons, A-4
Mouse icon, A-14
Mouse Keys, A-13
mouse pointer
   links, F-8
   moving, A-4
   resizing window shapes, A-9
   shapes, A-5
   speed, A-14
Mouse Properties dialog box, A-14
Move Here command, C-11, C-12, C-14
Move To Folder command, G-12
movies, B-18
moving
   files, C-10–C-12
   files to folder, D-12
   folders, C-10, C-12
   mouse, A-4
   mouse pointer, A-4
   shared files, H-12
   taskbar, A-9
   windows, A-8
MSN (Microsoft Network) Web site, F-14
multitasking, B-10
music CDs, B-16
music tracks, B-17
My Briefcase, A-3

My Computer, A-3, C-1
   formatting floppy disks, C-4
   moving files or folders, C-10
   toolbar buttons, C-5
   viewing files and folders, C-6
My Computer icon, C-4, H-16
My Computer window, A-8, C-4
   3 ½ Floppy disk icon, C-16
   previewing images and pictures, C-7
My Documents folder, A-3, B-4, B-10, D-14, D-16, H-8, H-16
My Documents link, H-8
My Network Places (Me), A-3, H-1, H-10, H-12, H-17
My Network Places icon, H-4, H-6, H-16
My Pictures folder, B-10, C-7

▶ N

naming files, B-5
navigating documents, B-6
Netscape Communicator, F-2–F-3
network and dial-up connections, H-2
Network and Dial-up Connections dialog box, H-5
network dialog box, H-4–H-5
networked computer icon, H-10
Network Neighborhood (98), A-3, H-1, H-10, H-12, H-17
Network Neighborhood icon, H-4, H-6, H-16
network password dialog box, A-2
networks, H-1
   benefits, H-2
   copying and moving shared files, H-12
   disconnecting network drive, H-16
   domains, H-4
   home, H-7
   mapping drive, H-10
   names and locations, H-4
   opening and editing shared file, H-14
   paths, H-16
   properties, H-4
   proxy server, F-5
   searching for computer on, H-6
   shared folders, H-8
   structure, H-6
   traffic, H-13

   viewing, H-6
   viewing and configuring for computers, H-5
   workgroups, H-4
Network window, H-6
New command, C-8, C-9, D-8, H-8
New contact Properties dialog box, G-7
New Folder folder, C-8, H-8
New Mail Rule dialog box, G-13
New Message window, G-8
New News Rule dialog box, G-16
newsgroups, G-1, G-14
   conversation threads, G-18
   deleting messages, G-19
   downloading messages, G-16
   filtering messages, G-16
   posting messages, G-18
   reading messages, G-18
   subscribing to, G-16
   viewing, G-16
   viewing unread messages, G-18
   watching exchange of messages and replies, G-18
Newsgroups Subscriptions dialog box, G-16
news servers, G-14
NICs (network interface cards), H-5
NSFNET, F-3

▶ O

objects, B-12
Online Services folder, A-3
Open command, B-10, C-15, H-14, H-17
Open dialog box, B-4, B-16, D-16
opening and saving documents, B-4
opening read-only files, H-15
Open Type fonts, E-10
Open With (Me) command, C-15
Open With dialog box, C-2
operating systems, A-1
option button dialog boxes, A-15
Options command, B-19
Options dialog box, G-19
Organize Favorites command, F-11, F-12
Organize Favorites dialog box, F-12
Outlook Express, A-3, G-1
   as default e-mail or newsgroup program, G-3

Index

displaying Inbox, G-10
help, G-5
Inbox, G-10
online Help system, G-5
starting, G-2
Outlook Express News, G-14
Outlook Express Start Page, G-3
   Inbox check box, G-10
   Open the Address Book link, G-6
   password, G-2
   Read News link, G-14, G-16
   Set up a Newsgroups account link, G-14
   toolbar button, G-5
   user name, G-2
Outlook Express Web sites, G-5

▶P

Page Setup command, B-14
Page Setup dialog box, B-14–B-15, F-19
Paint, B-10
Paint Toolbox, B-10–B-11
Paint window, B-10
panes, A-16
Paragraph command, B-9
paragraphs
   indenting, B-9
   selecting, B-6
paragraph tabs, B-7
Password Configuration dialog box, H-8
passwords, A-2
   protection, H-9
   screen savers, E-4
Paste command, B-13, C-10, C-11, C-15
Paste [Ctrl][V] keyboard shortcut, B-13
pasting selections, B-12
paths, H-16
patterns, E-4
peer-to-peer networking, H-2
Peet's Coffee & Tea Web site, F-9
permissions, H-3
Personalized Menus, A-6
Personal Letters folder, C-2–C-3
Personnel folder, D-4
phone list, printing, G-6

Phone List style, G-11
pictures, C-7
Play Entire Storyboard/Timeline command, B-18
playlist, B-16
pointing, A-4–A-5
pop-up menus, A-4
Portable/Laptop power scheme, E-12
Power Management (98) utility, H-9
power options properties, E-12
Power Options Properties dialog box, E-12–E-13
Power Options (Me) utility, H-9
power schemes, E-12
Preview (Me) command, C-15
previewing Web pages, F-18
Print command, B-14, C-15, F-18
Print dialog box, B-14, F-18
printer properties, B-15
printing
   business cards, G-6
   changing options, B-14
   documents, B-14
   fonts, E-10
   margins, B-14
   phone list, G-6
   Web pages, F-18
printouts, B-14
Print Preview, B-14, F-18
Print Preview command, F-18
Print Preview toolbar, F-18
programs, A-1
   active, B-12
   closing, A-18
   copying data between, B-12
   descriptions of, A-10
   starting, B-2
   starting as taskbar button, E-17
   switching between, B-12
Programs command, A-6, B-2, D-2, E-14, H-14
Programs submenu, B-2
Project Disk, copying, C-4
properties, E-12
Properties command, C-13, C-15, C-16, E-4, H-17
Properties dialog box, C-16–C-17, G-6
proxy server, F-5

▶Q

Quick Launch Toolbar, A-2–A-3, A-7–A-8, F-4

▶R

RAM (Random Access Memory), B-5
read-only files, opening, H-15
read permission, H-3
rec.food.drink.coffee newsgroup, G-16
Recommend Nelson file, C-10
recording video clips, B-18
Record Narration command, B-19
Recycle Bin, A-3
   checking for use of, D-14
   emptying, C-12, D-14
   properties, C-13
Recycle Bin toolbar, C-13
Recycle Bin window, D-14
Regional Settings dialog box, E-8
Rename command, C-15, D-8, H-17
renaming folders, C-8, D-8
Repeat command, B-16
resizing
   desktop, C-14, E-9
   taskbar, A-9
   windows, A-8
   windows in Windows Explorer, D-2
Restart in MS-Dos mode (98) option, A-18
Restart option, A-18
Restore button, C-12, C-14
Restore command, C-13, D-14, D-15
restoring
   deleted files, D-14
   files, C-12–C-13
   folders, C-12
reversing actions, D-14
right-clicking, A-4–A-5
right indent marker, B-9
right mouse button, A-4
rounded rectangles, B-10
Rounded Rectangle tool, B-10
ruler, B-7, B-9
Run command, A-6

Index

▶ S

Sales folder, C-2–C-4, C-10, H-8, H-12, H-16
Sales Properties dialog box, H-8
Save As command, B-4, B-10, F-13
Save As dialog box, B-4, B-18
Save Movie dialog box, B-18
saving
    e-mail, G-8
    files, B-5
    schemes, E-6
    Web pages, F-13
ScanDisk, E-14
Scheduled Task (98) command, E-14
scheduled tasks, E-14
Scheduled Tasks icon (Me), E-14
Scheduled Tasks window, E-14
Scheduled Task Wizard dialog box, E-14
schemes, E-6
screen fonts, E-10
screen savers, E-4
Screen Tip, A-10, D-6
scroll bars, A-12, A-13
scroll box, A-12
Search (Me) command, A-6, F-16, F-17
search engines, F-16, F-17
Search for Computer (Me) command, H-17
searching
    for computer on networks, H-6
    for people, F-17
    World Wide Web, F-16
Seattle's Best Coffee Web site, F-9
Select All command, H-12
selecting, A-4
    objects, B-12
    paragraphs, B-6
    text, B-4, B-6, B-8
selections, copying and pasting, B-12
Select Program Folder dialog box, E-18
Select Recipients dialog box, G-8
sending
    e-mail, G-8
    files and folders, C-10
Send Later command, G-8
Send To command, C-10, C-15
Send To folder, C-10

Sent Items folder, G-8
servers, H-2
services, H-5
Settings command, A-6, E-2, E-4, E-16, E-18
Settings submenu, A-6
Setup MSN Internet Access, A-3
shared files, H-12, H-14
shared folders, H-8
Sharing command, C-15, H-8
Shawn Brooks Properties dialog box, G-6
Shortcut menu, options for files and folders, C-15
shortcuts, C-14, E-18
Shortcut to Wired Coffee Logo file, C-14
Show Sounds, A-13
Shut Down command, A-6, A-18
Shut Down Windows dialog box (Me), A-18, A-19
shutting down Windows, A-18
skin, B-16
slider dialog boxes, A-15
slide shows, B-19
smaller icons, A-10
Small Icons command, A-10
software, adding, E-15
sorting
    e-mail, G-12
    files and folders, C-8, D-6
sounds, B-16
Sound Sentry, A-13
special characters, B-8
special-needs users, A-13
spin box dialog boxes, A-15
Spring Catalog folder, D-8, D-12, D-14
standby, E-12
Stand by option, A-18
Starbucks Coffee Web site, F-9
Start button, A-2, A-3, A-6, A-18, B-2
starting programs, B-2
Start menu
    commands, A-6
    customizing, E-18
    Find program, D-10
    rearranging items on, E-19
    shortcuts, C-14, E-18
status bar, turning off, A-10
Status Bar command, A-12

steaming media, B-16
Sticky Keys, A-13
stopping scheduled tasks, E-14
storing documents, B-4
storyboard, B-18
streaming media, B-17
submenus, A-6
Synchronize command, F-12
Synchronize dialog box, F-12
system folders, D-2
System Tools command, E-14

▶ T

tab dialog boxes, A-15
tabs, B-7
Tabs command, B-7
tab stops, B-7
Taskbar, A-3
taskbar
    Connect Icon, F-18
    customizing, E-16
    date and time, E-8
    hiding, E-16
    moving, A-9
    My Computer button, A-8
    Paint program button, B-12
    power option icons, E-12
    printer icon, B-14
    program button, B-12
    Quick Launch toolbar, A-7, E-16
    resizing, A-9
    Start button, A-2, A-6, D-2
    starting programs as button on, E-17
    status area, B-14
Taskbar and Start Menu Properties (Me) dialog box, E-16, E-18
Taskbar Properties (98) dialog box, E-16, E-18
Taskbar & Start Menu command, E-16, E-18
Task Scheduler, E-14
text, B-6, B-8
    finding, F-16
    highlighted, B-4
    selecting, B-4
text box dialog boxes, A-15
Text Labels (98) command, A-10, A-12

Index

threads, G-18
thumbnails, C-7, D-17
Thumbnails command, D-17
Tile Windows Vertically command, B-12
tiling windows, B-12, C-12
time, E-8
Timeline view, B-19
time-zone settings, E-8
title bar, A-8, C-4
To Do List file, C-10
Toggle Keys, A-13
toggles, B-8
toolbars
   Address Book button, G-6, G-10
   Attach button, G-9
   Back button, C-6, C-10, D-2, F-8, F-14, H-6, H-16
   Back button list arrow, C-6, C-10, C-16, F-8
   buttons, A-10
   Copy button, B-13
   Copy To button, C-11
   customizing, A-10
   Cut button, B-6, B-13
   Delete button, C-13
   Favorites button, F-10
   Forward button, C-6, D-2, F-8
   History button, D-13, F-15
   Home button, F-12, F-14
   Maximize button, G-18
   Move To button, C-11
   My Computer window, C-4
   New button, B-4, G-6
   New Mail button, G-8
   New Mail button list arrow, G-8
   Paste button, B-6, B-8, B-13
   Print button, B-14, F-18, G-11
   Print Preview button, B-14
   Refresh button, F-8
   Reply Group button, G-18
   Save button, B-6, B-8, B-12, G-8, H-14
   Save Movie button, B-18
   Save Project button, B-18
   Screen Tip, A-10
   Search button (Me), D-10, D-11
   Send button, G-8, G-18
   Send/Recv button, G-10
   text labels, A-10
   Undo button, B-8, D-14
   Up button, C-6
   Views button, E-2
   Views button list arrow, C-6, D-6
Toolbars command, A-10, A-12
Toolbars submenus, E-16
Toolbox, B-10, B-12
transitions, B-18
True Type fonts, E-10

▶ U

Undo button Toolbar, B-8
Undo command, B-10, D-14
undoing actions, B-8, B-10
up scroll arrow, A-12
URLs (Uniform Resource Locators), F-6, F-9–F-10
Using Windows Millennium Edition category, A-16

▶ V

vertical scroll bar, A-12
video clips, B-16, B-18
videos, B-17
viewing Clipboard, B-6
View menu, A-10
Virtual Private Network, H-2, H-11
visited links, F-8
visual effect, changing, B-16

▶ W

wallpaper, E-4
WANs (wide area networks), H-2
Watch Conversation command, G-18
Web addresses, F-6, F-9–F-10
Web browsers, F-2–F-3, G-3
Web items, adding to Active Desktop, E-3
Web pages, E-2, F-2
   adding to favorites list, F-10
   downloading, F-8
   finding text, F-16
   formatting, F-19
   frames, F-2
   headers and footers, F-19
   hyperlinks, F-2
   links, F-7–F-8
   next, F-8
   offline viewing, F-10, F-12
   opening, F-8
   previewing, F-18
   previous, F-8
   printing, F-18
   saving, F-13
   synchronizing, F-12
Web sites, F-2, F-9, F-15
Welcome to Windows dialog box, A-2
Win B-1 file, B-4
Win B-2 file, B-10
Windows
   changing system settings, A-6
   logging off, A-19
   shutting down, A-18
windows, A-1
   closing, A-8, A-18
   maximizing, A-8
   minimizing, A-8
   moving, A-8
   panes, A-16
   resizing, A-8
   returning to previous size, A-8
   scroll bars, A-12, A-13
   switching between, B-12
   tiling, B-12, C-12
   title bar, A-8
   as Web page, E-2
   without scroll bars, A-12
Windows 98
   backup program, C-17
   Help, A-16
   Internet mouse clicks, A-5
   My Computer toolbar buttons, C-5
   Network Neighborhood, H-1
Windows Desktop subcategory, A-16
Windows Explorer, C-1
   Address Bar, D-2
   changing folder options, D-3
   creating and renaming folders, D-8
   customizing, D-6
   customizing folders, D-16
   deleting and restoring files, D-15

Index

Details view, D-6
Explorer Bar, D-2, D-4
file hierarchy, D-4
finding files, D-10
Modified column indicator button, D-6
moving files or folders, C-10
Name column indicator button, D-6
opening and viewing files, D-4
resizing windows, D-2
status bar, D-7
toolbar, D-2
vertical bar, D-6
Windows Explorer toolbar, D-12
Windows Explorer window, C-7
Windows Help, A-16
Windows Help dialog box, A-16
Windows Me
   compressing files, C-9
   Help, A-16
   Internet mouse clicks, A-5

My Computer toolbar buttons, C-5
My Documents folder, B-10
My Network Places, H-1
My Pictures folder, B-10
Personalized Menus, A-6
previewing images and pictures, C-7
Windows Media Player (Me), A-3, B-16–B-17
Windows Media Player version 7, B-16
Windows Movie Maker, B-18–B-19
Windows networking window, H-6, H-12
Windows Update command, A-6
Wired Coffee Company page, F-8
Wired Coffee folder, C-3, D-8, D-16
   viewing contents, D-4
   viewing files and folders, C-4
Wired Coffee Logo file, B-10, D-12, D-14
Wired Coffee Logo shortcut, C-14
Wired Coffee window, C-10
WordPad
   document window, B-4

   editing text, B-6
   Format Bar, B-8
   formatting text, B-8
   opening and saving documents, B-4
   starting, B-2
WordPad toolbar, B-4, B-12
WordPad window, B-2, B-12
wordwrap, B-6
workgroups, H-4
Work Offline command, F-12
workstations, H-2
World Wide Web, F-2
   history, F-3
   Internet, F-3
   searching, F-16
   searching for people, F-17

▶ Y

Yahoo!, F-16

Project Files List

To complete many of the lessons and practice exercises in this book, students need to use a Project File that is supplied by Course Technology. Once obtained, the user selects where to store the files, such as to the hard disk drive, network server, or Zip disk or on floppy disk. Below is a list of the files that are supplied, and the unit or practice exercise to which the files correspond. For information on how to obtain Project Files, please see the inside cover of this book. The following list only includes Project Files that are supplied; it does not include the files students create from scratch or the files student create by revising the supplied files. Folders denoted by an asterisk (*) contain additional folders and files.

Unit	File or Folder supplied	Folder or File supplied	Location file is used in unit
Windows Unit A	No files		
Windows Unit B	Win B-1.doc Win B-2.bmp Coffee Cup.mpeg		Lessons
	AM Coffee.wav Win B-3.doc Better Coffee.wav		Skills Review
	Invitation Map.bmp		Independent Challenge 3
Windows Unit C	Wired Coffee folder	Advertising folder * Letters folder * Sales folder *	Lessons
	Lew's Books folder	2001 folder * 2002 folder * Employees folder * Letters folder * Store Locations *	Independent Challenge 1
	M&N Bakeries folder	Brownies.doc Icing1.doc Icing2.doc Passover & Easter Tore.doc	Independent Challenge 4
Windows Unit D	Wired Coffee folder	Advertising folder * Important folder * Letters folder * Personnel folder * Sales folder *	Lesson
Windows Unit E	Wired Coffee Logo.bmp		Lessons/Skills Review
Windows Unit F	No files		
Windows Unit G	No files		
Windows Unit H	Wired Coffee folder	Advertising folder * Important folder * Letters folder * Personnel folder * Sales folder *	Lessons

▶ 16 PROJECT FILES